THE CHANGING FACE OF ANTISEMITISM

THE CHANGING FACE OF ANTISEMITISM
From Ancient Times to the Present Day

WALTER LAQUEUR

OXFORD
UNIVERSITY PRESS

2006

OXFORD

UNIVERSITY PRESS

Oxford University Press, Inc., publishes works that
further Oxford University's objective of excellence
in research, scholarship, and education.

Oxford New York

Auckland Cape Town Dar es Salaam Hong Kong Karachi
Kuala Lumpur Madrid Melbourne Mexico City Nairobi
New Delhi Shanghai Taipei Toronto

With offices in

Argentina Austria Brazil Chile Czech Republic France Greece
Guatemala Hungary Italy Japan Poland Portugal Singapore
South Korea Switzerland Thailand Turkey Ukraine Vietnam

Copyright © 2006 by Walter Laqueur

Published by Oxford University Press, Inc.
198 Madison Avenue, New York, NY 10016
www.oup.com

Oxford is a registered trademark of Oxford University Press

Library of Congress Cataloging-in-Publication Data
Laqueur, Walter, 1921–
The changing face of antisemitism: From ancient times
to the present day / Walter Laqueur
p. cm.
Includes bibliographical references and index.
ISBN-13: 978-0-19-530429-9
ISBN-10: 0-19-530429-2
1. Antisemitism—History. 2. Christianity and antisemitism.
3. Judaism—Relations–Christianity. 4. Christianity and other religions—Judaism.
5. Judaism—Relations—Islam. 6. Islam—Relations—Judaism. I. Title
DS145.L325 2006 305.892'4009—dc22 2005030491

1 3 5 7 9 8 6 4 2
Printed in the United States of America
on acid-free paper

CONTENTS

Preface vii

ONE The New Antisemitism 1
TWO Interpretations of Antisemitism 21
THREE Ancient and Medieval Anti-Judaism 39
FOUR The Enlightenment and After 71
FIVE Racialism and Jewish Conspiracies 91
SIX Toward the Holocaust 107
SEVEN Contemporary Antisemitism 125
EIGHT Assimilation and Its Discontents 151
NINE Antisemitism and the Left 171
TEN Antisemitism and the Muslim World 191
ELEVEN In Place of a Conclusion 207

Bibliography 209
Index 215

PREFACE

HOW TO ACCOUNT FOR ANTISEMITISM? It has a very long history, but this history has been written only during the past century. There is no Thucydides or Plutarch of antisemitism; not one of the great historians and sociologists of the past has written about it in any detail. The endeavors to explain and interpret it are of even more recent date. Only after the Second World War and the disaster that befell European Jewry were the many attempts to analyze and understand it generated. Many questions remain open, and some will probably remain unresolved as far as one can look ahead.

They include the questions of whether there was antisemitism before the advent of Christianity or whether antagonism toward Jews at that time was no more than "normal xenophobia"; whether, as others argue, antisemitism can be traced back not to early Christianity but only to the late Middle Ages. This, in turn, raises the questions of whether and to what extent there has been continuity between the traditional, religious antisemitism that prevailed up to the second part of the nineteenth century and the racialist antisemitism that succeeded it and that led to the mass murder of the Second World War. A related debate concerns whether and to what extent contemporary antisemitism is rooted in the antisemitism of the past or whether it is mainly connected with the existence and the policies of the state of Israel as well as with anti-Americanism, antiglobalism, and other contemporary roots and movements.

While up to 1945 antisemites did not on the whole mind being called antisemites, there has been since that time indignation on the part of many, however hostile to the Jews, at being painted with the antisemitic brush. The question arises whether their angry feelings are justified. This also raises the question of whether what was historically predominantly a preoccupation of sections of Christian churches and right-wing movements has become in our time far more frequent among Muslim and left-wing groups; is this base calumny or undeniable fact?

The debate continues with regard to the questions of whether and to what extent economic and psychological motives are involved in antisemitism or whether historically antisemitism was simply the consequence of Jews rejecting Christianity and Islam. It involves the question of whether antisemitism is the more or less inevitable result of the anomalous social, economic, and political position of the Jews among other peoples which had a negative effect on Jews as a collective and as individuals.

This short review does not pretend to present yet another theory of antisemitism or to answer the many unresolved questions. Nor is it an apologetic or polemical statement; it merely attempts to summarize research and debates that have been going on for decades. It also deals with the present character of antisemitism and its future prospects.

One of the most renowned intellectuals of our time, Noam Chomsky, has stated that "antisemitism is no longer a problem, fortunately," and this could be quite correct as far as certain parts of the state of Massachusetts as well as some other regions of North America are concerned. But it is less certain that this statement still holds if one moves a little farther afield. Even a mile or two from the campus of

MIT, the president of Harvard, Lawrence Summers, has pointed to a widespread current of opinion that encourages a functional antisemitism marked by disproportionate preoccupation with Jews and the Jewish state: "serious and thoughtful people are advocating and taking actions that are antisemitic in their effect if not their intent." (And what of people who are less serious and thoughtful?)

The fact that Harvard's president was bitterly attacked for saying this shows that passions are still running high. Sixty years have passed since the end of the Second World War; the closed season on Jews is ending. Jews, it is argued, have been talking for too long and too intensely about the Holocaust as if mankind did not experience other tragedies too during the last century. On the other hand, Jews have been doing too well socially and economically and have been too influential politically and culturally to pass unnoticed. And then there is Israel, the greatest danger to world peace in the view of many in Europe. As the leading left-wing historian Eric Hobsbawm wrote, many of the gates which so widely opened to Jews after 1945 may half close. It seems premature to draw the final line under this chapter of human history.

A brief personal statement is called for. I belong to the last surviving members of a generation that lived through European antisemitism in its most extreme form, in contrast to later students of antisemitism for whom the subject was by necessity an abstract or at least remote phenomenon. It is unlikely that a member of this generation who lost his parents and family in this period will be inclined to treat antisemitism as a laughing matter as a professor in Canada recently suggested. On the other hand, having faced extreme antisemitism, he is unlikely to overreact, crying "wolf" at the appearance of every mouse or mosquito.

With a few specific exceptions (such as the origins of the *Protocols of the Elders of Zion*), antisemitism was not for a long time among the central issues preoccupying me on the scholarly level. But I was for thirty years director of what was then the leading institute for the study and collection of material on antisemitism, the Wiener Library in London. While I cannot claim that I studied every single publication on antisemitism that appeared in the world during these decades, I read (sometimes not without an effort) and pondered very many of them. The present long essay is the summary of my thoughts on the subject.

I would like to express my gratitude to Reinhard Kratz and Mark Cohen for a critical reading of one of the chapters and to Matthew Spieler for having acted as my research assistant in the work on this book.

Washington, D.C.
January 2006

THE CHANGING FACE OF ANTISEMITISM

Chapter One

THE NEW ANTISEMITISM

HOWEVER DEFINED OR CATEGORIZED, antisemitism, Judeophobia, or the hatred and suspicion of the Jews has appeared throughout history and in many parts of the world with various degrees of intensity. This did not end with Hitler and the Second World War. But the motivation, character, and manifestation of antisemitism have changed over the ages, and though widely studied especially in recent decades, much about it remains unclear and in dispute.

The first and obvious question in this context is what is different about Jews that may have attracted attack and persecution? The need for a scapegoat may be part of the human condition, but it does not explain why the Jews have been consistently cast in this role. The attempts to explain modern antisemitism as a mental aberration on the part of antisemites, even as a mental disease, have singled out, not quite convincingly, certain aspects of a far wider and more complicated phenomenon.

Historically, Judaism had rejected two of the major world religions, Christianity and Islam, and this was bound to generate hostility. The Jews lost their state and for two thousand years survived as a minority.

True, there were other ethnic or religious groups, some even more numerous than the Jews, that also did not have a state of their own, such as the Kurds, but these cases are hardly comparable. The great majority of the Kurds lived in contiguous territories and there was only a small Kurdish diaspora outside the region. The Jews, on the other hand, have been a minority presence in many countries and thus their difference has been reinforced across the globe.

Many branches of the tree of the Jewish people disappeared throughout history, some without trace, but others survived. What kind of communities are these outside the state of Israel? Many Jews are no longer religious, certainly not Orthodox. Most Jews living outside Israel do not regard themselves as a people except by way of origin. If they are a community, they are a defensive community, a community of fate—but as attacks against them decreased, this common tie also became weaker. Assimilation in Europe, where most Jews lived at the time, had not been very successful in the nineteenth century. But the fact that it had not been a success, and had not prevented the Holocaust, did not mean that it was always bound to fail—and this for obvious reasons. Today, the number of Jews has significantly declined and at the same time Western societies have become far less monolithic; or to put it more crudely, Jews are no longer the most bothersome minority.

Yet antisemitism continues, although there has been so much change in its character that the question of continuity itself is controversial. What is the nature of antisemitism? To what extent was Christian anti-Judaism connected with pre-Christian attitudes? What is the connection between the racialist antisemitism of the late nineteenth and early twentieth centuries and the earlier Christian anti-Jewish tradition? And is there a "new antisemitism" at the present time?

Xenophobia was a fairly frequent phenomenon in ancient Egypt, Greece, and Rome. Though Jews were not popular, the attitude toward them was not significantly different from attitudes toward other ethnic groups. Pre-Christian antisemitism had no obvious social or economic roots and it was not religiously motivated, except perhaps in the sense that while Jews had pioneered monotheism (and were proud of it), this was not considered by Greeks and Romans a great spiritual achievement. The Jewish religion was not more tolerant than others, nor had the Jews been in other ways in the forefront of human civilization. Compared to Greece and Rome, Judea and the Jews had not produced paramount cultural values other than the Old Testament. Yet, at the same time the Jews stuck to their own, isolated themselves, and (so it appeared to outsiders) considered themselves somehow better than others because of being the chosen people and having a special connection with their god. This caused resentment, and sometimes contempt, but it was not really one of the major issues of the ancient world. By and large, antisemitism was one of many national and ethnic antagonisms.

The situation radically changed with the advent of Christianity. While early Christianity had been a Jewish sect, it gradually distanced itself from Judaism and this turned into open hostility. In the beginning, competition might have been the predominant factor because both religions were looking for converts. But Christianity prevailed early on, and even after its victory, hostility between the two religions in no way diminished. The Jews, it was claimed, had been the main culprits in the death of the founder of Christianity; they had rejected him as they had rejected earlier prophets; the destruction of their temple, their country, and their dispersal among the nations was the just punishment.

European Jewish communities were subjected to frequent attacks, persecution, and deportation during the Middle Ages, and their legal status was regulated according to the church teaching that was designed to keep them alive—but in misery. Jews were limited to certain professions (such as usury, which made them even more unpopular) and eventually confined to ghettos. But years of acute persecution (1096, 1348, etc.) were followed by relatively "normal" years, and after the expulsion from a certain country they were often gradually readmitted. This would not have been the case if antisemitism had been purely doctrinal-religious. But social and economic motives were also involved, and they may help to explain in certain cases why persecution was more severe at some times than at others. What matters in historical perspective is the fact that the stereotype of the Jew created by the church—or the Muslim—theological establishment has lasted over the centuries and continues to be of importance to the present time.

Though traditional religious antisemitism has lasted until the contemporary period, most students of the phenomenon also point to the development of a new, modern racialist antisemitism that emerged in Central Europe during the second half of the nineteenth century. These scholars draw attention to the growth of the nation-state and nationalist ideology, to the social strains and stresses that accompanied the disintegration of feudal society, and to modernization. Jews were made responsible more often than not for these social ills. Because Jews were said to be the main benefactors of social change, they were also blamed for its negative consequences. In the twentieth century, and particularly after World War One, the socioeconomic decline of the middle class provided the background for the increased receptiveness to antisemitism.

But the break in continuity between modern and premodern antisemitism must not, for a variety of reasons, be overemphasized. Racialist antisemitism can be found (for instance in Spain) many centuries before its appearance in Central Europe. Furthermore, the political and ideological features that are characteristic for the emergence of modern secular antisemitism in Germany and Austria are by no means typical for antisemitism in Russia and Poland in the nineteenth and twentieth centuries. In these latter countries, where most Jews lived at the time, strictly racialist concepts never developed; there were no widely accepted theories about a Slavonic or Russian master race and the need to destroy racially inferior elements. But there was antisemitism and it was based as in the past on religious or quasi-religious elements. The same is true with regard to the Muslim and particularly the Arab world, where racialist theory always remained a marginal sectarian phenomenon and the main motivation in antisemitism remained religious or nationalist-religious. Seen in this light, it is not difficult to pinpoint chronologically the transition from traditional to modern antisemitism in Germany or perhaps in France, but it is quite impossible to do so in the East European context.

If there has been controversy about the continuity between the old mainly religion-inspired antisemitism and the new racialist theories, there has been a similar debate about the continuity between racialist antisemitism (of roughly speaking the period between 1880 and 1945) and the new antisemitism (or Judeophobia) of the period after World War Two. There certainly is an obvious if superficial difference: prior to 1945 few antisemites hesitated to call themselves antisemites, whereas more recently coyness has widely prevailed and open, outspoken antisemitism is restricted to sectarians of the extreme right. Post-1945 antisemites have been careful to stress that their hostility is limited to colonialist, capitalist, imperialist individuals and groups advocating racialist, aggressively militarist, and reactionary politics. Unfortunately, according to these contemporary critics, some or even many of these individuals happen to be Jewish (Zionist or pro-Zionist), but this should not give them immunity against justified criticism.

The term "new antisemitism" dates back to the 1970s when books with this title were first published. At the time, it referred simply to post-Nazi antisemitism emanating mainly from neo-Nazi groups in Europe and America. It did not imply a qualitative difference. At the beginning of the twenty-first century, however, "new antisemitism" refers to substantive differences as compared with earlier forms of antisemitism.

Some observers of the European and American scene argue that there is no "new antisemitism" and that antisemitism and anti-Zionism (or anti-Israelism) are two distinctly different tendencies that should not be confused. There is no demand for the expulsion of the Jews, not even for specific anti-Jewish legislation, and in this respect too, there is a basic difference between the present and the racialist antisemitism of the past. If this is antisemitism, they argue, there is as much, if not more, Islamophobia in the Western world, in Russia, and elsewhere. As long as Jews were persecuted, there was some sympathy for them on the left, but once Jews (or Israelis) became the persecutors, attitudes toward them were bound to change. Could it be that many Jews, suffering from the trauma of the Holocaust (or using the Holocaust as a propagandistic weapon), have been overreacting against justified criticism? In the Arab and Muslim world the situation is different inasmuch as the terms Israel, Zionism, Judaism, and the Jews are used as synonyms; if a difference is made, it is usually for outside consumption.

The fact that criticism of Israel is not per se antisemitism is so obvious that it hardly needs repeating once again. If Israel does not treat its non-Jewish citizens equally and humanely, if it persists in holding on to territories occupied in 1967 against the will of the local population, if it illegally seizes land elsewhere, if a racialist-chauvinist fringe inside Israel defies the law and elementary human rights and to a considerable degree dictates its outrageous behavior to a government, if some people in Israel are unwilling to accept the rights of others, such behavior invites condemnation.

But Israel does not border on Holland and Switzerland; how can it survive in a hostile surrounding if it does not play according to local rules? Is it not true that many, perhaps most countries outside Western Europe and North America behave in a similar way? Hence, we hear the Israeli and Jewish complaints about double standards being applied to them.

The complaint is correct, but it is based on the mistaken belief that there are equal rights for all. Israel is neither China nor India; it has not even a hundred million inhabitants nor oilfields or other vital resources. How can it conceivably expect to be permitted to get away with violations of norms forgiven to other, much bigger or strategically important countries? Russia may no longer be a superpower, but there has hardly been a murmur on the part of the other powers concerning the way the Chechens were treated, and in the Muslim countries too there have been no words of condemnation, let alone appeals for a jihad. There have been no United Nations resolutions and conferences condemning Russia, India, or China for persecuting Muslims.

What is the "new antisemitism"? The issue boils down to the question of whether antisemitism and anti-Zionism are two entirely distinct phenomena or whether anti-Zionism can turn into, in certain circumstances, antisemitism. Unfortunately, there is no clear border line. It has been argued that when criticism of Israel crosses the line from fair to foul it becomes antisemitic. But what is fair and what is foul? Some have argued that even the systematic vilification of Israel, singling out the Jewish state unfairly, may not necessarily be antisemitic, given the inflamed passions and the suffering the conflict has generated.

In the light of history, the argument that anti-Zionism is different from antisemitism is not very convincing. No one disputes that in the late Stalinist period anti-Zionism was merely a synonym for antisemitism. The same is true today for the extreme right which, for legal or political reasons, will opt for anti-Zionist rather than openly anti-Jewish slogans. It has been noted that in the Muslim and particularly the Arab world, the fine distinctions between Jews and Zionists hardly ever existed and are now less than ever in appearance. However, even if we ignore both history and the situation in other parts of the world and limit the discussion to Western left-wing anti-Zionism, the issues are not clear-cut.

About half of all Jews now live in Israel. Is the argument that the state of Israel is the greatest danger to world peace and has no right to exist anti-Zionist, anti-Israeli, or antisemitic? If it is based on the assumption that nation-states in general have caused more harm than good and should be dismantled, such a proposition cannot be considered antisemitic. But few of those who insist on the liquidation of the state of Israel share the conviction that all nation-states should be done away with. They believe that other states, not being such a danger to world peace, do have the right to exist.

There is a great deal of evil in the world and millions have perished within the last decade or two as the result of civil wars, repression, racial and social persecution, and tribal conflicts, from Cambodia to much of Africa (Congo, Rwanda, and Darfur). More than two billion people live in repressive dictatorships, but there is persecution too in countries that are free or partly free. National and religious minority groups have been systematically persecuted, abused, raped, burned, shot, gassed, and their property demolished, from Indonesia, Pakistan, and Bangladesh, to Central Asia and beyond. In fact, it would be difficult to think of countries outside of Europe and North America that have been entirely free of such suffering; and even Europe has had such incidents on a massive scale, as in the Balkans. But there have been no protest demonstrations concerning the fate of the Dalets (Untouchables) in India even though there are more than 100 million of them. The fate of the Uighur in China, the Copts in Egypt, or the Bahai in Iran (to name but a few persecuted peoples) has not generated much indignation in the streets of Europe and America.

According to peace researchers, 25 million people were killed in internal conflicts since World War Two, of them, 8,000 in the Israeli-Palestinian conflict, which ranks forty-sixth in the list of victims. But Israel has been more often condemned by the United Nations and other international organizations than all other nations taken together.

This takes us back to the issue of singling out Israel and whether this should be considered fair or foul, legitimate denunciation or antisemitism. Those singling out the Zionist misdeeds certainly do not do so because Israeli injustice has been on a more massive scale. Has criticism of Israel been harsher and so much more frequent simply because better was expected of the Jews? Or was it because Israel was small and isolated and there was prejudice against it?

Inflamed passions and the suffering caused could certainly explain Palestinian attitudes; their passions were indeed inflamed and the Palestinian people have suffered. This also explains why Palestinians in the heat of the battle have been attacking not just Zionism and Israel but Jews in general. But why should the passions be inflamed of people living thousands of miles away, who have never been to this part of the world, are not familiar with the circumstances of the conflict, or do not have particular emotional ties with it? If friends of the oppressed and humiliated were to protest in other cases of injustice, their case would be irrefutable. But if antiracialist protestations in defense of human rights are made selectively, the question arises why this should be the case. Neither antiracialist nor anti-imperialist emotions, however intense and sincerely held, can satisfactorily explain it. There must be something additional involved, and if this additional factor is not antisemitism, what is it? Is it a new form of post–racialist antisemitism masquerading as antiracism and anti-imperialism?

The "new antisemitism" has been explained as anti-Zionism or as hostility caused by the fact that Jews are perceived as representatives of Israel. Because it does not involve traditional stereotypes, it is claimed, it should not therefore properly be associated with the old antisemitism. This may be true in some cases but not in others. Moreover, anti-Jewish feeling among the left and the media in Western and in Eastern Europe has been generated only in part by events in Israel. There has been a transmutation and modernization of antisemitism in a more general way—"usury" has become "Wall Street" and the "Protocols of the Elders of Zion" have reappeared as the conspiracy of the neoconservatives aiming at world conquest.

Even if we assume that Israeli policies are the single most important factor with regard to the emergence of the "new antisemitism," the question still remains why Israeli policies, however wicked, should generate such strong passions in the first place among the likes of Mikis Theodorakis or "Carlos the Jackal"—in other words, people without a known personal stake in the Israeli-Palestinian conflict, who have not suffered from it physically or emotionally? Is it sympathy with the underdog, a feeling that injustice should be combated? But if so, why concentrate on one specific underdog and ignore the others? There is no clear answer to this question; it does appear, however, that there must be a specific aspect or dimension to this case of injustice that other cases do not have.

WHAT ARE THE PROSPECTS OF ANTISEMITISM in the contemporary world? Attempts to answer this question are bound to be speculative, but if there are no certainties, it is still possible to point to political, economic, social, and above all demographic trends that shed some light on these prospects.

Traditionally, Europe was the continent in which antisemitism had its strongest roots and most extreme manifestations. This is no longer so, partly because of the small number of Jews living there, but also because of the weakening of the traditional main pillars of antisemitism—the churches, the extreme right, and the fascist-Nazi movement. The political influence of the churches is weaker than ever before; furthermore, the churches have denounced antisemitism and engage instead in interfaith, ecumenical dialogue with the emphasis on amity and forgiveness. Individual churchmen continue to spread antisemitic propaganda (in Italy, Greece, Russia), but altogether this does not amount to much.

It would be premature to write off neofascism and neo-Nazism in Europe (and similar sects in America), particularly at a time when European power is shrinking, when the old continent faces economic and social strains, and, above all, when population pressure on Europe from the Muslim countries and the third world is increasing.

The facts and trends are well known and need not be adduced in detail. If the present decline in the birth rate continues, the number of people living in Germany will have fallen from 82 million at the present time to 32 million by the end of the century; the respective figures for Italy are 57 million and 15 million, for Spain 39 million at the present time and 12 million by the end of the century. On the other hand, the countries of the Maghreb will have 120 million inhabitants just by 2050, within one generation from now. Egypt will have 115 million and Turkey 100 million. The population of Iran will be larger than that of Russia. It is sometimes said that such projections are not reliable, but this is not true with regard to the period after World War Two; most serious projections have been correct with a margin of error of a few percentage points only.

In brief, the character of most European countries is rapidly changing and it will probably change even more quickly in future. Even at the present time between 40 and 50 percent of the young people in West German cities such as Cologne are foreign born; the same is true for the major Dutch cities (Amsterdam, Rotterdam, Utrecht). The percentage is almost equally high in the French regions of major Muslim immigration (Ile de France, Provence, Alsace, Languedoc) but lower in the United Kingdom (London, Bradford, Birmingham, Manchester). By the middle of the present century, between one-quarter and one-third of the population of France, Germany, and other European countries will be Muslim or of Muslim origin. Since the Jewish communities are also concentrated in the big cities, it means that in a few decades they will exist in a largely or even predominantly Muslim milieu.

The decline of "old Europe" is bound to strengthen political movements radically opposed to immigration. But such opposition is not limited to neofascism and the far right; it is shared even now by most political parties. The extreme right has not changed its fundamentally hostile attitude toward the Jews, but the "Jewish peril" is so much smaller now than the Muslim danger that they feel under pressure to adjust their policies accordingly. In fact, in parts of Europe such as Belgium, sections of the Jewish community are opting for the political parties most actively keeping the streets safe and preventing attacks—not because of any ideological affinity but for eminently pragmatic reasons.

How are European governments facing the demographic change? They are only partly aware of the huge problems facing them. The natural tendency of democratic governments elected for a period of four or five years is to ignore dangers that are farther ahead. But it could well be that it is too late even now to take effective measures, and chances are that there will be a sudden awakening that may well manifest itself in radical reactions and even panic. The policy that will be followed (and to a certain extent is already pursued today) is a mixture of a strong hand and appeasement. "Strong hand" means drastically cutting down on further immigration, opposing aggressive violations of the legal norms and cultural values of Western societies (for instance, the banning of the veil in France). But the situation is further complicated because of the fact that West European economies need new immigrants to get their industries and services running and to provide the social safety net on which the welfare state depends. But where will these new immigrants come from?

A policy of repression is bound to be softened by appeasement. While in some European countries only few immigrants from Muslim countries have the right to vote, this will change at the very latest within a generation or two. Even at the present time, the Muslim vote is significant in scores of British and French constituencies, and this will increase very quickly in the future. In the circumstances, political parties will try hard to show that nothing is farther from their minds than Islamophobia and there will be a readiness to make concessions to Muslim feelings on issues that are not of central interest to the non-Muslim majority.

It is in this context that the Jewish issue will very likely play a role. Given the anti-Jewish feelings in Muslim communities (less pronounced among German Turks than among French or Dutch North Africans), the policy vis-à-vis Israel (a country quite unpopular in any case) will be affected but also, inevitably, the position of local Jews, who will be well advised to take a low profile to escape attack. There are parts of Europe in which local Jews have been far less threatened than in others, and it is quite possible, even probable, that with the acculturation and integration of the Muslim element into European society, these tensions will become less acute with time. But this is unlikely to happen very soon.

In the meantime, European Jews will come under growing pressure. Britain exhibits such pressures, for instance, in the "anti-Zionist" speeches and articles of Ken Livingstone, the mayor of London, and the attacks against Jewish leaders of the Tory party. Each case is different and generalizations are bound to be misleading. In some cases, such attacks might be purely opportunistic, dictated by electoral facts; in other cases, there might be a genuine aversion toward Jews which will find expression more openly as the Holocaust recedes into the past and with it the bad conscience of European nations. In most cases, it is probably a mixture of the two trends. In any case, Jews are likely to be adversely affected.

A number of years ago, a leading left-wing French intellectual wrote in *Le Monde* that the political implications of the fact that there are ten times as many Arabs as Jews in France should not be disregarded. The writer in question was attacked—for saying out loud what everyone knew and many had accepted. In other European countries the discrepancy in numbers is much greater. These facts explain at least in part the shifts that have taken place in left-wing attitudes not just regarding Israel but also concerning the Jews. The domestic impact of the Muslim factor will be even greater in Europe in the future than in the past. Numbers do matter—Stalin's question: How many divisions does the pope have?

An exercise in counterfactual history: What if the Ottoman empire had collapsed one hundred years earlier than it did, and what if the majority of European Jews had decided to move and settle there? Given a birth rate similar to that of the Gaza strip, the region would now have a population of between sixty and eighty million inhabitants, perhaps even more. And, what if major oilfields had been discovered in this imaginary Greater Israel reaching from the Nile to the Euphrates?

Such a country would live in peace with its neighbors and be an honored member of the United Nations. There would be no debates about its right to exist, for no one would trifle with a country of such size, power, and geostrategic importance. Muslim religious leaders would invoke quotations from the Koran stressing the friendship and closeness of Muslims and Jews, children of the same ancestor— Abraham (Ibrahim). There would be no attacks against Zionism on the part of the antiglobalists and Trotskyites, only songs of praise concerning the miraculous renaissance of an old people.

These are, of course, mere fantasies that might have appealed to a visionary like Disraeli. But the Ottoman empire did not then collapse, and the Jews did not emigrate there. Israel is a small country that has not yet quite come to terms with its status in the world. Its existence has not yet been accepted by its neighbors. Small might be beautiful in all kinds of other contexts, but in international affairs, its drawbacks are obvious.

But it would be wrong to assume that attitudes changed only because of demography. The roots of the shift go back to the 1960s and 1970s, a period in which these demographic facts did not yet exist— or in any case were not fully perceived.

The shift also predates Ariel Sharon, the Intifada, and the coming to power of the conservative right in Israel. If so, why did left-wing attitudes change? To a certain extent the changes are connected with the anti-Americanism of the European left (but not only of the left). However, anti-Americanism was rampant in Europe well before Presidents Ronald Reagan and George W. Bush, and relations between Washington and Jerusalem were by no means close in the past. In other words, the estrangement between Europe and America goes farther back in time and to a deeper ideological shift, even though events since 1967 caused an aggravation.

While Jews were attacked in the 1920s and 1930s as destructive elements for their prominent part in Communism and other left-wing, revolutionary movements, the main attack at the present time comes from the populist left-wing, antiglobalist camp and the accusations are the very opposite of what they once were—now Jews are seen as the protagonists of international finance capital. Earlier on Jews were accused of being rootless cosmopolitans and internationalists. They are now singled out as the avatars of an anachronistic and reactionary nationalism, doubly reprehensible in view of the close alliance between Israel and America. A frequent antisemitic slogan in the streets of Europe in the 1930s was "Jews—move on to Jerusalem." Sixty years later they are called on to move out of Jerusalem.

Over the last few decades, there has been an ideological reorientation of what used to be the left. With the progressive disillusionment with Communism and the later breakdown of the Soviet empire, the sympathies of the left were transferred to the third world, the underdeveloped countries of Asia and Africa. If earlier on the (unofficial) slogan had been "no enemies on the left," the new guiding line became "no enemies in the third world." But Israel was not a third world country. The left, with only a few exceptions, had never been in favor of a Jewish homeland, which they considered a step in the wrong direction. And as the problems generated by the creation of a Jewish state multiplied, the erstwhile antagonism reappeared with additional vigor.

In an ironic twist of history, Israel had been admonished for decades not to be an outpost of the West but to become integrated culturally as well as politically in the part of the world in which it was located. In recent decades, such changes inside Israel have taken place with the growth of religious fundamentalism, religious nationalism, and the growth of the "Eastern" element (Jews from North Africa and the Middle East and their descendants). These changes did not help the integration of Israel in its surroundings in any way, nor did they affect hostility toward Israel. On the contrary, the "orientalization" of Israel only added to such enmity. As many Europeans saw it, Jewish support for Israel (and the assistance given by the American right) poisoned relations between Europe and the Middle East, endangered the oil supply, increased the danger of a new war, and, above all, added to the tensions inside Europe between Muslim new immigrants and the other segments of the population.

Such attitudes were by no means confined to the European left; they were increasingly shared by the mainstream European media. And as time went by, the hostility toward Israel was transferred to Jews supporting it—or at least to those not actively dissociating themselves from it. These explanations do not wholly account for the animosity toward European Jews who were neither Zionists nor indeed actively involved in Jewish life. On the other hand, it is also true that there was and is a tendency to exaggerate the intensity of the "new antisemitism" which, after all, is aimed not at the physical elimination of the Jews as per prewar racialist antisemitism, but merely at the reduction of the Jewish influence, real or perceived. The new antisemitism is aimed not at radical exclusion but at appeasement, and the Jews are expected to minimize their presence, and not to cause unnecessary and dangerous tension and conflict.

The situation of the Jews and the question of antisemitism in Russia and Eastern Europe are different inasmuch as the Muslim factor does not exist there or is perceived as basically hostile. This will not prevent the Russian government from trying to improve relations with Arab and Muslim countries, precisely in order to neutralize the political aims of the Muslim minorities at home. But this will not, in all probability, affect the Jews living in Russia. The fact that so many Jews emerged as super-rich oligarchs in the age of perestroika no doubt fueled native antisemitism, even though most of the oligarchs (like the Bolshevik leaders before them) had no connection with the Jewish community or had even formally distanced themselves from it.

On the other hand, the antisemitic impact of the appearance of these Jewish oligarchs was not as traumatic as might have been expected. The Russian antisemites had (falsely) argued for more than a century that the Jews were, among other things, dominating the Russian economy. And when for a number of years the oligarchs seemed to be in such a position, the shock was therefore much less than many assumed. In any case, the state-and-KGB bureaucratic apparatus soon started to squeeze out the super-rich. While Russian governments have no particular predilection for individual Jews or Jews as a group, they are not actively antisemitic. Given the small number of Jews surviving in these regions after the war and the great exodus from Russia and the Ukraine, the Jewish issue no longer figures among the most important on their agenda. The relations between Russia and its neighbors, the former parts of the Soviet Union, loom considerably larger.

Much depends, however, on the general climate that will prevail in Russia and Eastern Europe in the years and decades to come. If political and social trends and economic developments are relatively smooth, there will be peace on the home front. But if the politics and economic policy of the ruling stratum run into difficulties or fail, old enmities could reappear, and antisemitism could become official policy at least temporarily, affecting the Jews however insignificant their numbers.

Antisemitism in the United States as in Europe has appeared and will in the future be active both on the extreme right—especially the neo-Nazi sects and militias with their invocation of the ZOG (Zionist occupation government)—as well as on the far left. Both extremes share a belief in conspiracy theories and in the power of modern means of communication, especially in the Internet which has provided unprecedented access to many people. The neo-Nazis deny the Holocaust; the far left does not deny it but opposes the overemphasis on the murder of the Jews in World War Two because this can serve only the cause of Zionism and Israel. The antisemitism of the extreme right is traditional and racialist on the pre–World War Two pattern.

The anti-Zionism of the far left is post-racialist, mainly motivated by anti-Americanism and America's support for Israel, and counts not a few Jews among its spokespeople and followers. It is particularly prevalent on university campuses, and many of its followers take great pains to explain that they are by no means opposed to America per se, only to the wrong turn American domestic and foreign policy has taken of late. For this wrong turn, individual Jews and Jewish groups (the neoconservatives) are made responsible even though the majority of Jewish voters are traditionally found in the democratic left-of-center camp.

In its most radical form, the rejection of American values and of Zionism is absolute, as these principles are considered incurably reactionary and antihuman. In its milder form, the opposition to an activist (aggressive) American foreign policy has a far wider outreach. Shared by both the old right wing (paleoconservatives) and many liberals, this opposition is very influential in the media and has established itself as the new political correctness. It includes the belief that close association with Israel has caused far more harm than good and is not in the best interest of the United States. Hence, the all-powerful Jewish lobby in Washington is criticized and is made responsible for the fatal turn taken by American foreign policy.

How is all this likely to affect American Jews and at what point does anti-Zionism become antisemitism? This depends very much on events in the Middle East and the Muslim world in the years to come; American setbacks will create a constellation in which Jews could be blamed for having been responsible to a considerable extent for American involvement and defeats. But it is difficult to imagine that antisemitism, old or new, will become a crucial factor on the American political or social scene. America is a country of immigrants that has traditionally given a great deal of latitude to consecutive waves of newcomers. Muslims in communities in the United States are of different social and economic backgrounds than those in Europe and are more integrated. If there are fears concerning domestic ethnic tensions in the United States, they concern minorities other than Jews and Muslims.

Antisemitism in the contemporary world continues to exist in Europe and America, but it is far less important there than in the Muslim and Arab nations. The revival of antisemitism in Europe is predominantly Muslim in character. Is this likely to change in the foreseeable future and to what extent does it depend on Israel? Israel is considered an alien body in their midst by believing Muslims, the Jews a perfidious enemy according to the Koran. True, the Christians are an enemy too, but the Christians are many and for the time being powerful and they have to be accepted. The Jews are few and much less powerful, why not try defeating them? The jihad against them ought to be pursued to the end—the destruction of their state and the reduction of the survivors to the old status of "*dhimmi*-tude," that is, second-rate citizenship status. This is the desire of the religious and nationalist extremists. But such beliefs are not static and unchanging; their impetus does not remain forever equally strong. Just as Christianity has not engaged in crusades for a long time, there is no reason to assume that Islam will do so forever. For the Palestinians, the existence of Israel is bound to remain a trauma for as far as one can think ahead, the loss of part of their homeland being the greatest injustice which can be put right only by violence. It is only natural that they will want this state to cease to exist. Once they have a state of their own, however, problems of daily life will loom large and much of the energy will have to be invested in making this state work. The great urge to reconquer what was lost will not disappear, but it will not be pursued as in the days when this was the only issue.

The same is true in particular with regard to the other Arab and Muslim countries and the Muslim communities in Europe. Israel and the Jews will remain an enemy. But it is unlikely to remain the only or even the main enemy; these countries and communities, most of them remote in distance from Israel and the Jews, are facing great problems in every respect. Many of their complaints have nothing to do with the existence of Israel and the presence of the Jews, but with other factors such as the (perceived) discrimination of the young Muslims in France, or internal Arab relations, or the tensions between Shi'a and Sunni, or North African unemployment, or the conflict between India and Pakistan.

It cannot be taken for granted that Israel will follow a policy of accommodation to Palestine; the fundamentalist-nationalist extremism of the Muslim world has its counterpart in strong fringe groups of equal fanaticism inside Israel. Once the Palestinians have a viable state, however, and once Israel has taken other steps to accommodate Muslim interests—such as the internationalization of the holy places in Jerusalem—there is a reasonable chance that Arab antisemitism will decrease even though it will not disappear. On the other hand, mainly because of the deep-seated propensity of Arab and Muslim societies to believe in conspiracies, however far-fetched and unreal, there is no certainty that the deeply ingrained fanaticism will quickly fade. In a nuclear age such fanaticism could have devastating consequences.

Jews will be under pressure and attack in many parts of the world, mainly (but not entirely) because of their insistence that they have rights not only as individuals but also as a national group. That this is in no way comparable to the persecutions of the 1930s and 1940s goes without saying. Whether to call this pressure antisemitism or Judeophobia or post–racialist antisemitism or radical anti-Zionism is a fascinating semantic question that can be endlessly discussed. Hitler gave antisemitism a bad name and there is widespread reluctance on the part of even the most severe critics of the Jews to accept this label. A spade is no longer called a spade but an agricultural implement. But whatever terminology used, there is no reason to believe that the last chapter in the long history of antisemitism has already been written.

Chapter Two

INTERPRETATIONS OF ANTISEMITISM

"ANTISEMITISM" IS A RELATIVELY RECENT TERM. Most historians claim that it was coined in 1879 by Wilhelm Marr, a German journalist. This is only approximately correct, because the term was used for at least two decades earlier, even in contemporary encyclopedias. But it is true that Marr popularized the term and gave it wide currency. A radical in his younger years, he published an anti-Jewish pamphlet, "from a non religious point of view" as he put it. He argued that it was wrong to attack the Jews as Christ-killers and that the medieval accusations about the defilement of hosts and ritual murder were equally stupid—his attacks were directed against what he called the "Jewish spirit" and its nefarious impact on German culture and life in general. He was concerned with modern, not medieval, antisemitism.

But what exactly did antisemitism mean? It opposed and fought "semitism"—another neologism that has not survived. The term had been taken from the realm of linguistics, but the interest of antisemites in Akkadian (the oldest Semitic language) was as limited as in Phoenician or Tigrinya, the official language of Eritrea. They had nothing against Hannibal or Jesus Christ even though they were

Semitic language speakers. It was a synonym for racial Judeophobia as distinct from the earlier religious hatred of Jews.

But the radical antisemites of Marr's generation—such as Paul Lagarde, Eugen Duehring, and Richard Wagner—while no longer firm believers in Christianity, had not fully embraced a "scientific" racialist theory that did not yet exist at the time. Their concept was something like a halfway house between the old and the new antisemitism.

Even the Nazis for political reasons were not enamored with the term antisemitism; they did not want to antagonize their well-wishers in the Arab world, and during World War Two, Josef Goebbels, Hitler's propaganda minister, and others gave instructions to use the term as little as possible. On the other hand, strong elements of racialism can be found centuries earlier, as in Spain with its emphasis on the purity of blood (*limpieza de sangre*). More recently attempts to replace the term antisemitism with one or several other terms have been unsuccessful; the term had become too deeply rooted too long ago.

The literature about antisemitism is truly enormous; much of it has been polemical or apologetic. Until fairly recently, the attempts to explain the sources and motives of the phenomenon have been few and far between. With a few exceptions, these studies were written by Jews—the reasons are obviously that antisemitism was much more of a problem for Jews than for non-Jews—and this is the case even today despite the proliferation of academic studies on the subject.

Antisemitism is a difficult subject to discuss for a variety of reasons. Its character and manifestations have undergone changes over time and it has expressed itself in different ways in various countries and cultures. The study of antisemitism involves knowledge of both Jewish and general history and sociology—yet very few scholars were equally familiar with both. Most of the studies on antisemitism deal with one specific aspect—its ideological or social or psychological roots—at the neglect of other potential motives. There has been an enormous amount of literature on German (and Austrian) antisemitism, but most of the Jews prior to World War Two lived in Russia, Poland,

the United States, and Romania, and only few studies on these countries existed. The situation was similar even with regard to France;
an excellent work had been written in the 1950s about French
antisemitism—but it was virtually the only one in the field and the
second volume never appeared.

Among nineteenth-century Jewish liberals and their Christian
friends, it was generally assumed that with the spread of the Enlightenment and the emancipation of the Jews, it was only a question of
time until what some called the "Jewish question" would be solved.
They realized, of course, that there was considerable resistance against
the full integration of Jews into Western societies. But the spread of
antisemitic beliefs seemed to them an aberration which, given time
and good will on all sides, would sooner or later come to a halt. This
was, after all, the age of progress and it was unthinkable that medieval prejudice would persist indefinitely.

Events seemed to bear out these hopes to some extent. The
antisemitic parties that had emerged in Germany toward the turn of
the century had declined and disappeared before the outbreak of the
First World War. After the Dreyfus case, in France too there was a
significant decrease in political antisemitism. In other Western countries such as Britain and the United States, antisemitism was a social
issue but not one of great political significance.

There were still occasional attacks against Jews, and the question
was asked what could be done to dry out the antisemitic swamp? Liberal German Jews founded in the 1890s an association for the defense
against antisemitism which patiently tried to refute the accusations
against Jews—no, they were not bloodsuckers and parasites but honest, law-abiding citizens as much patriotically inclined as all other
Germans. The intention was laudable but the results meager. For the
antisemites were not primarily interested in facts and figures nor in
rational argument, and the fact that many Jews received the Nobel
Prize (adding to Germany's cultural prestige) did not greatly impress
them. They instinctively did not like them, did not regard them as

their kin, and had grave suspicions regarding them. Was it not true that there were no Jewish peasants but a great many businessmen, lawyers, and physicians? Did they not exert an influence quite disproportionate to their number in German cultural life—in publishing houses, the press, and the theater? Was not the German artisan and small trader squeezed out by the (often Jewish-owned) department stores? Some of these observations were quite correct—there were few if any Jewish peasants in Germany; others were untrue or irrelevant and they contributed little to the interpretation of antisemitism— there was no more antisemitism among German businessmen or lawyers or physicians than among the rest of the population.

The socialists and the nineteenth-century radicals were, if anything, even more optimistic with regard to the disappearance of the Jewish problem. With the victory of radical democracy and the social revolution, all other problems would disappear. They regarded antisemitism at best as the socialism of fools, or as a stratagem to distract the toiling masses from fighting their real enemies—the exploiters, capitalism, and the reactionaries. Among leading nineteenth-century socialists there was a great deal of anti-Jewish feeling and this refers not only to the (non-Jewish) so-called utopian socialists such as Pierre Proudhon and Charles Fourier but also to thinkers of Jewish background such as Karl Marx.

Marx's grandfather had been a rabbi but Judaism (the religion of usury, of egotism, of money as its fetish, as he put it) was for Marx an embarrassment, and he wanted to distance himself as far as possible from this despicable tradition. Marx wrote his "Jewish Question" (1844) when he was a very young man unencumbered by knowledge of Jewish history; he knew about the Rothschilds but knew little and cared less about the Jewish masses of Eastern Europe. In later life Marx did not deal with the Jewish question as such, though when he referred to Jews in private correspondence his tenor was almost always negative.

However, the socialist parties of Germany, Russia, and other European countries, while not paying much attention to the Jewish question, always rejected antisemitism. Neither the Jews nor antisemitism fitted well into the framework of Marxist ideology (historical materialism), and attempts to explain the relationship between Jews and capitalism were left to economic historians such as Werner Sombart. While Max Weber saw the Protestant ethic as the mainspring of modern capitalism, Sombart connected it also to the "Jewish spirit." To overcome this apparent contradiction, Sombart argued that the Puritan and the Jewish spirit were really one and the same, just as the Jewish Sabbath and the English Sunday were the same. The Jewish spirit was profit oriented and thus paved the way for the modern entrepreneur—the Jewish (and Puritan) merchant was the counterpart to the Aryan warrior-hero. As for America, it was totally *verjudet,* owing everything it was to the Jewish spirit.

While Sombart was a man of firm and often original opinions, his attitude to historical facts was not beyond reproach. He knew little about Jewish history and, like most of his contemporaries, he was not dealing with Eastern Europe, where the great majority of Jews lived at the time. He overrated the historical role of the court Jews, underrated the role of Christian bankers in history—be it Huguenot, German, or Italian (like the Fugger and Medici), or the Quakers or Dutch. He left out of his purview the entrepreneurs who had been instrumental in developing the American economy in the nineteenth and early twentieth centuries—and earlier the British—among whom there had been hardly any Jews at all. And he ignored that while at one stage the Rothschilds had indeed played a very important role in European commercial life, the private banks, Jewish or non-Jewish, had been squeezed out by much larger state banks or other entities that were not in the hands of a family or a clan or tribe.

Sombart's study of the origins of capitalism and its connections with antisemitism was too complicated for much use by the political antisemites, even though Julius Streicher of *Stuermer* fame used to quote him. For a while Sombart found more interest in his theses among Jews than among non-Jews.

But the most radical attempts to explain the rise of antisemitism came from different quarters—namely from Jews who did not share the optimism of their coreligionists who firmly believed in the coming blessings of emancipation. Leon Pinsker, a Russian physician, had early in his life been among those who fought for full emancipation of the Jews of his homeland; he had believed that the spread of education among Jews and non-Jews alike would bring more or less automatically a solution of the Jewish question. But the rise of antisemitism in Western and Central Europe, and above all the major pogroms of 1881 in Southwest Russia, taught him that such optimism had been misplaced.

In a short pamphlet entitled "Autoemancipation," published in Berlin in 1882 in German (Pinsker had studied in German universities), Pinsker argued that the Jews were a distinctive element among the nations and as such could not assimilate and be digested. In what way were Jews different from others? They were not a nation and did not have a state of their own. They had renounced their nationality but this had not given them equal status. Their position was abnormal, ghost-like, and it was pointless to blame the antisemites. Judeophobia was demonopathy (as he put it), a psychic aberration like other superstitions and idiosyncrasies. But it was hereditary and incurable, part of the human condition; polemics against it were useless, a waste of effort, for prejudice could not be removed by rational argument. No people liked foreigners and the Jew, having no country and being the foreigner par excellence, would not be able to change this in the foreseeable future. Perhaps one day in the distant future national barriers would no longer exist and all mankind would live in brotherhood and concord. But no previous civilization had been able to achieve this and the world had yet to wait for eternal peace. Hence, he called on the Jews to become a nation.

Pinsker traveled to Western Europe and talked about his ideas with Jewish leaders but found little sympathy—they were far more optimistic concerning the future of Jews in Europe. They advised him to publish his thoughts, which he did in "Autoemancipation." He died soon after and did not clarify how he envisaged the Jews becoming again a nation; his appeal was made years before political Zionism appeared on the scene.

Pinsker's views became part and parcel of official Zionist ideology —the assumption that, while reprehensible, antisemitism was in some ways a "natural" phenomenon given the anomaly of Jewish political and social existence in the diaspora, the prevailing xenophobia, and social and economic tensions. And it was also true that the conditions of Jews in Eastern Europe where most of them lived were miserable and Jewish existence undignified. Persecution and oppression over many centuries had had a negative impact on Jewish character and behavior. There was an objective "Jewish question" in countries such as Poland; this was not the invention of malevolent antisemites. Radical Zionists advocated the "negation of the diaspora," the exodus of European Jewry, at least from those countries where the Jewish question was most acute. But in practical terms, given the limited absorptive capacity of Palestine, this was not a practical proposition.

Such pessimism was, for obvious reasons, more frequent among East Europeans Jews than in Western and Central Europe. There were, after all, no pogroms outside Russia but merely resistance against full emancipation. True, antisemitism had a major revival toward the end of the century and France had its Dreyfus scandal. The Dreyfus case induced Theodor Herzl to work for the establishment of a Jewish homeland and state. The Dreyfus case also persuaded Bernard Lazare, a French Jew whose family had lived in France since time immemorial, to change his views concerning the character of antisemitism.

While not a historian or sociologist or student of politics by profession, Lazare was one of the first to engage in a systematic study of antisemitism (*Antisemitism: Its History and Causes*, 1894). He disliked antisemitism, he said in his foreword, because it was a narrow and one-sided view, but he sought to account for it. It was after all not born without a cause. Following his research, he reached the conclusion that these causes resided in the Jews themselves, not in those who attacked them, because the Jew wherever he lived was a reclusive and unsociable being. According to their own law they could not accept the law of the land. Furthermore, the policy of the Talmud made them sullen, unsociable, and haughty; in the words of Spinoza—by their external rites, they had isolated themselves from all other nations, even to the extent of drawing upon themselves the hate of all mankind.

True, anti-Judaism from the seventeenth century on had changed its character inasmuch as the social motivation became gradually stronger than the religious hatred. In their majority the Jews remained "unproductive"—brokers, money lenders, usurers, and they could not be otherwise, given their habits and the circumstances under which they had lived. Lazare wrote his book with German and French Jewry in mind; his knowledge concerning Eastern Europe was scanty and third-hand; he believed, for instance, that while the Russian government was antisemitic, the Russians were not.

Thus, the real causes of antisemitism were political, economic, and social. However, as Lazare saw it, the Jewish personality tended to disappear when freed from hostile legislation and obscurantist Talmudism. Jews no longer believed that they were destined to remain a people having an eternal mission to fulfill. This could be a long process and in the meantime antisemitism was against its will acting as a progressive factor. Originally reactionary, it had become transformed and was acting for the advantage of the revolutionary cause. It stirred up the middle classes, the small tradesmen, and sometimes the peasants against the Jewish capitalists. In doing so, it gently led them toward socialism, infusing in them a hatred of all capitalists and, more than that, for capitalism in the abstract.

These then were Lazare's views in 1894 and it should not come as a surprise that his book is still sold even today in antisemitic bookshops in France, Britain, and other countries—a Jew, revealing the truth about his own people.

But only a few years later, Lazare became the first, and for a while most prominent, fighter for the rehabilitation of Captain Dreyfus, and he no longer believed in the progressive role of antisemitism. He was shocked above all by the fact that the attacks of the antisemites were directed not primarily against the new Jewish immigrants to France from Eastern Europe (whom he had earlier called contemptible and useless) but against those fully emancipated Jews who had lived in France for many generations. It showed that emancipation was not working and that the Jews, scattered among other peoples, were bound to attract hostility. This led him to the belief in a Jewish nation and even in Zionism.

At about the same time that Lazare suffered his bitter disappointment, a document was fabricated (possibly in France) to which we shall have to return later on—*The Protocols of the Elders of Zion*, which became the bible of antisemitism in the twentieth century. This document had little to do with religious hatred and did not propagate a racialist science; it revealed, no more and no less, the idea of a Jewish conspiracy to conquer and rule the world. However, it is also true that before World War One the influence of the *Protocols* was limited to certain circles in czarist Russia—no one outside of Russia had heard about it or would have been ready to give much credence to its message. In the years before 1914 there was (as pointed out earlier) the general belief among Jews in Europe and America that gradually reason and harmony would prevail; only a very few accepted the analysis of antisemitism shared by Pinsker, Herzl, and Lazare.

Pogroms again took place in Russia from 1904 to 1906, but even there the belief prevailed that the "objective" Jewish question would somehow be resolved—by emigration, the gradual emancipation of the Jews, and their ensuing transformation into a "productive people."

In the writings of the antisemites at the time there was a tone of despair—why was there so little willingness on the part of the population to accept their message and to realize how great the Jewish peril was? Only the war changed all this; in Germany the Jews were accused of shirking their patriotic duties fighting at the war front, but above all it was the impact of the Bolshevik revolution in Russia and the threat of further Communist revolutions in Central Europe (Hungary, Bavaria) that gave a great impetus to the spread of antisemitism.

The stories about a Jewish world conspiracy which had been dismissed a few years earlier now received much greater credence. Many of the leaders of world revolution were of Jewish origin; the fact that they had wholly distanced themselves from their religion and community mattered little. These revolutionary leaders did not regard themselves as Jews but as soldiers in the army of world revolution, yet this was not the way others saw them. Nor did it matter that in the 1920s and 1930s, with the victory of Stalin over Trotsky, Jews were squeezed out of the leadership of the Communist party. The stereotype of the Jewish revolutionary as a ferment of decomposition had grown deep roots and, if need be, Stalin could be made a Jew or at least a hatchet man of Lazar Kaganovitch, allegedly the real force behind the scenes.

There was a new wave of pogroms immediately after the First World War especially in the Ukraine, and later on radical antisemitic parties appeared, such as the Nazis in Germany but also in countries such as Romania and Hungary. Anti-Jewish legislation was passed in several East European countries.

Even though antisemitism became a political factor of great importance after World War One, there were no significant new attempts at trying to explain it. A few fine books were published about the demonization of the Jews in the Middle Ages (see J. Trachtenberg, *The Devil and the Jews*). The Zionists continued to point to the existence of an "objective Jewish problem" in Eastern Europe and, with the establishment of the British Mandate in Palestine, suggested emigration to that country. The Communists continued to argue that only with the world revolution would the Jewish question be solved; until then, they suggested Biro Bidzhan, a Soviet district in the Far East, as an alternative place for Jewish settlement. The liberals continued to hope that the upsurge of antisemitism, which after all had not affected all countries, would pass in due time. A few Christian theologians (James Parkes, Lukyn Williams, Peter Browe) showed interest and competence dealing with premodern antisemitism but their work did not have a great echo at the time.

A few historical studies on antisemitism and apologetic books and articles were published, but it was only with the Nazi takeover in Germany that a new impetus was given to the study of antisemitism. Hugo Valentin, a Swedish-Jewish historian, published a historical and sociological study that was translated into English and pirated by the Japanese in Manchuria; it became something like a standard text in the absence of other serious books.

Interest in the antisemitic phenomenon was displayed in other quarters hitherto not preoccupied with this topic, such as the circle later called the Frankfurt school of critical theory. This was a group of enlightened Marxists who found the Communist party line on the Jews too simplistic but still believed that the roots of antisemitism had to be found in the capitalist mode of production and bourgeois society. The Jews were mainly occupied in the sphere of circulation (they had been merchants and bankers) rather than production, and for this reason it was easier to make them responsible for all the shortcomings and sins of capitalism. These ideas were not altogether new; they had been expressed by the Zionists calling for the normalization of the Jewish social structure, the "return to the soil," etc. They were expressed in more academic language by Max Horkheimer and Theodor Adorno in a number of articles before and during the war and also in the framework of a general study of National Socialism by Franz Neumann (*Behemoth*).

How to explain that the Enlightenment had not made it clear who the real culprits were and why the antisemites had succeeded in deflecting the hatred of the oppressed from the real causes of their misery (displaced aggression)? For these questions historical materialism did not have an answer, hence the gradual turn from a Marxist "primacy of economics" point of view to psychoanalysis. This manifested itself above all in the famous study of the authoritarian personality undertaken by members of the Frankfurt school during the Second World War.

This study claimed that people tending toward antisemitism had a weak ego and felt dependent on authority of various kinds; they were conventional, repressive, and archaic in their attitudes, aggressive against strangers; they gravitated toward superstition and paranoia and believed in power and toughness. These findings were influential among a certain public but were not, however, accepted by leading students of antisemitism, who rejected them as too crude or simplistic and not in accordance with the historical facts. One of the weaknesses of the Frankfurt school interpretation was that, with a few exceptions such as Erich Fromm (who in the beginning was at its margins), they knew little about Jewish history and sociology; they had concepts and theories but not the factual knowledge to deal adequately with a complicated and multilayered subject. Furthermore, their knowledge was limited to a few countries—not those where most Jews lived. The study's yardstick, the baseline for the definition of an authoritarian personality, had been constructed in such a way as to show that antisemites were often found on the political right. This was true but had been known earlier; in addition, the Communists were also great believers in authority, as were many orthodox Jews and non-Jews. In brief, these findings on an authoritarian personality were not of great assistance on either a theoretical or a practical level.

An ambitious attempt to explain antisemitism was undertaken by Hannah Arendt, a German Jewish refugee, who was neither a Marxist nor a staunch believer in psychoanalysis. In earlier years she had shown little interest in Jewish history and antisemitism, a subject that she found boring. But the Nazi rise to power and her escape to France and America taught her differently, and in her magnum opus *The Origins of Totalitarianism* antisemitism became the cornerstone of her theory. Arendt dissociated herself from the two prevailing theories of antisemitism—the Jews as a scapegoat version on one hand and the eternal antisemitism concept on the other. Arendt argued that antisemitism was, at least partly, the fault of the Jews who had not resisted the attacks against them. But Arendt's idea that the Jews need not have become a scapegoat had they taken political action is not readily acceptable. How could the Jews take political action facing a hostile majority? How could they fight for their rights if they did not have armed forces?

"Eternal antisemitism" was something of a strawman because few serious scholars had ever argued along these lines. Herzl and the Zionists had not a priori excluded the possibility of a world without national conflicts and had conceded that, given a few generations of peace, assimilation might succeed in many countries. But they strongly doubted whether in Central and Eastern Europe the Jews would enjoy a closed season that long.

Hannah Arendt saw a basic difference between the earlier antisemitism of the nation-state and the far more dangerous and deadly antisemitism of the age of imperialism and the pan-movements. This thesis was widely discussed for a while but had little impact on the study of antisemitism. As John Gager, a leading scholar of early Christianity, wrote, the notion of an "unbridgeable chasm" between the modern world and antiquity or the Middle Ages ran against the grain of common sense and sound historiography. Furthermore, in the imperialist country par excellence (Great Britain) there was little antisemitism, and the connection between, for instance, Cecil Rhodes (who figured prominently in Arendt's work) and twentieth-century antisemitism was not readily obvious.

Nor was Arendt's critique of Sartre's existentialist interpretation of antisemitism quite convincing. Writing in 1944, Sartre had argued that a Jew was someone regarded and defined by others as a Jew. This, Arendt claimed, was the mirror image of what the Jewish parvenu thought: he wanted to be accepted by a society that rejected him. Success meant that he ceased to be a Jew the moment others no longer regarded him as such. But in many ways Sartre had only stated the obvious. And it was also true, as Sartre argued, that democrats were not unconditional friends of the Jews in their struggle; they were ready to support Jews but only if the Jews were willing to give up their Jewishness, be it religious or the feeling of belonging to a certain community. As Sartre put it, the democrat was willing to save the Jews as human beings but only if the Jew ceased to be a Jew.

While émigré political philosophers were speculating about the mainsprings of antisemitism, investigations by non-Jewish academics were infrequent. A rare exception was a volume published in the United States in 1942 whose contributors included Carl Friedrich and Talcott Parsons. Friedrich (like Hannah Arendt a few years later) stressed that the new antisemitism was different in character from the old, traditional religious intolerance and persecutions—but he had in mind its racialism rather than imperialism. The same point was emphasized by another book widely read during World War Two, Maurice Samuel's *Antisemitism*; Samuel pointed out that the earlier anti-Jewishness had its roots mainly in thinking badly of Jews whereas modern antisemitism was largely based on fear, suspicion, and even hallucinations of Jews as international plotters and corrupters.

Friedrich singled out several factors that were in his opinion of paramount importance—first, antisemitism as a manifestation of cultural decadence, that is to say the wearing thin of faithful belief in ethical norms—or to put it more starkly, a relapse into barbarism. This also referred to the profoundly anti-Christian nature of Nazism and its hostility toward civilization. Friedrich also mentioned the rise of pseudoscientific dogmas of a materialistic type (i.e., racialist theory) and the increasing dominance of the Jewish businessman in capitalist countries on one hand and the prominent role of Jews in left-wing revolutionary movements on the other.

Talcott Parsons emphasized the rabid character of German nationalism and the fact that the lower-middle class was particularly prone to embrace antisemitism. He based his theory in considerable part on the findings of the French sociologist Emile Durkheim concerning the "anomie" of modern society, meaning the disintegration of traditional social structures leading to a feeling of uncertainty and the urge to establish a close tie to the national collective (the folk, the nation). The Jews were everywhere in a minority (and minorities were never gladly received); the Jewish religious belief in being the chosen people had never contributed to their popularity.

Much of the academic effort at the time was descriptive in nature and centered around such questions as how to define the Jews—if they were not a people or a race, what were they, and also what could be done about antisemitism after the war? All this did not contribute greatly to clarifying why the new antisemitism had arisen in the first place and why it had been far more virulent at some times (and in some countries) than in others—questions that confront the experts to this very day.

It is not surprising that the study of antisemitism during the war and the early postwar period focused on Germany, simply because it had been in that country that modern antisemitism had received its ideological underpinnings and that antisemitic practice, i.e., the Holocaust, had been most murderous. Thus, the debate about antisemitism turned into a debate about the mass murder of Jews carried out by Nazi Germany. This produced some pioneering studies about the origins of antisemitism in nineteenth- and early-twentieth-century Germany and Austria; over the years hardly a stone remained unturned in this field. The impact of the Holocaust on the study of antisemitism was obvious, probably inevitable, but there had been antisemitism both before and after, and there was the danger that the study of the Holocaust would not only overshadow the study of antisemitism but simplify and even distort it. It was only toward the end of the twentieth century that attention was again given to antisemitism in other parts of the world, including in the Islamic world, and to the analysis of the problem in general. There was a veritable explosion of studies on antisemitism. A bibliography on antisemitism published in the

1930s or 1940s would have comprised a few pages; a list covering the last ten years (1995–2004) enumerates 40,000 items.

As long as there has been antisemitism, attempts have been made to investigate its causes, though these were usually neither systematic nor very sophisticated. The earliest school of thought was the theological—the explanation of Jew hatred against the background of Jewish obstinacy and exclusiveness: they had crucified Jesus and refused to accept his teachings; they had refused to listen to Muhammed and accept Islam. This was a crucial factor over many centuries but it hardly explains antisemitism in modern times.

Social tensions and economic rivalries—the fact that Jews in many countries were on the margins of society and engaged in economic activities bound to provoke hatred and envy—were factors of undoubted importance. One obvious example from early modern history is the opposition and resentment of the non-Jewish urban population against Jews in Central and Eastern Europe who tried to enter the cities from which they had been expelled and to compete in urban occupations such as commerce and handicrafts.

Social tensions may explain antisemitism in nineteenth-century Russia and Poland. But antisemitism affected Jews irrespective of whether they were rich or poor, usurers or beggars. It explains neither the expulsions from Spain, France, Britain, and other countries nor the persecutions in Nazi Germany. It is not surprising that the rise of a wealthy court Jew such as Joseph Suess Oppenheimer in early-eighteenth-century Germany generated envy and ill will. But it has been estimated that at this time one-third of the Jews in Germany were peddlers and perhaps one-quarter were beggars, and they were not popular either even though no one wanted to share their fate.

Demographic factors have to be taken in account, such as the influx of Jews into big cities in the nineteenth century. In 1850, 9,000 Jews lived in Berlin but in 1925 their number had risen to 180,000; the figures for Vienna were even more striking—about 2,000 in 1850 and 200,000 in 1925. Vienna was a center of antisemitism, but Berlin was not, nor was Frankfurt, which had the second largest Jewish community in Germany. Antisemitism often received a fresh impetus at a time of economic crisis but even more frequently in a political crisis. And very often social and political crises had little or no effect on the fate of the Jews.

The psychological approach to explaining antisemitism (Jews as strangers, the dislike of the unlike, the authoritarian personality) is helpful in some instances but not in others—Jews were disliked when they were weak and when they were strong, when they made an effort to assimilate and when they stuck to their traditional beliefs and way of life. Nor does that approach explain the great intensity of antisemitism in some countries and ages and its weakness or absence in others. Sigmund Freud came to believe late in life that Jews were hated because there was much jealousy of the people who had committed prehistoric patricide (killing God, the father), pioneered monotheism, and believed themselves chosen by God. But this concept was not shared by many students of antisemitism, and what some of Freud's disciples had to say about narcissism and antisemitism, about the role of the superego and other analytical concepts was more or less ignored by students of antisemitism.

Was the key to antisemitism perhaps found in the specific (negative) character of a Jewish race? It is true that life in the ghetto and the *shtetl* produced certain common attributes and that oppression did not bring out the best in people. But the Jews are still not a race in any meaningful sense; the differences among them are enormous in every respect after two thousand years of life in the diaspora. Stereotypes about peoples and national character are seldom true, and they are even less true concerning the Jews.

All this does not mean that antisemitism is an impenetrable mystery and that there is no way to account for it. (It is a mystery only to the extent that the existence of peoples in general is.) But it does mean that there is no monocausal explanation, that in different times and places different factors were at play. At times anti-Jewish hostility was predominantly irrational, at other times it was quite rational, and usually there was interplay between these two. The motivation of the great medieval pogroms in Central Europe of 1096 (the First Crusade) and 1348–49 (the Black Death) was predominantly religious in character. But this does not explain why the Jewish communities in the Rhineland were attacked and those in France, where the movement had originated, were not. In both instances there was widespread plundering which tends to show that economic motives must have been involved. And since the crusaders also killed many thousands of other people on their way—Christians and Muslims—is it correct to consider the massacres of 1096 manifestations of antisemitism?

In Spain Jews could escape persecution by conversion, whereas in the massacres in the Ukraine in 1648–49 conversion made no difference. Were the attackers out to capture the souls of the Jews or their money? It is certain that in the two great pogroms (more perhaps in 1348 than in 1096) both religious fanaticism and social tensions were involved, but no one can say for certain how much of one and how much of the other.

The murder of millions of Jews in Europe during the Second World War had a crucial impact on the concept and interpretation of antisemitism. But this is a topic to which we shall return later on in this study, following a survey of the origins of antisemitism; more recent manifestations of this phenomenon cannot be understood without going back to its roots, the constant factors, and the mutations that occurred over the ages.

Chapter Three

ANCIENT AND MEDIEVAL ANTI-JUDAISM

THE HISTORY OF THE JEWISH DIASPORA begins a century or two before the destruction of the first temple (586 BCE), and the history of antisemitism dates more or less from that period. But historians have quarreled for a long time about whether it is appropriate to use the term "antisemitism" with its medieval and modern connotations when dealing with the pre-Christian era. There is very little we know about these early centuries and the sources are virtually all Jewish, such as the book of Esther in the Old Testament, which reports a failed intrigue by Haman to have all the Jews liquidated: "And Haman said unto king Ahasuerus: There is a certain people scattered abroad and dispersed among the people in all the provinces of thy kingdom; and their laws are diverse from all people; neither keep they the king's laws: therefore it is not for the king's profit to suffer them." The accusation was to occur many times throughout history.

Nor has a single text reached us in the original and there is, to put it cautiously, at least a strong suspicion that those who copied them over the ages "edited" or even rewrote them. The first recorded incident of a major anti-Jewish action is the destruction of the Jewish temple in Elephantine, the Egyptian military colony in 410 BCE. But we know only that the temple was destroyed and can only speculate why. It could have been a political-religious conflict. The Egyptian priests were opposed to the burnt offerings in the Jewish temple and to the Jewish cult in general. It could have been that the Persians, the undisputed masters of the region, treated the Jews living in Egypt more leniently and that this provoked resentment among the Egyptians. But it is equally likely that the Elephantine accident had mainly to do with property conflicts.

That Egypt certainly remained the focus of anti-Jewish feeling during the following centuries emerges from the writings of two historians of the third century BCE—Theophrast, a Greek from the island of Lesbos, and Manetho, a priest at the Egyptian temple at Heliopolis. The former refers to the sacrifice of living animals by the Jews; the latter had been commissioned to write a Greek history of Egypt (of which only a very small part has survived) in which he refers to the age-old Egyptian-Jewish hostility. Manetho deals with the story of the expulsion of Jews from Egypt in a counterversion to the book of Exodus. The Jews were shepherds, a savage people with strange, intolerant customs such as praying to one god only, ignoring or rejecting the Egyptian gods. They did not accept Egyptian customs, kept to themselves, and were lepers. Here the exodus was not a flight for freedom as the Bible described it but an outcasting of negative, impious, and diseased elements.

But Manetho wrote some seven hundred years after the event and what we know about his writings are paraphrases quoted by Josephus Flavius who wrote yet another three hundred years later. Josephus had been a leading politician and military commander in Judea and later joined the Romans and became the chief historian of his period. Nonetheless, according to these paraphrases, many essential questions remain open—whether these lepers were Egyptians or foreigners, and if they were foreigners, were they Jews? Was it a case of xenophobia and ethnic cleansing, to use the language of a later age? These and many other issues are unresolved.

Most historians agree that antisemitism during the whole Hellenistic period existed but was not a paramount issue.

It was only during the Roman period that more detailed and apparently more reliable news has reached us—again through the good offices of Josephus Flavius—and it concerns the city of Alexandria, in which there was a sizable Jewish community. The main antisemitic ideologue of the period was a certain Apion who claimed that the Jews were praying to the head of a donkey displayed in their synagogues. This story may have been based on an even earlier legend that appears in the writings of a Greek historian, Diodorus Siculus, according to whom there was a statue in the holiest Jewish temple in Jerusalem that depicted a bearded man (Moses) on a donkey.

Be that as it may, hostility toward the Jews probably had little to do with the donkey or with the observation of the Sabbath or the ritual of circumcision (which at the time was by no means limited to the Jews) that Apion derided. The hostility has to be interpreted against the background of Jewish relations with the Romans ruling Egypt at the time. The Jews, temporarily at least, enjoyed better treatment from the rulers than the Egyptians and this was bound to create resentment. There were pogroms and riots in Alexandria in the time of the emperor Caligula (38 CE). It is also true that the citizens of Alexandria and above all the Greeks refused to grant the Jews full citizenship rights. The Roman emperor Claudius told the Jews that they should be satisfied with the freedom to live and pray and work but should not claim the rights of fully fledged citizens.

By and large, however, antisemitism during this period was mainly literary in character. The question then arises whether what we know about attacks verbal, literary, and sometimes physical against Jews during the pagan period amounts to more or less normal xenophobia or whether there more was involved.

We do know about a number of Greek writers such as Lysimachus, Posidonius, Apolonius Molon, and Haecateus of Abdera who wrote about the Jews (Haecateus allegedly wrote a whole book). Apolonius

Molon called Moses an impostor and noted that the Jews had contributed nothing to human civilization. But again all we have from him
are a few fragments; by and large it is astonishing that the Greek
historians and geographers (except those living in Egypt) who wrote
about small and distant ethnic groups wrote so little about the Jews
whom they undoubtedly encountered—not only in Egypt. In these
writings the same themes always recur and there is much reason to
believe that these writers copied each other. The exodus from Egypt
was a common thread (the Bible had been translated into Greek in the
meantime). Jews were described as lepers and suspect strangers because they did not pray to the same gods as others but exclusively to
their own. They were considered misanthropic because they disliked
and hated all people outside their community. They were also attacked
because of human and animal sacrifices.

Negative judgments about other people can be found at random in
the ancient world. As the historian Zvi Yavetz notes, natives of Crete
(and of Sardinia) were described as inveterate liars, Egyptians as vil-
lains, Boeotians as drunkards. Syrians were said to have a slave
mentality, those from Abdera were referred to as fools. All of them
were barbarians and the question arises whether the Jews were somehow depicted in a more negative light than the other barbarians. On
this opinions diverge; some historians of antiquity maintain that up to
the Maccabean struggle and the rise of the Hasmoneans (that is to
say, the expansion of the Jewish state in the second century BCE),
there was virtually no negative anti-Jewish comment in Greek. Others find this interpretation too categorical.

In Roman literature the Jewish religion is consistently described as
a form of superstition (principally by Quintilianus and Tacitus). Cicero
also feared that the Jews had too much influence and that their religion
was incompatible with the Roman values and traditions and would bring
about general degeneration. Seneca (the younger) expresses contempt
for the Jews and was worried about Jewish missionary activities. Traditionally Jews did not go out of their way to make converts; but

apparently—also according to other authors—there were Jewish missionary activities in Rome and conversions to the Jewish religion even in the higher strata of Roman society, and these caused Seneca's misgivings. He was particularly annoyed by the ritual of the Sabbath; this meant that the Jews were wasting one-seventh of their lives doing nothing.

Petronius was a satirist, and he poked fun at the ritual of circumcision and at the Jewish custom of males letting their hair grow longer than Romans and Greeks did. He claimed that the Jews were praying to a "pig god"; why he should have believed this is not clear—perhaps he thought that since Jews were not eating pork, the animal must have been sacred to them. Other satirists, Martial and Juvenal among them, also focused on circumcision—which they found comic—and they referred as well to the attempt of some crypto-Jews to hide the fact that they had been circumcised. Juvenal wrote that there was a secret book originating from Moses and according to which Jews should not show a traveler the way unless he was a Jew too, nor should anyone but a coreligionist be guided to a water place. The Jews kept themselves apart from society and they were a strange element and therefore suspect.

By and large the attitude of the Romans was less hostile than that of the Egyptians and the Greeks. Tacitus, for instance, who had no liking for the Jews at all (calling their institutions sinister and shameful) put more of the responsibility for the rebellion of the Zealots on the local Roman proconsuls than on the Jewish insurgents. Tacitus and other Roman writers even showed some respect vis-à-vis the Jews for sticking to their old customs and traditions and knowing their meaning and origin—apparently in contrast to other Eastern cults.

The Romans thought the Jews a little stupid, willing to believe almost anything in contrast to the far more sophisticated and skeptical Greeks. It is certainly true that ancient Greece had produced a higher civilization, and that there was little in the Jewish heritage at the time comparable to Greek literature, science, and philosophy. There were, of course, the books of the Hebrew Bible but they were less widely known than Greek philosophy. The Romans were not impressed by Jewish monotheism; on the contrary, they regarded it is as intolerant and regressive.

They were not altogether certain about the origin of the Jews, for which Tacitus reports no less than six different versions. But Tacitus tended to subscribe to the story of the lepers' exodus from Egypt and even the adoration of the donkey's head. He believed, perhaps correctly, that Jews did not eat pork because the Jews suspected that pigs were transmitters of diseases from which they had once suffered. What bothered Tacitus above all was the clannishness of the Jews, the fact that they behaved well to each other but not to outsiders. They were lustful according to his account but did not sleep with non-Jewish women.

The fact that they refused to worship the Roman emperors and, generally speaking, refused to accept Roman customs only aggravated the situation. But Tacitus seems to have been perfectly willing to tolerate the Jews if they would accept the blessings of Greek and Roman civilization. Educated Jews willing to assimilate were welcome but not the others. All things considered, the Jews constituted a certain danger to Roman society, its values and traditions, because for reasons not entirely clear some Romans seemed to be willing to accept Jewish customs and rituals, such as observing the Sabbath and circumcision.

Intellectual anti-Judaism apart, Jews were for a long time not badly treated in Rome, with some notable exceptions such as the expulsion of 4,000 of them under Tiberius, following the rebellion in Galilee. But the Jewish zealots in Palestine were anti-Roman fanatics, and the Romans, who were well aware of this hostility, suspected and disliked them. Thousands of Jews in Alexandria were killed by Roman soldiers, although earlier on Rome had shown more benevolence toward Jews than Greeks in that city. Roman Jews had to pay a special tax, the *fiscus judaicus*. Such fines were not unusual and, generally speaking, persecution of Christians on the part of both the authorities and the plebeians was far more pronounced. Economic rivalry did not play a role; there were hardly any Jewish bankers at the time. Contemporary historians of Jews and anti-Judaism in the ancient world are divided in their overall judgment. One ("functionalist") school of thought tends to believe that there was a basic difference between pagan (Egyptian, Greek, Roman) antagonism vis-à-vis the Jews and that later generated by Christianity, and that on the whole its importance should not be overrated. In fact, the question arises whether the term antisemitism is not misleading if applied to the pre-Christian world. Their hostility was neither extreme nor consistent; where it appeared in a rabid form (such as in Alexandria), it was political in character. The other ("essentialist") school of thought believes that the hostility went deeper and had to do with the very character of the Jews and the essence of Judaism. Some Greek authors, after all, regarded Jewish separateness not merely as a harmless and quaint affair but as a dangerous conspiracy against all mankind.

Seen in a wider perspective, however, these differences of opinion concern nuances rather basic issues. There is no doubt that the advent of Christianity and in particular its subsequent interpretation present the turning point in the history of antisemitism and the Jews.

Jesus Christ was a Jew and so were the apostles; originally he wanted to change Judaism, albeit in a radical way, not to create a new religion. He was the head of one of many small apocalyptic Jewish sects that existed at the time. There was no break with Jewish religious rituals, such as the observation of the Sabbath; this came only with the appearance of Paulus, who had not known Jesus. From this point on, Christianity was the new Israel. There was systematic vilification of the Jews beginning about a hundred years after the death of Christ, as in the work of Justin Martyr, who claimed that the destruction of the temple (by the Romans) was just punishment for the sins of the Jews and their perfidy. But the question that has preoccupied historians and theologians was and is to what extent the New Testament was anti-Jewish from the beginning or whether it was only interpreted as such by the church fathers several centuries later.

A few examples will have to suffice. Matthew relates how Pontius Pilate was quite literally washing his hands when confronted by the multitude demanding that Jesus be condemned to death: "And washed his hands before the multitude saying I am innocent of the blood of this innocent person, see ye. Then answered all the people and said: his blood be on us and our children" (Matt. 27:24-25). This seems to be a wholly conclusive self-condemnation, if the account was correct. But it is not wholly convincing. Pilate was known as a severe, harsh ruler and it is unlikely that he would have a Jew crucified just because some others wanted it, especially if he thought him innocent. In addition, the text is not entirely clear—a few words are missing and the expression "his blood be on us" was not meant to be an eternal curse. It appears more than once in the Bible and not necessarily in consequence of a murder. Nor does it concern all Jews but merely those assembled that day in Jerusalem.

Another example is Luke 13:34-35, which has been interpreted as a condemnation of all of Israel: "Oh Jerusalem, Jerusalem which killest the prophets and stonest them that are sent unto thee, how often would I have gathered thy children together, as a hen her brood under her wings and ye would not. Behold your house is left unto you desolate. . . ." This, too, has been interpreted as an eternal curse by later commentators, but such threats (or predictions) can be found by earlier prophets such as Jeremiah. Prophets in Israel were seldom received with open arms and Stephanus, a follower of Jesus, was not quite wrong when he said "which of the prophets have not your fathers persecuted? Ye stiff necked and uncircumcised in heart and ears. Ye do always resist the Holy Ghost . . ." (Acts 7:52).

These inner Jewish disputes were exceedingly bitter and the language ("murderers," "betrayers," "followers of Satan") very abusive. Of all the sections of the New Testament, Revelation is the most outspoken, with frequent references to the "synagogue of Satan." In the gospel of John, Pilate is exculpated as far as the crucifixion is concerned, and the guilt is put on the Jews. The idea of a Jewish Antichrist, which played such an crucial role in the Middle Ages, goes back to John and his later interpreters. According to them, the Jews were a useless people, odious to God; furthermore, the Antichrist which would compel the whole world to obey the Jewish law would arise from among them (the tribe of Dan, to be precise). Other interpreters have argued that the original reference was not really to Jews but to those who claim to be Jews but really were Satan's followers, and that the church fathers hated heretics even more than Jews. But this is not quite convincing since there were too many references to the Jew as the enemy, the synagogue a congregation of animals. The church fathers certainly did make an enormous contribution to the development of Judeophobia.

Hostility became sharper with every generation of early Christian interpreters: God had rejected the people he had originally selected; the Torah was no longer legitimate; the Jews had sinned and fallen; in brief, God hated them. This appears most strikingly in the writings of the church fathers from the third to the fifth century after Christ. Many of them are forgotten today; others, like St. Augustine, are considered central figures in Christian theology.

Mention has been made of Justin Martyr, the first in a long row of such churchmen; he was followed by Origen, bishop of Alexandria, who preached that the Jews had committed the most abominable crimes and that as a punishment the city where Jesus had suffered was destroyed and the Jews dispersed. The most violent language was used by John Chrysostom in the fourth century. The synagogue, he said, was worse than a brothel and a drinking shop; it was a den of scoundrels, the repair of wild beasts, a temple of demons, the refuge of brigands and debauchees, and the cavern of devils, a criminal assembly of the assassins of Christ. It was an abyss of perdition. Following these and similar pronouncements, it came as no surprise when he finally declared that he hated the synagogue and the Jews. The Jews alone, not the Romans, were responsible for the murder of Christ; they were killing children (Socrates of Constantinople); they were pigs, stinking of garlic (Efraim the Syrian). Absolving Pilate from guilt may have been connected with the missionary activities of early Christianity in Rome and the desire not to antagonize those they wanted to convert.

But even more moderate churchmen, such as St. Augustine of Hippo (North Africa), showed little of Christian love and charity; he wrote, "How I wish that you would slay them (the Jews) with your two-edged sword, so that there should be none to oppose your word . . . Gladly would I have them die to themselves. . . ." St. Augustine also wrote that Judas Iscariot, the traitor, was the true image of the Hebrews and that the Jews would forever bear the guilt for the death of Jesus.

These pronouncements became in later centuries a source of inspiration to antisemites and also to the Nazis who otherwise had not much patience with Christianity. St. John Chrysostom was frequently quoted and reprinted in the Third Reich as a witness for the prosecution; after the Holocaust, this became an embarrassment for the church and attempts were made to explain their words in the historical context. It was said that the general discourse at the time was aggressive, brutal, and extreme. At a time of struggle for survival and recognition, Christian forgiveness and salvation were not in demand. These anti-Jewish attacks continued and grew even sharper after Christianity had become a state religion in the Roman empire.

It was also argued that these attacks were frequently directed not against Jews but Judaizers, that is, Christian sectarians who had not completely broken with the Jewish religion and continued to pray in synagogues. But more often the Jews were directly attacked. And it was said that the Talmud, which was composed between 400 and 600 CE, contained outspoken anti-Christian statements. This issue will occupy us later in this study because the Talmud was to play a crucial role in subsequent ages in antisemitic propaganda. That such statements can be easily found in the Talmud is perfectly true but they were mainly defensive, prescribing that no help should be extended to their persecutors and tormentors.

Could the attacks of the church fathers against Judaism and the Jews be explained as a result of political rivalry? Both groups were engaged in missionary activities among the pagans and the Christians, and the early Christians felt the necessity to distance themselves as much as possible from the religion from which they had originated. This could well have been an important motive albeit not the only one. For Jewish missionary activity ended with Constantine's edicts and the laws of 315 to 339 which made Christianity the state religion, and as a result, Jewish missionary activity became a criminal offense.

John Chrysostom, the most aggressive of the anti-Jewish spokesmen with his eight sermons against the Jews, belongs to a later period in which there was no competition to fear. Some authors believe that the anti-Jewish propaganda was somehow connected with the fact that, in a few instances, Jews may have made common cause with the pagans (the Romans) in the persecution of the early Christians. But it is doubtful that such cooperation took place on a significant scale; on the contrary, there are more references to common Jewish-Christian interests during the age of Roman persecution.

Yet other theologians stress that among the church fathers not a few obscurantist statements can be found, for instance with regard to women, but that this should be interpreted not by modern standards but against the general cultural level of a dark age. Even if most of the church fathers became saints, they were not infallible; it would have been easiest to dissociate Christianity from the Old Testament—as the "Deutsche Christen" did in the Nazi era. But this for a great variety of theological reasons was quite impossible, not only because the Messiah had arisen from the house of David but because Christianity was so deeply rooted in the Old Testament. And so a consensus was reached that, with all their shortcomings and sins, the Jews had been the chosen people up to the time of Christ but that they forfeited the role by rejecting Jesus and his message.

Lastly, it was argued that even if Christian writers denied that Jews were human beings but were, instead, wild beasts, as did Peter the Venerable, (who nonetheless was called by his contemporaries the meekest of men), they should not be killed but only consigned to a life worse than death—greater torment and ignominy. This leads to a central question, namely whether and to what extent did the anti-Jewish preaching lead to violence and ultimately to murder.

There had been physical persecution of the Jews under the Roman emperors; reading the Torah, practicing circumcision, etc. were banned in the year 135 CE, and Judaism ceased to be a legal religion. But these strictures were limited and temporary, and were restricted to the land of Palestine. This changed in the fourth century; under Constantine— Jews were forbidden to live in Jerusalem (315 CE). Even earlier, mixed marriages and sexual intercourse had been forbidden, and in 337 these became punishable by death. The first case of burning a synagogue following a local anti-Jewish campaign occurred in 388 in Kallinikon in Mesopotamia. Emperor Theodosius wanted the culprits punished and to pay for the restoration. But Ambrosius, bishop of Milan, persuaded the emperor that this had been an action pleasing to god, something akin to divine punishment.

St. Cyril, bishop of Alexandria, had the Jews expelled from this city, and the Byzantine emperor Justinian I prohibited reading the Bible in Hebrew, building synagogues, and Jews' assembling in public. The Synod of Claremont in 535 decreed that Jews could not hold public office; in the fifth century Jews were expelled from parts of France, and in 613 Jews in Spain had to either embrace Christianity or leave the country. Pope Leo III outlawed Judaism and in 855 the Jews were exiled from Italy.

The list could easily be prolonged. But it is also true that, in part, these decrees remained a dead letter, because some Jews did stay on and the old orders had to be restated from time to time. If the church

council of Toledo in 697 decreed that Jews were to be held in perpetual slavery, this was not general practice in reality. In any case,
following the spread of Islam, most Jews lived under Islamic rather
than Christian rule.

Furthermore, while the rulers had become Christian, Christianity
had not yet become the religion of the masses and there were few
instances of popular anti-Judaism. Seen in historical perspective, the
situation of the Jews in Europe was not too bad up to the First Crusade. From the seventh to the eleventh century, there were attacks
against Jews on the part of popes and bishops, some Visigoth kings
were inclined to be friendlier than others, and there were various forms
of pressure such as compulsory conversion. But by and large, the
position of Jews in Western and Central Europe under the Carolingian
dynasty improved as manifested in the spread of Jewish communities
in various countries. Jews fulfilled an important function as international traders and bankers. In many places, they had special rights
and enjoyed the protection of ecclesiastic and secular authorities. There
was a fair amount of intermarriage, and they could own land and carry
arms. Their numbers were not large but they were needed in society
as merchants and bankers, and while the road to leading positions in
public life was barred, there were not a few wealthy Jews who caused,
as far as can be established, resentment on part of the bishops rather
than the common people. Generally speaking, there is little evidence
of popular antisemitism during this period.

What concerns us in the present context, however, is not the effi-
ciency of the persecutors but their intentions, and in this respect there
can be little doubt. Anti-Jewish preaching continued. Some of the
bishops, such as Agobard of Lyons, complained that the Jews were
living too well, that they had domestics and other servants who were
observing the Sabbath with the Jews and violating Sunday. There
was even a danger of conversion because Judaism still had a certain
attraction. There were physical attacks against Jewish communities
in France and Germany when news spread that Jews collaborating

with Muslims were responsible for the persecution of Christians in the Holy Land, the destruction of the Holy Sepulcher, and the beheading of the patriarch of Jerusalem.

But these were short-lived, sporadic interludes. Only with the First Crusade in 1096 did a rapid and dramatic deterioration set in. Pope Urban II called in November 1095 for a religious military crusade to liberate the holiest places in Christendom that had been conquered and desecrated by the Muslims. This appeal had an enormous echo; masses of people were shouting "*dieu le veut*" (It is God's will). But the crusade proceeded not quite in the way the pope had envisaged. Instead of an orderly army under papal command, all kinds of private militias gathered. Obscure rabble-rousers like Peter the Hermit were preaching to the masses in Germany and enlisted people quite unsuitable for any military expedition. Once they confronted Islamic regular forces, they were defeated in no time. Subsequently there was an even more ill-starred children's crusade and a French shepherds' crusade.

As the crusaders made their way from France to the Holy Land by way of Germany, Austria, and Byzantium, they killed thousands of Jews. Some of the motivation was theological, for they had been told that anyone who killed a single Jew would have all his sins absolved. But there was also the element of blackmail and plundering. French Jewish communities paid the priest Peter the Hermit protection money and were left in peace. In the Rhineland the Jews were less lucky; whole Jewish communities such as those in Cologne, Mainz, and Worms were destroyed, and three thousand people were killed. Many Jews committed suicide rather than fall into the hands of the murderous bands. Some of the authorities—the local bishops and citizens (burghers)—tried to give some protection but often half-heartedly and not effectively. For the Jews of Central and Western Europe, these attacks became a great trauma, perhaps because they had been so sudden and unexpected, or perhaps because earlier persecution had been mainly in the form of bans and restrictions imposed from above. The massacres of 1096 were seemingly spontaneous, not instigated by the authorities but carried out by the mob.

What was the place of these attacks in the history of anti-Jewish persecutions? Only a tiny part of the Jewish people lived in Northern Europe at the time and the communities that had been destroyed were reestablished in the years thereafter. The pope had certainly not intended to initiate mass pogroms at the time, and the key figure in the Second Crusade, Bernard of Clairvaux, denounced anti-Jewish violence. If so, what caused these anti-Jewish attacks?

Some Christian historians have stressed that the Middle Ages were a violent age and that mass murder (for instance, of Christian heretics such as the Waldensians) was not infrequent. In the course of the crusades, not only Jews but a great many others, including Christians, were killed. All this is true and it stands to reason that the Jews, being marginal people in society, were an obvious target. It is also true that the later Middle Ages were a time of great political and social tensions, of a struggle for power between the papacy and the secular rulers, between the central power and the towns. It was an age of natural calamities, such as the Black Death, of mass migration, of religious fanaticism and superstition, and of all kinds of strange quasi-religious beliefs.

But the general climate created by the church also played an important role. According to church dogma, with its concept of Jewish servitude caused by their sins, the Jews were slaves of the Christians. The emperors usually interpreted this injunction by regarding Jews as "serfs of our Chamber" (or as in Spain, the property of the royal treasury), which meant they had to pay protection money and special taxes. Still, this attitude could be regarded as too liberal by the church. The popes were not in favor of the murder of Jews and on occasion spoke out against it. From a theological point of view, the survival of Jews was necessary—as a proof of the essential rightness of Christianity; their misery was to help to let the glory of Christ shine all the more.

Yet among the clergy, there were not a few who thought that the Jewish remnant was too large.

From time to time, the popes would declare that some of the grosser libels against the Jews—such as the ritual murder of Christian children and the poisoning of wells—were false. But the church also believed that love for the church had to manifest itself in hatred of the Jews. For a variety of reasons the church pressed for stricter and stricter discrimination against Jews, which was evident in the imposition of laws aimed at their further isolation. The Fourth Lateran Council in 1215 decided that Jews and Muslims should wear special dress—yellow badges in some places, horned hats in others. Pope Innocent III in 1205 wrote that the Jews through their own guilt were consigned to perpetual servitude, and Pope Gregory IX in 1236 ordered the confiscation of Hebrew books.

On the other hand, various popes insisted that Jews were not lawless but should be treated according to Roman law. The Jews were subservient and should not be attacked, unlike the Saracens, according to Alexander II early in the eleventh century. Nicholas IV, late in the thirteenth century, demanded strict punishment for Jews who aided conversion to Judaism, but at the same time denounced Christian attacks against Jews as long as Jews stuck to the rules, meaning as long as they accepted living in a state of servitude, wore the distinguishing marks imposed on them, and did not eat at a common table. Pope Clement VI even published a papal bull in 1348 against the persecution of the Jews that said the Black Death was not the fault of the Jews but divine punishment of sinning mankind.

There was a certain inconsistency on questions of detail: some Catholic theologians were in favor of forced conversion of Jewish children; others were against it. Some churchmen favored the expulsion of Jews from Belgium (1261), England (1290), France (1306 and 1394), Spain and Portugal (1492 and 1507); others did not make a stand on this issue. Some radicals (Capistrano for one) demanded the abolition of all rights to the Jews or fomented and carried out pogroms (the Flagellants); others distanced themselves from the violent persecution of the Jews.

Some Christian scholastics engaged in interesting hairsplitting—whether God, being all powerful, was responsible for the actions of the devil, whether Lucifer was a fallen angel or whether he had been evil from the creation, whether the Passion of Christ broke Satan's power. But these debates were far too abstract for the common people who knew from the New Testament that the Jews were children of Satan (whether the Antichrist himself was a Jew was a question left open). The Jews were not the only ones to be demonized by the church: witches, sorcerers, and various heretics were also included but the Jews usually took the place at the top. The devil had a far more central position in Christian religion than in most others, and his story appeared in countless sermons, books, plays, and medieval works of art on every level of sophistication. It was only natural that those receiving this message would reach the conclusion that if the devil was the creator and incarnation of evil, he had to be permanently fought. If Satan had to be expelled, so had his children—the Jews.

The church, in brief, created a certain image of the Jews that dominated the Middle Ages and that led to persecution, murder, and expulsion. The devil was taken by some as a metaphor, by others—including Luther—as a personal devil, just as there was a personal God. Other features of this image of the Jew in popular religion to which we next turn included the blood libel and the poisoning of wells.

The blood libel was the accusation that according to the Jewish religion, Christian infants or young children had to be abducted, abused, tortured, slaughtered, and their blood consumed (especially on the occasion of Passover) for religious purposes. One of the first recorded cases of this libel was that of St. William of Norwich (England) in 1144. According to Theobald, a former Jew who had become a monk, leading Jews (the forerunners of the Elders of Zion perhaps?) assembled each year in Narbonne, France, to decide what child should be killed. In the Norwich case, several local Jewish leaders were arrested and executed. Even more famous was the case of Hugh of Lincoln (England) in 1255. The body of a little boy had been found in a cesspool near the house of a Jew, who was arrested, tortured, and confessed. As a result, about a hundred Jews in the town were arrested; some were killed outright, some were tried and killed, others paid a ransom and were freed.

Altogether, there have been about 150 recorded cases of blood libel (not to mention thousands of rumors) that resulted in the arrest and killing of Jews throughout history, most of them in the Middle Ages. Initially, most cases occurred in England (Bury, Bristol, Winchester); they were subsequently also reported in France, Spain, Germany, and other countries. In almost every case, Jews were murdered, sometimes by a mob, sometimes following torture and a trial. The story of the murder of Christian children entered folklore (it appears in *Grimm's Fairy Tales*) and was exported to countries outside Europe; in the famous Damascus trial of 1840, the alleged victim was, however, not a child but an elderly Italian monk. We shall later return to the cases of blood libel that took place in the nineteenth century.

Pope Innocent IV appointed a committee to study the issue in 1247, and it was established that there was no truth to these allegations— and not only because Jewish law strictly forbid the consumption of blood. Gregory X in 1275 published a letter ordering that no Jew should be arrested under such silly pretexts. He further demanded that no Christian should "stir up anything against the Jews." He noted that blackmail had been involved in many cases—that the parents of these children or some other Christian enemies of these Jews had secretly hidden the children in order to injure the Jews so that they might extort money from them.

Pope Nicholas IV in 1291 issued a bull entitled "Orat mater ecclesia," announcing that the church would not tolerate Christian injury to Jews. Four other popes denounced the blood libel, but others took a more lenient view of overzealous preachers such as Capistrano, who continued to spread the malicious tale. In this age, the church was very powerful and if the popes would have threatened the Christian evildoers with Draconian punishment, they could have stopped the blood libel. But they did not want to go that far. During the centuries that followed, some of the alleged child victims of the Jews were beatified and canonized.

As late as 1881 *Civilta Cattolica*, the Rome-based Jesuit organ, tried to demonstrate that ritual murder was, after all, an integral part of the Jewish religion; the main innovation on this occasion was that the murder took place on Purim rather than on Passover. Some of the blood libel charges continued to the twentieth century. Such was the case with the martyrdom of Anderl von Rin, allegedly killed in 1462 near Innsbruck. In the seventeenth century this legend became the subject of a cult; pictures in the local church showed how the little child's throat was slit and the blood collected in a bowl. The pictures were finally removed five centuries later, in the 1990s, on the instructions of the local bishop. A similar, even better known, case was the one of St. Simon of Trent, Italy, where a Jewish doctor was said to have killed a two-and-a-half-year-old boy. The cult that grew around this tale was at last suppressed by the clerical authorities in 1965.

Another frequent reason for attacks against Jews was the alleged desecration of the Host, the bread or wafer used in the mass. The Fourth Lateran Council of 1215 adopted the doctrine of transubstantiation, i.e., the bread and wine used in the mass actually become converted into the body and blood of Christ. Groups of Jews in various European countries such as Germany, Poland, France, and Belgium were accused of stabbing the Host, forcing a nail through it, or misusing it in other ways. Arrested and tortured, they confessed and sometimes were burned. Persecutions on this charge, however, were less frequent than the blood libel cases and they occurred only infrequently after the Middle Ages.

Far more important for the history of antisemitism is the gradual development of the concept of the "Talmud Jew," which dates back,

broadly speaking, to the thirteenth century. Following the denunciation of a converted Jew named Nikolas Donin of La Rochelle, Pope
Gregory IX was informed in 1239 that the Jews were guided in their
practices not by the biblical injunctions and taboos as transmitted by
Moses in Sinai but by a monstrous collection of books entitled Talmud. Various committees were appointed, mainly in France; various
rabbis were invited to explain the charges against them. Eventually the
Paris theologians and jurists decided that the accusations were true and
the Talmud was ceremoniously burned in 1242. Parts of the Talmud
were translated into Latin and reissued, reprinted, and translated many
times; all these publications were approximate and incomplete simply because there were few experts at the time capable of dealing
with texts in Hebrew, let alone Aramaic—the language in which the
Babylonian Talmud had been written.

Over four centuries later, in the year 1700, a professor named Eisenmenger at the University of Bonn published a massive work (2,120
pages) in which he claimed to have unmasked the monstrosities of
the Talmud Jews. Eisenmenger knew the languages concerned and
his book became the bible of religious and post–religious antisemitism
for two centuries and more.

What were the specific accusations? Mainly, it was alleged that
the Talmud was full of blasphemous statements about God, Jesus, the
holy Virgin, and Christianity in general. It superseded the Bible and it
claimed that the rabbi-interpreters were wiser and cleverer than God.
Furthermore, it was alleged that the Talmud justified any crime committed by Jews against non-Jews. Jews were not only permitted to
defraud, betray, and even kill the gentiles, it was their sacred duty.
Nor was it sufficient to refrain from helping non-Jews in an emer-
gency; one should actively work toward their perdition. Everything
should be done to deceive the dumb gentiles who were outside the
protection of the Talmudic law. It was allegedly written in the Talmud
that Adam had sexual intercourse with every animal in the garden of
Eden and that the Jews should eat excrement as a medicine against

pleurisy. Even the best of the gentiles should be killed—one who was observing the Sabbath deserved death, as did one who was studying the Bible (this, despite the fact that Eisenmenger had been greatly helped in his work studying the Bible by a variety of rabbis, who were not aware of his intentions). All strangers were Amalekites, the most bitter enemies of the Jews. In brief, the Jews were permitted to lie, to perjure themselves, to be disloyal to every non-Jew, to cheat authority, to steal, to rob, to commit every possible crime, to defraud others, to cause the greatest possible harm to non-Jews, according to Eisenmenger.

It was obvious that a book containing such monstrous teachings should be destroyed and that the persecution of the people who had accepted these criminal guidelines should be intensified. The Jews were the enemies of God and of mankind. The church had not initiated the "Talmud Jew" concept, but it accepted it since it confirmed all their suspicions about the Jews. The lower clergy was particularly active in spreading the message about the enemies of Christ and the Christians that had allegedly been uncovered.

In the present context all that need be said about the Talmud, written between the fourth and sixth centuries, is that it contains many statements that seem outrageous or ridiculous from today's perspective but not more than other theological works of that period. Equally outrageous statements can also be found in the works of the church fathers and in the hadith, the interpretations of the Koran. In any case, the Talmud was never a secret document; although it was banned and burned on various occasions by the church, it was published in 1520 by Daniel Bomberg in Venice under the protection of papal privilege. The Talmud was also published in Switzerland in 1578–81, as well as in Wilna, Lublin, and in other European cities. Some of these editions from the late Middle Ages were expurgated, omitting, for instance, attacks against Christianity—but they were expurgated also because of the very length of the Talmud; modern editions such as the Soncino run to more than 12,000 pages, and fill many CD-Roms.

Whatever the sins of commission or omission of the Talmud, secrecy was not among them.

This image of the Jew created (or rather refurbished) in the late Middle Ages provides the general background of the particularly violent persecution that took place during the period of the Black Death (1347–61) which felled about one-third of the population of Europe and virtually destroyed German Jewry. The plague was endemic in various parts of the world such as the Far East, and it was believed to have been brought to Europe by Genoese ships sailing from the Far East to Messina. In 1348 it reached France by way of Marseilles, and in the summer months of that year it spread to London, Germany, Hungary, and other countries. It had a disastrous effect, killing some twenty-five million people in Europe. In the larger cities the death rate is estimated to have been between 30 and 60 percent; elsewhere the death rate estimates range between 20 and 100 percent.

No one had the faintest idea what caused the epidemic and how it spread, and there were of course no drugs to prevent or stem it (the plague bacillus would not be discovered until the middle of the nineteenth century). It was an unprecedented trauma—physicians refused to attend to the sick, priests refused to give the last rites to the dying. There were mass flights from areas that had been infected, often to no avail. Jews were suspected of having caused the disease even though Jews suffered as much from it as the rest of the population—and the pandemic continued even after Jewish communities had been destroyed. Jews were arrested and tortured, and admitted everything the authorities wanted to hear.

One well-known incident was the evidence of Agimet, a Jew from Geneva, who confessed that he had been sent to Venice by Rabbi Peyret of Chambray, who had given him a parcel of poison to spread in the wells, cisterns, and springs in and around Venice. From Venice he went to Calabria and Apulia to cause further damage. He also said that he had spread poison in the wells of Toulouse and other places in the South of France.

There had been earlier accusations of "poisoning the wells" during the age of the crusades, but since there were no epidemics at the time, these had been isolated cases. Nor had Jews been tortured and forced to confess that they had committed these acts out of hatred against Christianity and the Christians. There had been no confessions that all Jews knew about the plot and that it was planned and administered by a committee of twelve. In parts of the world where no Jews lived, other minorities were accused of spreading the disease, including Muslims and Christians, and in some cases priests and monks. But the Jews were by far the most numerous and most often accused. According to a more sophisticated version of the accusations, the Jews had perhaps not caused the outbreak of the disease, but they were certainly involved spreading it. This period became known in Jewish history as *emek ha'bacha* (the valley of tears).

The number of Jewish deaths is unknown but probably the majority of Jews of Central Europe, including whole communities, perished. They succumbed not only to the disease but as victims of persecutions that ensued. A few thousand Jews were killed in Mainz, two thousand in Strasbourg. Sixty large Jewish communities were destroyed; altogether 350 massacres were counted. This wave of mass murder caused the migrations from Western and Central Europe to the east, where earlier there had been few Jewish communities.

The church as such had no hand in these persecutions. In the regions where papal authority was strong (Avignon and Italy), Jews were not attacked, and in many cities the local authorities also tried to defend them albeit often ineffectually. Pope Clement VI spoke out several times against the popular belief that the Jews were to blame for the pestilence and he called it a divine punishment.

The attackers were what contemporary chroniclers called the "common people," that is, the poor and the riffraff. They were incited by the itinerant Flagellants, whipping themselves and torturing the flesh in a frenzy of fanaticism and hysteria. The Flagellants were not merely radical religious fanatics; they despised the priests who, they thought, lived a life of sin. The pope had initially taken a benevolent view of this movement, but he later declared them heretics because they placed themselves beyond the control of the church and rejected parts of the church ritual, such as the Eucharist.

There is much evidence that those attacking the Jews were motivated, as in the First Crusade, not only by fear and religious fervor but by greed and envy; there were countless cases of robbery and spoiling. As a contemporary chronicler wrote, the money in the hand of the Jews was also the poison that killed them. Had they been poor, they would not have been burned.

There were no mass attacks against "Jewish poisoners" after the period of the Black Death, but the accusation became part and parcel of antisemitic dogma and language. It appeared again in early 1953 in the form of the "doctor's plot" in Stalin's last days, when hundreds of Jewish physicians in the Soviet Union were arrested and some of them killed on the charge of having caused the death of prominent Communist leaders. Only the death of Stalin put an end to this campaign. Similar charges were made in the 1980s and 1990s in radical Arab nationalist and Muslim fundamentalist propaganda that accused the Jews of spreading AIDS and other infectious diseases.

AFTER THE TRIBULATIONS of the Middle Ages had passed, there was little change in the status of the Jews, certainly none for the better. There were fewer sporadic attacks from the general populace than in earlier centuries but more repression from the powerful authorities. In 1394 Jews were exiled for the second time from France. And 100,000 Jews were expelled from Spain in 1492 following the Christian reconquest of the Iberian peninsula, and later also from Portugal.

This period marked the establishment of ghettos, closed districts to which the Jews were confined, beginning in Venice in 1516. The Catholic Church took a leading part in the establishment of these ghettos. It was the age of the Inquisition which was set up to determine, among other things, whether conversions to Christianity were genuine. Jews were further restricted in their work and the professions they were permitted to exercise—trade with agricultural products and peddling in the countryside were not permitted—and it was perhaps no accident that Rome's ghetto was the last in Europe to be abolished in 1870.

Early in the sixteenth century, a baptised Jew named Johannes Pfefferkorn appealed to the clerical and secular authorities to ban and destroy the Talmud which, he argued, was the source of all evil motivating Jewish behavior. He denied, however, that Jews had engaged in ritual murder, and he protested against other forms of persecution of the Jews. Pfefferkorn's publication "The Mirror of the Jews" (1516) and his activities encountered the opposition of some Renaissance humanists such as Johann Reuchlin and Erasmus, who advocated greater religious tolerance. But the debate that raged for more than a decade made no difference as far as the legal and social status of the Jews was concerned. Nor did the advent of Protestantism have a positive impact.

Martin Luther at the beginning of his career had entertained hopes that the Jews would be converted to his new creed and stressed in particular that Jesus had been born a Jew—a fact frequently ignored in church discourse. But he did not win converts among the Jews and in later years turned sharply against them. His views are of considerable importance because they helped to shape the outlook of the Protestant churches up to the twentieth century, and his pamphlet entitled "The Jews and Their Lies" (1543) was frequently reprinted during the Nazi era.

Luther was a high-strung man who felt persecuted all his life by various kinds of demons; he believed in the power of prayer to make Satan disappear. But to be quite safe, he also threw inkpots at the satanic apparitions that came to visit him. No wonder therefore that Luther turned against the children of the devil, the Jews.

What shall we do, he asked, with this damned, rejected, blasphemous, accursed, evil, poisonous race. He observed that the Jews had been punished "a thousand times more than we might wish them," but all this seemed insufficient, and he made a number of practical suggestions about how to deal with them in his 1543 pamphlet. Their synagogues should be burned and whatever did not burn should be covered with dirt. Their homes should also be destroyed and they should all be put under one roof or stable so "that they realize that they are not masters in our land as they boast but miserable captives." They should be deprived of their prayer books and the Talmud, and their rabbis should be forbidden under threat of death to teach any more. They should not be given travel permits for they had no business to take them into the countryside. All roads should be closed to them and they should be forced to stay at home. Jews should not be protected by the authorities and everything should be done to free the world of this insufferable, devilish burden—"our plague, pestilence and misfortune."

Luther mentioned that he had heard about the poisoning of wells and the kidnapping and murder of children, and he tended to believe the allegations even if he was well aware that the Jews denied it. Hence, in conclusion, he proposed that the Jews be sent to parts of the world where there were no Christians for "the Turks and other pagans do not tolerate what we Christians endure from these venomous serpents."

The attitude of other Protestant reformers toward the Jews was more positive. For the Calvinists, the seed of Abraham was part of the body of Christ. The Jews were God's first-born, and the grace of divine calling could not be made void. On occasion, Calvin even expressed "great affection for the Jews" and said that "our differences with them were purely theological" (Calvin, *Commentaries*, vol. 19).

It was no accident that under Oliver Cromwell Jews were again permitted to settle in Britain—albeit against the resistance of the clergy and the merchants—and they found a shelter in the Netherlands after their expulsion from Spain.

No major changes occurred in the life of Central European Jewry between the sixteenth century and the emancipation in the nineteenth century. Although Jews had been originally merchants and bankers, they were squeezed out of these fields and engaged in marginal trades such as peddling their wares in villages and small-scale money lending and currency changing. A few Jews rose to wealth and prominence as court Jews (*Hofjuden*), helping kings and dukes to increase their revenues—which did not endear them to the population in general. They could not own land and most of the professions were closed to them by the town guilds.

Expulsions continued from time to time—for instance, the Bohemian Jews were expelled in the eighteenth century by Empress Maria Theresa, who suspected them to be enemy agents of Prussia. Even though the number of Jews in Germany was small, and even smaller in France and Britain, attitudes toward Jews did not change and antisemitic literature continued to appear. Whereas in the early Middle Ages there had been social intercourse between Jews and non-Jews in Europe (hence the papal injunctions against it), there was little if any after the fourteenth century.

The situation was different in Poland, where many Jews from Central Europe had found refuge following the persecutions. Until about the eighteenth century the situation of Jews in Poland was considerably better than in other European countries, despite attempts by religious radicals (such as Capistrano) to persuade the kings of Poland to abolish the rights and privileges of the Jews. To a large extent, the Jews in Poland constituted the urban middle class and were engaged in all kind of professions other than trading, including craftsmanship and even agriculture. According to a popular saying, Poland in the sixteenth and seventeenth centuries was a heaven for the Jews, a paradise for the nobles, and hell for the serfs. In the mid-seventeenth century about half a million Jews lived in Poland, more perhaps than in the rest of Europe taken together.

Jews served the Polish nobility, acting as their business agents and advisers. This made them vulnerable; in the Ukrainian Cossack uprising against the Polish overlords (1648) headed by Bohdan Chmielnicki, tens of thousands of Jews were killed because as close collaborators with the Poles, they had also become an object of hatred. The situation of the Jews in Poland began to deteriorate in the second half of the eighteenth century, resulting in their gradual impoverishment. They were gradually squeezed out of banking and also from major trade activities by the rising Polish urban middle class. The frequent wars taking place in Poland in the eighteenth century also played a negative role, compelling them to live in smaller communities and engage in more marginal professions. Eventually this led to mass emigration to Western Europe, and then mainly overseas in the nineteenth century. Accusations of blood libel and profanation, which had been rare earlier, began to appear.

By and large, it seems to be true that—as Leon Poliakov, the historian of antisemitism, put it—there was a considerable difference between antisemitism in Western and Eastern Europe. Whereas antisemitism in countries such as Germany was primarily theological in character, its roots in Poland were to a larger extent social. This has to do with sheer numbers—even before the persecutions and expulsions, the number of Jews in Germany (and *a fortiori* in France, Britain, and Italy) had been quite small; the Jews had been scapegoats rather than competitors. In Poland, the Ukraine, and Western Russia, on the other hand, the number of Jews was considerable. To put it in another way, while antisemitism in Western Europe was an ideological issue, in Eastern Europe it was, or became, an objective problem in view of sheer numbers. That the church—Catholic in Poland, Uniate in the Ukraine, Russian Orthodox in Russia—was not enamored with the Jews goes without saying, but the decisive factor was their sheer number—Jews in Western and Central Europe were counted in the thousands, whereas in Eastern Europe they numbered in the hundreds of thousands and later millions.

THIS SURVEY OF THE SOURCES of antisemitism has taken us to early modern history. Until fairly recently many historians tended to disregard the fact that during much of the Middle Ages, the majority of Jews lived not in European Christian societies but under the rule of Islam. With the spread of this new religion in the seventh and eighth centuries, Muslim rule extended from Spain to India and Central Asia, and eventually included the Balkans. To the extent that Jewish historians dealt with the fate of Oriental Jewry—the sources are not abundant—they did so to juxtapose the persecutions of Europe with the more fortunate experience of the Jews in the Orient. It is true that, for the most part, Jews under Muslim rule fared better than in Europe; there was a cultural flowering in Spain and Baghdad, the social and economic situation was better, and there were no massacres on the scale of the Black Death pogroms.

But this is not to say that Jews could feel free as citizens with equal rights, that Jews were not persecuted, and that there was no anti-Jewish feeling. This leads back to the basic Islamic writings, the Koran and the hadith. The Jews had committed no basic sin as in Christianity—the founder of the religion had not been killed by the Jews (even though, according to some later-day Islamic interpreters, Muhammad thought that he might have been poisoned by a Jewish woman). There was also the story of the Banu Qurayza, a Jewish tribe in Medina, who had refused to accept Muhammad's message and turned against him—he had them all killed. But mostly the Jews played a far smaller role in Islamic thought than in Christianity; they had been hostile to the prophet according to the Koran, but they had not killed him.

It is impossible to summarize the attitude of the Koran toward the Jews simply because the evidence is contradictory. It states repeatedly that Allah has cursed them on account of their unbelief, and that Allah is the enemy of the unbelievers. It says that the Jews of Medina, where Muhammad had taken refuge, had not only been defeated but humiliated, and that they were afflicted with humiliation and poverty and felt the wrath of God. The Jews were weak and were bound to remain weak: there was no particular reason to worry about them.

(The main enemy of Islam over the centuries was Christianity.) The Koran says that the Jews (and the Christians) falsified the message God had given them. It warns that most of them are evildoers and "you shall always discover treachery in them except a few of them." It says "do not take Jews and Christians for friends" and mentions in passing that Allah has transformed some of them into monkeys and pigs. It calls for the killing (beheading) of Jews and Christians (Sura 47:4–5). There is in the hadith the famous, often quoted story about the final struggle between Muslims and unbelievers, when a Jew will be hiding behind a rock and a tree and the rock will say "O Muslim there is a Jew behind me—come and kill him."

But it is also true that Islam accepted much of the Old Testament (as they interpreted it) and that there was less bitterness in Muslim polemics against Jews than against Christians, perhaps because, as Bernard Lewis has pointed out, the Jews were less significant and less of a competitor than the Christians. They were powerless and no danger. Jews and Christians much of the time enjoyed a protected status as People of the Book (the Bible); as dhimmis they had something like second-class citizenship. They had to pay a poll tax, something akin to protection money. But the hadith also said that according to the prophet, "He who robs a dhimmi or imposes on him more than he can bear—will have me as his opponent."

Jews could not as a rule attain public office (as usual there were a few notable exceptions), and there were occasional pogroms, such as in Granada in 1066. They had to dress in a certain way to make a clear difference between them and the Muslims. They were (in theory, if not always in practice) forbidden to ride horses and to bear arms— but this also applied to Christians. They were, however, permitted to ride on donkeys provided they did so side-saddled. They were persecuted under the Fatimids in Egypt and Palestine, under the Almohads in North Africa, and temporarily in Spain. There were expulsions from the Arab peninsula but fewer than in Christian lands.

There was nothing in Christian Europe comparable to the Golden Age in Spain, with its flowering of the arts and sciences in which the Jews played a prominent part. Or, to be precise, some Jews played a prominent part; the goldenness of the Golden Age and the extent of the Arab-Jewish symbiosis were often exaggerated in the nineteenth and early twentieth centuries. General attitudes toward Jews changed little over the centuries, at least on the level of doctrine. The Jews had their legally defined, rightful place in the society; there was a degree of tolerance as long as the Jews did not try to rise above their inferior status.

In reality, there were considerable differences as far as their treatment was concerned. Harsher attitudes prevailed in times of crisis and Jews fared on the whole less well among the Shi'a than among the Sunni. Their lot was better in Spain and the Near East than in North Africa and Central Asia. But one would look in vain for the sources of modern antisemitism in the medieval Islamic world. Persecution of Jews and massacres became more frequent in modern times—beginning in the late eighteenth century from Morocco to Persia. This had to do with the decline of the Muslim world (the decline also in self-confidence and tolerance), which strengthened xenophobia in general. It had to do with sudden outbursts of fanaticism (of which there had always been a strand in the Islamic tradition), but it had also to do with the importation of European antisemitic propaganda into Muslim lands.

IN SUMMARY, the persecution of the Jews in Europe continued throughout the late Middle Ages and beyond, while the situation of the Jews in Eastern Europe was better at the time than in Western, Central, and Southern Europe. The Chmielnicki massacre in which tens of thousands perished was not an exception; there simply was no systematic, state-supervised antisemitism in Eastern Europe as in Spain and Portugal. The Spanish persecutions culminated in the expulsion of 1492, when about 300,000 Jews were forced to leave the country unless they were willing to be baptized; Portugal followed suit a few years later. The Jews in these countries emigrated to Turkey, the Near East, and also to the Low Countries.

Conversion alone, however, did not necessarily solve the problem in Southern Europe. The Inquisition spent much time and energy—it continued to be active into the early nineteenth century—investigating whether conversions had been sincere and punishing the insincere. But even if the conversions had been sincere, Jews and their descendants were still barred from many professions, including public office, and from attending universities. This was based on the principle of purity of blood, a forerunner of the racialist antisemitism of the late nineteenth century. True, political and social practice at the time was not always in conformity with the doctrine. Ignacio de Loyola appointed a *converso* as his successor, and it was not too difficult to forge genealogies. In any case, only those of high birth had been registered in church and even among the nobility there had been a great deal of intermarriage over the ages. What matters in the final analysis is the fact that hatred of Jews came from both above and below and continued for a long time, even after no Jews were left on the Iberian peninsula.

Chapter Four

THE ENLIGHTENMENT AND AFTER

SLOW BUT IMPORTANT CHANGES took place in the social status of the Central European Jews in the late seventeenth and eighteenth centuries. Wealthy Jews could move out of the ghettos in Germany, and some of them became influential, the so-called Court Jews. Elsewhere in Europe, there were only a few ghettos in France, and none in Britain. During the age of the Enlightenment, voices were heard in Britain, France, and Germany advocating the emancipation of the Jews. The majority of European Jewry had moved from west to east at the time of the persecutions in the late Middle Ages; their fate would be determined by different forces.

While the leading thinkers of the Enlightenment fought for tolerance, their attitude toward the Jews was at the very least one of reserve. Voltaire had nothing but contempt for the Jews who, as he saw it, were intolerant and fanatical. As he put it on one occasion, "I would not be in the least surprised if these people would not some day become deadly to the human race." Attempts have been made to explain Voltaire's antisemitism against the background of his enmity to all established religion. What he wrote about Muhammad would certainly be interpreted in our time as an extreme case of Islamophobia.

Some commentators have argued that when Voltaire attacked the Jews he was really aiming at the Catholic church—but for political reasons could not be as outspoken. His general attitude toward the church establishment—*ecrasez l'infame*—is well known. But it does not explain the additional animus against the Jews, including the utter contempt for the Old Testament. Other leading figures of the Enlightenment were ready to make an exception for the educated Jews but not the bearded ones. There were, however, not many Jews at the time who had a good secular education.

By and large there was a built-in limit to the antisemitism of the French philosophers, for while preaching tolerance and humanism, they could not totally exclude the Jews. But they included them with a feeling of great disdain; as Paul-Henri Baron d'Holbach wrote, the Jewish character had been shaped by certain historical conditions, climate, and environment, and for the most part, these people were hopelessly foreign to Europe. He clearly underrated the eagerness and capacity of European Jewry to assimilate. The antisemitism of Voltaire—and other philosophes—was in some respects influenced by his attitude toward the Greeks and Romans, whom he admired and who had disliked this strange and zealous tribe which kept to itself and always emphasized its exclusivity. The Jews had remained, it was always pointed out, a state within a state, a nation within a nation. Voltaire's anti-Judaism was also based on Spinoza's critique of the Jewish religion. Spinoza and later rationalists had maintained (to simplify it) that the biblical stories were not to be trusted and that the Jewish religion in particular had become ossified.

Seen in historical perspective, the ideas of the Enlightenment led to the emancipation of the Jews, but they also contributed to the emergence of modern antisemitism, particularly in France. Count Clermont-Tonnerre in a famous speech declared that the Jews as individuals deserved everything, Jews as a nation, nothing. This was in part a concession to the members of the Assembly from Alsace Lorraine where most of the Ashkenazi Jews lived. The Assembly had argued that full rights should be given to the Jews only after they had adapted themselves to the norms of the society in which they lived. The emancipation of the Jews encountered resistance on the part of the Catholic church, the reactionaries, and some Jewish apostates who had become ultraorthodox Christians (such as the brothers Ratisbonne), but it became the law of the land under Napoleon, albeit with some delays. However, political and intellectual hostility to the Jews and their emancipation continued throughout the nineteenth century; it reached its apogee in France at the time of the Dreyfus trial.

Very often attacks against the Jews were combined with a campaign against Freemasons. Thus a new ideology was born—that of a conspiracy of evil carried out by Jews and Masons in close collaboration. This doctrine found supporters not only in France but also in Eastern Europe, even though there was little in common between these two groups. The Masons had no particular predilection for the Jews, and for orthodox Jews, adherence to a Masonic lodge was an abomination.

If there had been resistance to the emancipation of the Jews in France, there was considerably more of it in Germany and the lands of the Austro-Hungarian monarchy. The Napoleonic wars and the age of romanticism generated modern nationalism in Europe. Although there had been voices in Germany during the eighteenth century advocating the emancipation of Jews—Gotthold Lessing was the best known—there had been even more opposing it. Some of these were mainly theologically inspired; others expressed the fear that the character of the Jews was so negative as to make them virtually not reformable. Yet others adduced socioeconomic arguments—the Jews were incapable of engaging in productive labor and they would be a burden on society. Nor would Christian merchants be able to compete with the Jews in view of their close ties with other Jews inside and outside the country. Seen by these critics, Jewry was not so much a religious group but an exclusionist company that, being alien to society and the state, had no desire to give up its specific character.

These negative views about the Jews were shared by both populist pamphleteers and the leading German philosophers of the age. They were not in principle opposed to giving rights to the Jews, but they doubted whether the Jews were capable (as Johann Fichte put it) of changing their nature, as formed by their religion and their past, to achieve love of justice, love of man, and love of truth. He thought that the only way to achieve this was to decapitate them and to give them heads that did not contain Jewish ideas. Fichte claimed that the Jews were a state within a state and a very powerful one at that.

Kant was a milder man and less influenced by Christian religion (even though he defended it and thought it superior to all others). Still, he thought that old-style Judaism was not compatible with the morals of civilized society. He regarded Judaism as basically amoral: "The Palestinians living among us," he wrote, "have acquired not without reason the reputation of swindlers." However, he did not exclude the possibility that Jews could become full-fledged citizens if they underwent a basic, wholesale reform—in other words, if they gave up traditional Judaism and adopted Christianity, in practice if not in doctrine.

At the same time, other great German philosophers had their doubts about the consequences of conversion and assimilation—Judaism as they saw it was both less and more than a religion.

Hegel, the third of the great philosophers of that age, also thought Jews contemptible, beginning with Abraham, the first of the patriarchs. Judaism, according to Hegel, was not only unnatural and inhuman but had resulted in a petrified social system. Even Jesus had failed to liberate the Jews from their self-imposed limitations through his love. If the Jews had remained pariahs, it was simply a consequence of their beginnings as a group and their basic religious concepts.

Although in his later writings Hegel did not oppose the inclusion of Jews in society on the basis of equal rights, this was connected with his belief in the Prussian state, which had to treat all its subjects more or less equally. Neither Hegel nor Kant proposed that the Jews should be sent back to the ghetto forever, and they had esteem for a few emancipated Jews. Yet, on the philosophical level, their attitude remained hostile—the Jews were, as Johann Herder put it, an alien, Asian element in Europe. Herder called them corrupt, parasitic, and without honor. For this reason, even if the Jews were to be given equal rights, they should probably not become state officials or exercise any kind of authority over non-Jews. The day might come, Herder wrote, when no one in Europe would ask anymore whether a person was a Christian or a Jew—but this day was quite obviously in the very distant future.

The anti-Judaism of the great German philosophers was restrained by the impact of the principal ideas of the Enlightenment—human rights and tolerance. Such restraints applied to a much lesser extent (if at all) to the generation of romantic thinkers that followed them; their ideology was German-Christian, and while Jews, as they saw it, could change their religion, there was no such thing as conversion to being a German.

Among both the French philosophes and the German thinkers of the time there were some who took a less hostile attitude—Rousseau among the French, Schelling among the Germans—but they were the exception. To what extent was this negative judgment of the Jews explicable and justified? The condition of the Jews after centuries of persecutions and ghetto life was miserable, their contribution to European civilization, nonexistent. The accusations of the petrification of Jewish religion, of the unchanging ritual having all but squeezed out true religion and the religious impulse, were not unjustified; nor was the observation that Jews kept to themselves and tended to help and defend each other. Without such solidarity, the feeling of responsibility for each other, they would not have survived.

For most of these thinkers—Voltaire and Fichte perhaps excepted—Judaism was not a major issue. What surprises is the absence of Christian charity vis-à-vis a persecuted minority on the part of people who,

Deists or true Christians, prided themselves not just on a rational approach in contrast to the dark Middle Ages but also on their humanity and their love of their neighbors. The question of responsibility for the misery of the Jews did not occur to them.

With all this skepticism, the emancipation began even during the last days of absolutist rule. The most prominent instance of this was Austria, where Emperor Josef II had decreed his tolerance edict in 1781. This gave the Jews all the duties and some of the rights of other citizens. Following Josef's death, many of these laws were revoked and the Jews were given full equal status only after the revolutions of 1848. In Holland and England, emancipation had proceeded without much fanfare, though in England Jews could not enter state service or parliament prior to the abolition of the "Jewish oath" in 1832, and in Holland the guilds refused to give them membership for a long time. In the United States the constitution stated that no religious test should ever be required as a qualification for any office or public trust.

In Germany the emancipation of the Jews as decreed by Napoleon suffered severe setbacks during the era of reaction following the 1814 Congress of Vienna—in some cities, such as Frankfurt, Jews had to return to the ghetto; from a few others they were expelled. Anti-Jewish pamphlets mushroomed. There were small-scale riots (the Hep Hep disturbances of 1819—the origins and the meaning of the antisemitic Hep-Hep slogan remains unclear to this day); opposition by the church and the various professional associations and ideologues manifested itself in many ways. Only after the revolutions of 1848 did a decisive change in the legal status of the Jews take place.

There was opposition to the emancipation also in Slovakia and Hungary, where comparatively many Jews lived, and even the liberals there thought that emancipation was premature. Switzerland banned the presence of Jews in the country (except in the canton of Aargau, but there, too, Jews had no civil rights), and a plebiscite as late as 1862 overwhelmingly rejected giving citizen rights to Jews; these were granted eventually, in 1874, after a new constitution was adopted. It is difficult to think of a single European country with a significant Jewish presence in which emancipation passed without resistance.

What were the reasons underlying the physical attacks against the Jews in the first half of the nineteenth century? They were not widespread and could not possibly be compared with the pogroms in Russia in later years. There were local attacks against Jews in Italy (in Toscana and Livorno in 1799–1800); in France in 1848 and 1898; in Odessa in 1821, 1849, and 1871; in South Wales in 1911. The mood prevailing was nationalist-patriotic and the Jews were considered strangers, even more than in the age of absolutism when everyone had been a subject of a monarch or ruler. At the same time, with the downfall of the walls of the ghetto, Jews entered various trades and professions that had been closed to them before. As a result, the Jew was considered a competitor—all the more so since some had grown quite rich after leaving the ghetto.

In some German universities students demonstrated against Jewish writers who in their books had shown an unpatriotic spirit; elsewhere students helped to protect Jews who had been attacked in the riots. It was during this period, particularly during the revolutions of 1848, that Jews actively entered European politics, but the revolutions often also witnessed anti-Jewish manifestations and the birth of political antisemitism. The Jews became a target in some cases because of their role in the revolutionary movement (they were attacked as "destructive elements"), but in other cases, on the contrary, they were considered enemies of the people because of the protection they had previously enjoyed by the hated authorities.

Generalizations are difficult. Attempts to explain these riots mainly against the background of social tensions (as a "displacement of social protest") on the whole have not been very convincing for a variety of reasons. There were attacks also against other minorities; furthermore, it is difficult to think of periods in the nineteenth century when Europe was entirely free of social conflict. The year 1819 was not a year of economic crisis in Germany—nor was 1881 in Russia. Had these been years of crisis, it can by no means be taken for granted that economic strain had led to fear and aggression and that this aggression, because of the stupidity of the masses (their "false consciousness"), had been directed against the perceived enemy (the Jews), who were not really responsible for the crisis. The Hep Hep riots of 1819 began in Würzburg in Franconia, but there were no obvious reasons that predestined Würzburg. They could have equally originated in nearby Bamberg or anywhere else.

There was a considerable upsurge of antisemitism in Austria in the 1880s and a decline in the influence of the antisemitic parties after the turn of the century. Since the 1880s witnessed an economic depression and since the economic situation improved later on, it would be tempting to see a correlation in these processes, but this is by no means certain. The upsurge of antisemitism probably had more to do with demographic change, with the fact that Jews moved into positions of influence in various fields in Austria, and, last but not least, with the presence of a charismatic antisemitic leader in Karl Lueger.

Local political incitement was a factor of considerably greater importance—as in later Eastern European pogroms such as the Kishinev pogrom in 1903. If the authorities suppressed the riots early on, employing strong forces and strict measures, riots did not spread; if they failed to do so, there was a good chance of repeat performances elsewhere. (There is an interesting parallel with the spread of militant Islamism in our time; its teachings lead to terrorist activities, not in regions that were particularly torn by social strife but in districts where radical preachers could spread their message without hindrance.)

The first half of the nineteenth century also witnessed the emergence of the socialist movement in Western Europe. While Catholicism continued to oppose the liberation of the Jews from the shackles of earlier ages, and the right wing was against the Jews because they did not truly belong to the nation, the early socialists, such as Charles Fourier and Pierre Proudhon, were hostile to the Jews because they regarded them as agents of capitalism, of commerce, speculation, and exploitation. The fact that the same period witnessed the rise to prominence and riches of some Jewish families such as the Rothschilds only strengthened these convictions. The anti-Jewish feelings of the young Marx have been mentioned; the fact that Jews took a leading role among the Saint-Simonians, part of the socialist movement, and were also counted among the Marxist Social Democrats mattered little in this context.

IF SOCIOECONOMIC REASONS played a limited role in Western and Central European antisemitism, the situation was quite different in Eastern Europe, where it was of greater importance. The number of Jews in Russia had been minimal up to the eighteenth century; furthermore, all Jews had been expelled from Russia and the Ukraine following imperial decrees in 1727 and 1747. When Empress Catherine II invited new immigrants in 1762, this applied to everyone but the Jews. Early anti-Jewish feeling was almost exclusively religious-theological in inspiration—Jews were feared because of their false teachings that might corrupt god-fearing Christians.

The situation radically changed as the result of the first division of Poland in 1772 when the Jewish population of Russia suddenly grew by 200,000, which made it the largest concentration of Jews in Europe. Many more Jews became part of the Russian empire after the later divisions of Poland. Jews had migrated from west to east during the Middle Ages, despite the resistance of the Catholic church in Poland, and had found there a safe haven. They were of considerable use to both the monarchy and the nobility as traders and as the representatives of absentee landlords, managing feudal estates as leaseholders. This was bound to bring them into conflict with the peasants and other parts of the population. They had to maximize profits in order to fulfill their obligations to the landlords, thus opening themselves to charges of exploitation and "bloodsucking." The peasants felt exploited not by the owners of the estates, absentee landlords whom they never saw, but by the Jews whom they made responsible for their misfortunes.

In the towns, Jewish artisans competed with Christian craftsmen and merchants, which also led to considerable tension. Jews took a leading part in the production and the retail sale of wheat-based alcohol, and most of the inns were in Jewish hands; this too was to play a central role in anti-Jewish charges in Poland and Russia. There were even accusations that Jews added poisonous herbs to the alcohol.

A concatenation of circumstances contributed to the spread of antisemitism. Poland, once a major power, was falling behind Western Europe economically and politically; modernization and reform did not make much progress. The Jews, lacking secular education, could not adjust to changing circumstances and play a significant role in the development of industry and other branches of the economy. At the same time, the number of Jews located in Poland and Lithuania considerably increased—there were more and more people and fewer work opportunities. The Catholic church, never particularly well-disposed toward the Jews, intensified its attacks; at a time when blood libels in Western and Central Europe became rare, they began to appear in Poland and the Ukraine. As was to be expected, Catholic militants (and also the Russian Orthodox church) found a few converted Jews who confirmed their suspicions that Jews needed the blood of Christian children for religious purposes.

There was also criticism of the Jews on the part of the Polish Enlightenment and its more progressive thinkers when the question of equal rights for Jews was discussed. Jews, it was argued, had shown idleness and hypocrisy; they had become in their majority backward and useless; unlike their coreligionists in Western Europe, they had not lived up to the moral standards of the society in which they lived. They had made no effort to learn the language of their neighbors and stuck to their antiquated clothing and their conspicuous beards.

Whereas in earlier times Jews in Central Europe had been compelled to wear their own specifically marked garb, in Poland, on the contrary, they were expected to conform to the rest of society. Disputes about the granting of civic rights raged for a number of years, beginning in 1789, and ended inconclusively. Freedom of worship was given but little else; the Jews were legally nonpersons, excluded from public law, and could not own land, only rent it. They were considered by and large an unproductive and backward element, and they were at least in part blamed for the general decline of the country. For their part, most Jews, immersed in their community's own internal problems and living in the religious world of the Middle Ages, made little effort to adapt to modernity. Enlightenment among the Jewish community was slow and encountered much resistance. Poland stagnated and the Jews were made responsible for the stagnation.

The situation in Russia was different in as much as prior to the divisions of Poland, the Jews were permitted to visit on business for short times certain places such as Riga and White Russia. The attitude of the czars and the ruling class toward Jews was one of suspicion and hostility, even though few of them had ever met a Jew in the flesh; this situation persisted well into the nineteenth century. The Russian government had decided early on to confine the Jews to the Pale of Settlement, which consisted of Poland, Lithuania, parts of White Russia and the Ukraine (but not Kiev), but excluded Russia proper. Only a very few Jews were permitted to live outside the Pale, such as merchants of the first class and those who had served in the army for nearly a lifetime. In 1827 Czar Nicholas I, in an attempt to force the Jews to convert, had introduced military conscription beginning at the age of twelve. This did not lead to many conversions but to a great deal of suffering. Given the general climate of corruption, Jewish communities managed in many cases to circumvent this requirement.

The socioeconomic situation of Jews in the Pale of Settlement was so bad and degrading that more-enlightened individuals among the Russian authorities developed various schemes to solve the Jewish problem, mainly through education (teaching secular subjects) but also by the reorganization of the economic and social life of the Jewish communities. Attempts were also made to induce Jews to work in agriculture, but given the miserable conditions of the peasants, this was not very successful.

Under Czar Alexander II, who ascended to the throne in 1855, various liberal reforms such as the abolition of serfdom were carried out, and Jews too benefited to a certain extent. Juvenile conscription was abolished. As a result of these somewhat friendlier measures, the Jewish Enlightenment (the Haskalah) made certain progress. By and large, however, the hopes that had initially been raised among Russian Jews were disappointed: the Pale of Settlement was not abolished; civic rights were not extended to the Jews. In fact, the general climate toward the Jews changed for the worse even among the intelligentsia after the Polish uprising of 1863; there was increasing distrust and hostility toward all non-Russian nationalities in the empire.

The 1860s witnessed the spread of ideological antisemitism, and Iakov Brafman's *Kniga Kahala* became the bible of this new wave of Judeophobia. Brafman, a convert, served as a professor at a Russian Orthodox seminary in Minsk. His book played the role that Eisenmenger's had in Germany in an earlier period, and that the *Protocols* would at a later date. He claimed that there was an all-embracing Jewish conspiracy, that the Jews were a state within a state, that in every city there was a Jewish executive committee which, based on the prescriptions of the Talmud, was trying to enslave and exploit the non-Jews.

The authorities who originally had been pressing for the Russification of Russian Jewry began to change their policies and introduced quotas—a *numerus clausus*—for Jews in schools and universities. This in turn induced young Jews who had turned their backs on orthodox religion and the traditional way of life, and who were only too eager to become submerged in a secular culture, to turn to the revolutionary movement as the only way out of the ghetto. For it was only among these groups of often-violent oppositionists that they saw a way to emancipation and assimilation. While Jews had not been among the founders of the Narodniki groups and not among its leading ideologues, they figured prominently among its militants. They were even more strongly represented among the Social Democrats (Mensheviks and Bolsheviks) and the Social Revolutionaries of the last decades of the czarist period.

The presence of Jews among the revolutionaries fueled antisemitism among the nationalists and the right-wingers, but it did not play a paramount role as far as the pogroms of 1882 were concerned; there had been only one person of Jewish extraction among the revolutionary group who had assassinated Alexander II. She had been a minor figure and the antisemitic press had hardly mentioned her.

Generally speaking, the pogroms had not been incited or organized by the authorities as was frequently believed at the time. Most of the leading officials (and the new czar) disliked and even hated the Jews, but they believed that the Jewish question should be solved by imposing laws from above rather than by popular riots—which could well get out of control and turn against other targets. The authorities feared popular violence and the pogroms were an embarrassment, for they painted Russia in a bad light abroad; during the second half of the nineteenth century it was widely believed in Europe that a more civilized spirit had prevailed in human relations and the pogroms were a throwback to bygone ages.

The security forces were understaffed when the riots broke out and pogrom activists who were apprehended were given only mild punishment. But if the government played no active role in fomenting the riots, who did? This is not easy to answer, for frequently various circumstances merged. The pogroms of the 1880s were on the whole limited to certain towns in the southern Ukraine (with some notable exceptions—such as Warsaw, Homel, and Nizhni Novgorod); they seldom spread to the countryside. They started, as so often in Russian history, at Easter, a time of processions and other church activities in which the role of Jews in killing Jesus was emphasized by militant preachers. While most Jews still lived in dire poverty, some had become relatively wealthy in the 1860s and 1870s and were the subject of envy. Often it was heard that the Jews were no longer humble but had become "impertinent," that although they were inferior people, they claimed to be treated as equals. However, the Jewish victims of the attacks, as far as can be established, were poor people, not the rich. At the same time, there had been an influx to the cities of occasional laborers from Russia and the Ukrainian countryside, which constituted an element of instability and ferment. They were frequently involved in brawls that easily turned into pogroms.

All together, the wave of pogroms of the 1880s was much smaller than the later ones of 1904–06 and 1918–19, and its main impact was political and psychological. It was a fatal setback for the Russifiers among the Jewish community, who had believed in a gradual rapprochement with the Russian people and Russian society. It also greatly helped to trigger emigration of Jews from Russia on a small scale to Palestine and on a much larger scale to America and South Africa.

During the two decades after the pogroms of 1881, the antisemitic policy of the czarist government became more intense; the "Temporary Rules" of 1882, which had severely restricted the rights and movements of the Jews, became permanent, and antisemitic propaganda, official and unofficial, greatly increased. If the government had a concept of how to solve the Jewish question, it was the formula presented by Pobedonostsev, the procurator of the Holy Synod: one-third will die out, another third will emigrate, the rest will disappear without leaving a trace—that is, become Christian. This was the period in which the Black Hundreds came into being, a radical right-wing, populist political movement, largely inspired and financed by the government. This group played a leading role in the pogroms of 1904–06 and under one name or another continued to wield political influence for years thereafter. This period should be regarded in many ways as a transitional stage between traditional, old-fashioned antisemitism and modern, Nazi-style antisemitism, even though the role of the church was still quite prominent and it fervently supported the monarchy.

This was also the period in which the *Protocols of the Elders of Zion* was composed, the bible of modern antisemitism, which is still sold in millions of copies in many countries. But it should also be mentioned that the *Protocols,* fabricated apparently in the 1890s in both Russia and France, had no significant political impact at the time inside Russia or in any other country. Its political impact only followed the revolutions of 1917, the civil war, and the emigration of millions of Russians. Even though a great deal of research has been invested in the origin of the *Protocols*, there is no absolute certainty as to its authors and origins to this day.

A series of major pogroms began with the massacre in Kishinev, the capital of Moldavia, in early 1903. It lasted for two days and left more than forty Jews dead. While accusations against V. K. Plehve, the Russian minister of the interior, of having instigated and organized the pogrom were unjustified, the local security forces certainly failed to react—partly because they were outnumbered (some 1,500 to 2,000 rioters confronted 350 police), but mainly because their commanders had no particular desire to protect the Jews. The Kishinev pogrom caused a worldwide scandal; it also created much heart-searching in the Jewish community—why had there been no resistance in a city a third of whose inhabitants were Jews? ("The sons of the Maccabeans were hiding like mice," Haim Nahman Bialik wrote in a famous poem.) The reasons for Kishinev were sustained anti-Jewish incitement by *Besarabets*, the only daily local newspaper; rumors about ritual murder; and accusations against the Jews that they were taking a prominent part in the revolutionary movement and that, at the same time, they were exploiting the native population, which was Moldavian rather than Russian in its majority.

The Homel pogrom occurred in September 1903; it started with a brawl between a fishmonger and a peasant on the town's market square.

The difference between Kishinev and Homel was that there was determined resistance on the part of the local Jews and, as a result, the number of victims was about equal. But the fact that the Jews defended themselves enabled the authorities to claim later that Homel had been a Jewish pogrom against Russians as an action of revenge for Kishinev. In the beginning, railway workers took a leading part in the Homel riots; later on peasants from the neighborhood joined in and there was a great deal of robbery and plundering. The reasons given by the czarist authorities were the usual ones—it was the conduct of the Jews that had provoked the native population.

But the great wave of Russian pogroms came only in the wake of the war against Japan in 1904–05, which had taken an unprepared Russian government by surprise. This wave can be divided into two subwaves—the minor one that began in the fall of 1904 and comprised about 40 riots, mainly inside the Pale. As usual it is not easy to establish a clear pattern of the pogroms during the earlier phase, except that they did not last long and were limited in scope wherever Jewish self-defense was strong and/or the authorities were determined and capable of stopping the rioting. There seems to be little doubt that there was a connection between these disturbances and the indiscriminate conscription policy of the government. But subsequently the conscription policy became more sensitive and the pogroms nevertheless continued.

A connection with the Russian fortunes in the war became even more obvious. After a few months, even before the surrender of the Russian garrison in Port Arthur in December 1904, it had become clear that the war was not going well and that the military and political leadership was ineffective. This caused political and social unrest and the usual polarization. While the liberals and the leftists blamed the incapacity of the government and the general lack of freedom and backwardness of the country, the right-wingers and the reactionary forces found the culprit in the seditious, unpatriotic forces, and the Jews were an obvious target.

There was the usual antisemitic propaganda, reinforced by rumors that Jewish international financial capital was conspiring to effect the downfall of the Russian government. In 1904–05, in contrast to 1882, the Black Hundreds movement, politically and materially supported by the government, served as the organizing force behind many—probably most—of the pogroms and it also provided the foot soldiers. As the authorities lost control in a chaotic situation, however, the Black Hundreds achieved a momentum of their own and even independence. George Louis, the French ambassador, wrote at the time, "the Black Hundreds are ruling the country and the government obeys them because it knows that the emperor is inclined to sympathize with them." (This was an understatement—the czar had called them a "shining example of order and justice to all men.") Alexander Dubrovin, their leader, mobilized mass support through sympathizers in the clergy and patriotic organizations as well as in the police and the local administration.

The social base of the Black Hundreds was often called Okhotny Ryad—a small road in central Moscow which at the time housed Moscow's game and meat market and other small shops owned usually by first generation Muscovites. These were people with little education, bewildered by the pace of social change and the rapid economic ups and downs, staunch believers in the monarchy and the church, enemies of the intelligentsia and the non-Russian nationalities.

Comparing the Black Hundreds with the Action Française, the main pillar of antisemitism in France at the time, one finds striking differences. The Action Française was predominantly middle class or upper-middle class and included the lower nobility, with considerable influence in the academic world. The Black Hundreds had a few aristocrats and professors among its supporters but considerably more hooligans and plain thieves, to quote Count Witte, a former prime minister. They engaged in riots but also individual acts of terrorism.

The Black Hundreds were populist and in this they resembled the Nazi party; they advocated limiting the working week and raising the living standard of the peasants. These demands and the unruly character of the movement became an embarrassment to their backers in the government, and official support for them dwindled once the danger of a revolution had passed. Internal squabbles in the Black Hundreds leadership as well as the temporary political stabilization in the country weakened the movement, and in 1908 they split and lost much of their momentum. But the tradition of the Black Hundreds survived, and its successor groups again became a political force in the civil war following the revolutions of 1917 and in the Russian emigration.

Lastly, it should be remembered that the whole climate of those years was one of political protest, mass strikes, demonstrations, and clashes such as the massacre of Bloody Sunday in St. Petersburg in 1905. The first phase of these pogroms, in which about a hundred Jews were killed, was part of a much larger historical development— the revolution of 1905.

Under considerable popular pressure and following the impact of the general strike of October 1905, the czar was compelled to announce far-reaching political reforms in his October 1905 manifesto. But the political climate did not immediately improve. On the contrary, during the three months following the publication of the manifesto there was an unprecedented wave of pogroms (between 600 and 700), which resulted in the murder of about 3,000 Jews; many more were wounded, and there were many cases of rape and plunder, with whole quarters burned. The worst pogrom was in Odessa, where some 800 men, women, and children were killed; there were 200 victims in Bialystok, 100 in Kiev, 100 in Minsk, and many more in smaller places.

The October Manifesto had been hailed as a victory by the left and the liberal forces. There had been mass demonstrations welcoming it, and the pogroms were part of the backlash by the unhappy extreme right. The authorities had not organized the pogroms, except in a few instances on the local level such as in Odessa; there was no need to because the Black Hundreds fulfilled this role. As the czar wrote to his mother, "the revolutionaries have angered the people . . . and because nine-tenths of the troublemakers are Jews, the people's whole anger turned against them. That is how the pogroms happened . . ."

Nine-tenths of the troublemakers had not, in fact, been Jews, but the Jews were undoubtedly the easiest targets for the counterrevolutionary forces. The backlash was directed in principle not solely against them, but the democratic and liberal forces were more difficult to locate and to combat, while the Jews were dispersed and defenseless. The socialists were even more difficult to confront, only because their political demands were quite popular and the Black Hundreds quite liberally borrowed from them.

The pogroms had been preceded by a massive propaganda campaign supported by the monarchist forces, including the church. They came to an end after order in the country had been reestablished by the government. The immediate danger to the czarist regime had passed. Antisemitic forces were represented in the Duma (the lower house of parliament) but were not a significant force in the political life of the country.

The one major antisemitic affair that occurred in the following years was the 1911 Beilis trial in Kiev. A young Jewish tailor had been accused of killing a Christian boy for ritual purposes. The local authorities knew that this was a fabrication—they even knew the real killers—but they thought they were acting in accord with the wishes of the central government. This enterprise backfired, however; public opinion in Russia was overwhelmingly in favor of the man who had been falsely accused (less so in Russian Poland), and in the end Beilis had to be acquitted. Beilis left Russia with his family for Palestine just before the outbreak of the First World War. He did not find work there and went on to the United States. He died in the Bronx, New York, in 1934.

Chapter Five

RACIALISM AND JEWISH CONSPIRACIES

RELIGION DECLINED IN THE NINETEENTH CENTURY but antisemitism did not; the doctrine of antisemitism gradually changed its character. It had been almost exclusively religious and this was found more and more unsatisfactory by staunch antisemites. Why, they asked, should a Jew who converted to Christianity be regarded as an equal? This issue had arisen in sixteenth-century Spain when the doctrine of the purity of the blood (*limpieza de sangre*) had been made a statute; Jews could not be trusted even if they abjured their religious faith. Perhaps their conversion was genuine and perhaps it was not. And even if it was genuine, radical antisemites would argue that the character of the Jews was such that they could not be considered equal to the "old Christians." There was something beyond their religion that made their assimilation difficult and perhaps impossible. Ironically, it was also argued that Jews or descendants of Jews were behind the religious sectarianism that had been so influential in Germany and France at the time—in other words, Jews were believed to have been behind the advent of Protestantism.

Limpieza de sangre laws prevailed even though they were opposed by many high-ranking churchmen, including the Jesuits. But the doctrine of the purity of blood was restricted at the time to the Iberian peninsula, where it applied also to the Moors. Furthermore, it was whittled down gradually over the ages and dismissed altogether in the middle of the nineteenth century.

Modern race theory has its origins in the work of philologists and ethnographers from the late eighteenth century onward. For some time it was believed that the cradle of Western civilization and religion (such as Zoroastrism) had been in the Caucasus, but subsequently the opinion prevailed that their beginnings must have been somewhere in Northern India, Central Asia, or Persia.

One of the leading protagonists of the concept of the importance of race in history and of the inequality of races was Count Gobineau, a French diplomat whose influential work on the subject was published in 1853. Joseph Gobineau also believed that the mixture of races was fatal and that it had caused the decline of nations and civilizations. Gobineau was not of much use to the antisemites, however, because he only rarely referred to the Jews and what he said about them was by no means always hostile.

Nor were the findings of linguists such as Max Mueller, a German professor teaching Sanskrit in Oxford, or of the French historian Ernest Renan, of much help to the antisemites because these precursors put the emphasis on cultural rather than biological concepts. Mueller, who coined the term "Aryanism," declared that there was no such thing as an Aryan race. Nor was it acceptable for German racialists to subscribe to a theory that claimed that their origin should have been somewhere in Central Asia; the Nordic race that had produced all that was great in civilization including the Renaissance and the French Revolution surely must have originated in Northern Europe.

Human biology and genetics had not really come into their own at the time; this would happen only later with the work in Britain of Francis Galton and, above all, Karl Pearson. When race theory initially emerged, it was largely based on speculation. Among its early protagonists in Germany, where it was most popular, were not scientists but economists such as Eugen Duehring, composers such as Richard Wagner, students of the Bible and oriental languages such as Paul Lagarde, amateur historians and philosophers such as the Englishman Houston Stewart Chamberlain. They were quite aware of the uncertain foundations on which their theories rested, and Chamberlain wrote that while there might not have been an Aryan race in the past, the task ahead was to create one. Some of them vaguely talked about a "religion of the future," but hardly anyone wanted a total confrontation with Christianity—as advocated by Nietzsche, who had, however, no sympathies for the racialist antisemites. Most of them thought it possible to de-Judaize the Bible by ignoring the Old Testament and declaring Jesus Christ an Aryan rather than a Jew (for the Jewish people could not have possibly produced a figure like him). Still others were dreaming of a future German national religion, but even the Nazis at a later period preferred not to press this divisive subject.

The early racialist antisemites had no clear program concerning the treatment of the Jews. Wilhelm Marr, who had coined the term "antisemitism," thought that it was too late to do anything about that. The Jews were already dominating the economic and political life of the country (Germany) as well as the cultural scene, and he concluded his book with the words "Finis Germaniae," the end of Germany. We do not know whether this pessimism was genuine or sham. Lagarde and, in particular, Duehring regarded the Jews as parasites that had to be exterminated one way or another. At the very least they wanted a reghettoization, but deportation would have been preferable in the view of many. Some suggested the island of Madagascar as a possible haven for the Jews, an idea that was taken up for a short time by the Nazis before they opted for physical extermination. Emperor Wilhelm II in his Dutch exile advocated the murder of the Jews by means of poison gas. But the kaiser was not a stable and consistent thinker; his antisemitism did not prevent fairly close relations with leading Jewish industrialists and bankers such as Albert Ballin and

Max Warburg. While in office he had always opposed anti-Jewish legislation.

Race doctrine received a fresh impetus toward the end of the nineteenth century when social Darwinism and eugenics became fashionable and the specter of "degeneration" was conjured up. These ideas were very much part of the Zeitgeist. The supporters of Houston Stewart Chamberlain included the German emperor as well as Teddy Roosevelt and George Benard Shaw. Chamberlain, it should be noted, lived until 1927 and managed to meet Hitler at the beginning of his political career; in a letter written after this meeting, Chamberlain hailed him as the savior of Germany.

But the preoccupation with race did not necessarily lead to antisemitism. The leading book about "degeneration" was written by a prominent Jewish essayist, Max Nordau, and he saw the root of the evil not in biological factors but in a variety of cultural modernist fads and fashions. Not all the critique of modernism was reactionary and unjustified; eugenics at the time probably had more supporters among the left, including the Social Democrats, than among the Conservatives, and among its proponents were also Jewish sociologists and ethnologists. In other words, while these biological and genetic concepts could become part of a new antisemitic "German ideology," this was by no means the only possible political consequence.

By and large, racialist antisemitism had only limited political impact during this time. Various antisemitic leagues and parties sprouted in Germany and to a lesser degree in neighboring countries. The leaders of these parties spent as much time fighting each other as fighting the Jews. They were instrumental in convening two international antisemitic congresses in the 1880s, but few participants came from outside Germany and these meetings were largely ignored.

The German antisemites succeeded in getting a few of their own elected to local parliaments and even the Reichstag, mainly in Saxony (where few Jews lived) and in Hesse (where a somewhat larger percentage of Jews made their home, mainly in the countryside). They had their greatest success at the general elections of 1893, when sixteen of them were elected to the Reichstag. But there was no unity among them and in later elections they did not achieve remotely similar results. The racialist antisemites continued to be active in various fields, and they created something like a political subculture with social clubs, youth and student groups, as well as newspapers and a literature of their own. They exerted some indirect influence, for instance on the Conservatives, but generally they were not taken seriously and simply not considered respectable in a society such as Wilhelmian Germany. They focused their propaganda on certain social issues, such as the influx of Jews from Eastern Europe following the pogroms. But most of these emigrants had no wish to settle in Germany and were merely in transit to the United States, Britain, or South Africa. Another issue was the appearance of department stores that emerged around the turn of the century; many of them were in Jewish hands and they constituted serious competition and even a threat to the survival of small shops.

More important perhaps than the impact of racialist doctrine on the development of modern antisemitism was the idea of a Jewish world conspiracy. This concept goes back a long time; some have traced it to King Solomon and the days of the Bible. In the Middle Ages there had been rumors about an executive of leading rabbis meeting once a year in France and deciding what crimes to commit to cause maximum harm to the hated Christians. The Jews were miserable, downtrodden, and isolated, however, and it was difficult to persuade anyone that they constituted a serious danger. It was only in the wake of the French Revolution that some reactionary clerics claimed that the great upheaval had been the result of a plot by Freemasons and, above all, the Illuminati. The Illuminati were a Bavarian Masonic group founded in the eighteenth century by one Adam Weishaupt about whom little is known; it is doubtful whether they still existed in the nineteenth century. However, the Jews could hardly be made responsible for the French Revolution since they were not involved in the political life of France or any other country. It was only toward the middle of the following century that political conspiracy theories became truly fashionable. One typical example was the so-called speech by the chief rabbi in a novel entitled *Biarritz* (published in 1869) by the German journalist Hermann Goedsche, who wrote under the pen name of Sir John Retcliffe. According to Goedsche's novel, the Sanhedrin, the supreme Jewish body consisting of representatives of the twelve tribes of Israel, meets every hundred years near a certain grave on the Jewish cemetery in Prague. At this meeting, the planning of a world revolution aimed at creating a global dictatorship is discussed. This is to be achieved by means of international financial intrigues as well as revolutions to overthrow religion, the monarchy, and the army first of all in Prussia and Russia. However, two unwanted observers somehow penetrate the meeting, a German named Dr. Faustus and an Italian converted Jew named Lasali. This chapter of the novel was reprinted countless times in various countries; the antisemitic ideologues who used it did not deny that its origin was in a trashy horror novel, but they argued that it must have been based on some real events.

The historical role of *Biarritz* was that, together with an obscure pamphlet by Maurice Joly (published in Brussels in 1865), it became one of the two main sources of inspiration for the *Protocols of the Elders of Zion*. The *Protocols* were the main text and the basis of modern antisemitic propaganda and have remained so with countless modifications to this day. Although its origins are still murky, it is believed to have been fabricated by agents of the czarist secret police (the Okhrana) in France before the turn of the twentieth century, but this has never been conclusively proved. They were first published in a St. Petersburg newspaper in 1903 and subsequently reprinted many times, by the Russian government printing office and mainly by one of Russia's leading monasteries just outside Moscow.

There are many divergent versions of the *Protocols;* sometimes the Jesuits are brought in, very often masonic lodges as well as various

revolutionaries and representatives of finance capitalism and an ar-
ray of subversive secret societies. In contrast to the chapter of *Biarritz,*
the *Protocols* text is not a speech but the alleged verbatim record of
twenty-four sessions of the heads of a Jewish world conspiracy that
outlines both their plans and their intentions. Sometimes it was explained that this body is identical with the Alliance Israelite Universelle,
a Jewish defense organization founded in Paris in 1860; at other times
it has been claimed that it refers to the Zionist movement, whose first
congress took place in Basel in 1897. Yet other commentators have
explained that neither of these bodies was involved, but that it was an
organization so secret that most Jews did not even know about its
existence. Their declared aim is to overthrow all existing thrones,
institutions, and religions; to destroy all states; and to build on their
ruins a Jewish world empire headed by an emperor from the seed of
King David. Included is a section that could be entitled "Machiavelli
for Backward Students": he who would rule must act with slyness,
cunning, and hypocrisy—there is no room for moral values, honor,
and honesty, let alone openness in this field. The masses are blind,
unable to understand what is good for them.

To achieve their ends, the document alleges, the Jews use all kinds
of secret organizations, and their main tools are democracy, liberal-
ism, and socialism. They have been behind all upheavals in history,
supporting the demand for the freedom of the individual; they are
also behind the class struggle, all political assassinations, and all major
strikes. The plotters induce the workers to become alcoholics and try to
create chaotic conditions by driving food prices up and spreading infectious diseases. There is also a swipe at nefarious "society ladies."

The Jews already constitute a world government, the document
claims, but their power is as yet incomplete and they incite the nations against each other to trigger a world war. There is a great distance,
however, between their proclaimed and their real aims. These fictional leaders are by no means liberals and democrats. Real happiness
will be brought not by democratic principles but by blind obedience

to authority. Only a small part of the population will receive education, for the spread of learning among the lower classes has been one of the main causes of the downfall of the Christian states. It will be the honorable duty of all citizens to spy and inform on all others. The rulers will put down without mercy those who oppose them; other conspiratorial groups such as the Freemasons will be liquidated, some killed, others exiled to punitive settlements overseas.

But what if the non-Jews discover this diabolical conspiracy in time? What if they attack the Jews once they have understood that all the disasters and intrigues are part of a gigantic Jewish master plan? Against this last eventuality the Elders have an ultimate horrible weapon which is revealed in the ninth protocol. All the capitals will be undermined by a network of underground railways. In case of danger, the Elders will blow up the cities from the underground tunnels, and all government offices and all non-Jews and their property will be destroyed.

This ultimate weapon was too much even for the credulity of the Russian—and later the German—editors of the *Protocols*. The Russian editors added a footnote to the effect that while at present there were no such underground tunnels in Russia, various committees were at work to establish them. The German editors (after the First World War) said that common sense revolted against this idea, and that it was probably a mere manner of speaking or a figure of speech used to emphasize that the Jewish plotters would not be deterred by using even the most horrible weapons to attain their aims.

The *Protocols* were widely distributed in Russian during the decade before the outbreak of the First World War but their political impact was limited. The Russian government, with all its anti-Jewish feelings, rejected it as unsuitable for propagandistic purposes and it was not initially translated into other languages. The great acceptance of the *Protocols* began only after the Russian Revolution and the end of the First World War.

The Russian empire, which many believed would last forever, disappeared without a trace after the Russian Revolutions of 1917; the new leaders were people few had ever heard of, including many Jews from Trotsky downward in the new hierarchy. Revolutionary coups were attempted in other parts of Europe, such as Hungary and Bavaria, and they too were headed by Communists of Jewish origin. That these Jewish revolutionaries had fought against and dissociated themselves from their communities was of no interest to the purveyors of the *Protocols*—perhaps it was a mere stratagem.

The *Protocols* were brought to Europe during the White Russian emigration, probably by an army officer named Shabelski-Bork. Alfred Rosenberg, a Baltic German and later the chief ideologist of the Nazi party, made a name for himself as a leading early commentator on the *Protocols*. But the influence of the *Protocols* was no longer restricted to fringe groups; leading German and British newspapers published them in installments, and the ex-kaiser Wilhelm II, then in his Dutch exile, sent copies to all his friends. True, the London papers were also the first to admit that their correspondents had been taken in by a forgery, but this did not greatly affect the triumphant success of the *Protocols*. Within a few years they were translated into most languages, including Japanese and Chinese. The Latin patriarch of Jerusalem, Barsalina, called on his flock to purchase the Arab translation of the pamphlet. Henry Ford sponsored the publication in the United States, where it sold hundreds of thousands of copies.

The *Protocols* were neither the first nor the last literary product of its kind, but it was certainly the most successful. How to explain its phenomenal success? The postwar environment was of decisive importance. After years of peace and prosperity, the general optimism of Europe had been rudely shaken. To many, the war had come like a bolt out of the blue; millions had died in the senseless slaughter, and there had been unprecedented material destruction. Millions of those who survived found themselves at the end of the war without means and without hope. The war was followed in many countries by further unrest and economic disasters such as inflation and unemployment. In these circumstances, many were looking for an answer, if possible a clear and easily intelligible explanation to their searching questions about the cause of these disasters and the global unrest in general. And now a document had emerged from the very country in which these apocalyptic events had first happened—sufficient reason for many to accept these startling explanations. So many disasters could not possibly have been unconnected and unplanned; surely there must have been a hidden hand behind all this.

That the forgeries were primitive and unconvincing did not really matter. As one contemporary observer wrote, "The ignorant believed them because they were ignorant and the semi-intelligent because it was for the good of the reactionary cause."

If the *Protocols* were widely read and partly believed in the countries that had emerged victorious from the war, their success in the camp of the defeated, from the White Russian emigrés to Weimar Germany, is all the more understandable. Who had brought about the downfall of the czarist empire? Who had stabbed in the back the German armies previously undefeated on the field of battle? A scapegoat had to be found. Russian and German right-wingers discovered that they did not have to blame themselves and their own shortcomings for these traumatic defeats. The explanation of an outside enemy had psychologically much to recommend.

But the *Protocols* offered more than an explanation; they were also a political slogan, a battle cry. Whether Hitler truly believed in the *Protocols* is doubtful, but he was shrewd enough to realize the enormous propagandistic potential of the basic idea of the *Protocols*. Some observers have gone further and argued that Nazi Germany and Stalinist Russia with their dictatorships, propaganda, terror, and ideas of a totalitarian welfare state owed more than a little to the *Protocols*. But whether Hitler was indeed a pupil of the Elders of Zion is a moot point; he had no need for the *Protocols* in his struggle against the Jews or as a blueprint for Europe's future.

The *Protocols* and kindred literature belong to the species of conspiracy theory of history, a genre of political philosophy and literature that has had enormous attraction since time immemorial. That there have been plots and conspiracies throughout history goes without saying, but the theories that have attracted so many people do not belong to this category. This species consists of conspiracy theories that are manifestly absurd, have nothing to do with the real world, and appeal not only to individuals with an inclination toward paranoia but to a far wider public. They can be found in virtually every part of the world, though a world map of conspiracy theories would show that they are more widespread and popular in some countries and cultures than in others. It has been argued that the high tide of conspiracy theories was in the Middle Ages with its obscurantism and mass hysterias, but this is doubtful in view of the enormous revival they have had in modern times, especially in the last century. This revival is, of course, connected with the fact that the world has become infinitely more complex and difficult to understand and is also related to the revolt against obvious "official explanations" in politics, science, and other fields.

The enormous success of conspiracy theories in literature and the cinema tends to show that the belief in abstruse explanations must be part of the human condition and corresponds to a human need. Some of these theories are entertaining and harmless (the UFOs or the Bermuda Triangle); others are far from innocent because they are used as political weapons against groups of people deemed hostile. They certainly have become an integral part of contemporary antisemitism, adapting themselves to new developments and circumstances, and we shall again have to deal with them later in this book.

Before World War One conspiracy theories played only a minor role in antisemitic propaganda; they existed but their appeal was limited. True, Jews were considered disloyal to their respective countries by the antisemites, but this did not amount to a giant global conspiracy. The details of the Dreyfus case, for example, need not be recounted in detail. A captain in the French general staff, Alfred Dreyfus was arrested in October 1893 and accused of having passed military secrets to the Germans. In December of that year a military tribunal behind closed doors sentenced him to life imprisonment on Devil's Island, where he spent four years in solitary confinement. However, following some investigations by a few courageous writers, first Bernard Lazare and later Emile Zola, it appeared that the evidence against Dreyfus had been faked by two fellow officers—one of whom committed suicide, the other escaped abroad.

This should have been the end of the case, but the general staff tried to maintain a cover-up at all costs and in 1899 Dreyfus was again found guilty by a military tribunal. A few days later he was paroled by the French president. It took another seven years for Dreyfus to be restored to the army and to be awarded the Legion of Honor.

The case split the country and led temporarily to riots and outbreaks of antisemitism. It was not so much the question of whether Dreyfus was guilty that motivated the anti-Dreyfusards, but the conviction that the good name of the army should be protected at any cost. French Jews were accused by the antisemites of trying to save one of their own even though he was guilty. In fact, French Jewry had not shown great courage and hesitated a very long time to join the defenders of Dreyfus, as did the socialists.

The Catholic church and the traditional right were heavily involved in the affair and were bound to suffer as the intrigue against Dreyfus collapsed. It led to a strict division between church and state; antisemitism in France was weakened but continued to exist. Edouard Drumont, the leading antisemitic writer of the period, and his disciples continued to publish books and articles according to which the goal of the Jews was the downfall of France. But the echo they had was limited. Even while Dreyfus was deported, Jews continued to serve as senior officers in the French army—posts closed to them in Germany.

During the early years of the twentieth century, it was widely believed in enlightened circles that antisemitism was a thing of the past. True, from time to time rumors about ritual murders would occur in distant rural places such as Tisza Eszlar in Hungary, in Konitz and Xanten in East Germany, as well as in some Bohemian villages. But these throwbacks to the Middle Ages quickly led to protests and were dismissed. There was social and cultural antisemitism: Edward, Prince of Wales, was derided by part of the British press because he surrounded himself with Jewish financiers. Some Jewish businessmen in South Africa were accused of having provoked (or at least assisted) the outbreak of the Boer War. But these were marginal events. Antisemitism as a central issue existed only in czarist Russia and a few other backward regions of Eastern Europe and the Balkans, such as Romania.

All this changed with the outbreak of the First World War. The war had various causes but it was difficult to attribute it to Jewish intrigues. During the early months, even antisemitic newspapers in Russia, France, and other belligerent countries refrained from continuing their propaganda because internal peace (*Burgfrieden*) had been declared. But once it appeared that the war would last years, antisemitic attacks reappeared. In Russia hundreds of thousands of Jews were expelled from the regions close to the front line, especially in Lithuania and Northern Poland. Many thousands died during and as a result of the deportations. Tens of thousands of Jews from Austrian Galicia fled to Vienna to escape the advancing Russian armies; this sudden influx added fuel to tensions in a city in which antisemitism had been deeply rooted for a long time.

In Germany antisemites spread rumors that while Jews had enlisted in the army like everyone else, most of them had found safe jobs in the rear. The military authorities decided to carry out a "Jewish census"; the results were never published, partly perhaps because of political pressure or because they did not bear out the allegations. All that is known is that the number of Jewish war dead in Germany—12,000—was proportionally the same as that of the non-Jewish victims. However, neither this fact nor the many second- and first-class Iron Crosses awarded the Jewish soldiers were of any help to the Jewish community twenty years later when Hitler came to power.

The Russian Revolution of October 1917 led to a bloody and prolonged civil war. Although many Jews were represented in the Communist leadership, from Trotsky on down, and although these Jews had emphatically dissociated themselves from their communities, the Jews were still widely equated with Bolshevism in the popular mind. For the volunteer White armies, particularly the Cossacks, the Jews were the enemy par excellence. In a major civil war, a great many people tend to be killed, but Jews suffered more than all other groups in this conflict. Pogroms were carried out not only by the Whites but by Ukrainian nationalist groups, by quasi anarchists, and also by the Bolsheviks for whom the Jews were capitalists, the class enemy. The high tide of the pogroms came during the second half of 1919; it is estimated that about 10 percent of Ukrainian Jewry, between 150,000 and 200,000 people, perished.

While the earlier waves of pogroms in 1881 and 1905 had taken place predominantly in the cities, the pogroms of 1918–19 were also in the countryside; one of the greatest massacres was in Proskurov, a small town in the Ukraine, in which 1,700 Jews were killed and thousands injured. Although there had always been a good deal of plundering in the earlier massacres, this became even more pronounced in the civil war pogroms. The White armies were supported not only by the political right but also by the centrist and liberal parties. Their commanders refused to condemn the anti-Jewish persecution, for antisemitism seemed so deeply ingrained that they thought any such attempt would be fruitless. The Ukrainian leadership, especially Symon Petlyura, was in theory more liberal—they advocated the emancipation of the Jews and there were a few Jewish advisers among them. But they had no control over their armed gangs and the same was true of anarchist groups such as the one headed by Nestor Makhno. The supreme leadership of the White armies did not specifically call for pogroms nor did they oppose them; as General Anton Denikin once said, if he had done so he would be accused of having sold out to the Jews.

The Russian officer corps was traditionally antisemitic and the revolution had reinforced these feelings—the Jews were responsible for the Russian tragedy; they had to be punished and eliminated from Russian public life. The political and propaganda branches of the White volunteer armies were particularly active in spreading antisemitism; they brought the *Protocols* to Central and Western Europe and continued their struggle against the Jews from their new homes in Paris, Berlin, and other centers of the emigration.

Originally there had been few if any sympathies for Bolshevism in the Jewish street; the percentage of Jews among the political émigrés from Russia after 1917 far exceeded their numbers in the general population. But for those who remained, Soviet power, however unfriendly to specific Jewish concerns, constituted the best hope in a hostile world—the Bolsheviks reimposed order and the pogroms came to an end.

To what extent did the presence of many Jews among the Communist leadership contribute to antisemitism? It certainly played an important role in antisemitic propaganda, and it is certainly true that during the 1920s Jews were heavily overrepresented in the ranks of party and state officials. With the rise of Stalin, Jews were removed from key positions and very often "liquidated." The fact that other minorities were also disproportionately highly represented did not greatly matter—there was no tradition of anti-Latvianism in Russia, nor were Latvians found in the very top positions. Nor did it matter that Jews were equally strongly represented among other anti-Communist parties of the left such as the Mensheviks and the Social Revolutionaries, or that the anti-Stalinist opposition was to a considerable extent of Jewish extraction. The Jews were the destroyers of Holy Russia.

Young Jews were attracted by the most radical groups in Russia because of traditional Russian oppression of Jews. The liberals attracted the Jewish middle class, but the Jewish middle class was weak since most Jews in the czarist empire had been poor. And for young people from such a background, the revolutionary party that promised total national and social liberation and equal chances for everyone was bound to be very attractive. This, in briefest outline, was the background of the "Judeo Bolshevism" that played such a crucial role in antisemitic propaganda in the 1920s and later, despite the fact that the Jews had become a prominent scapegoat of the Communist regime.

Chapter Six

TOWARD THE HOLOCAUST

THE MAIN SCENE OF ANTISEMITISM between the two world wars was Eastern Europe even though the situation in Germany became more and more critical with the rise of the Nazi party during the late 1920s. The Jewish presence in Eastern Europe was much stronger than in Western and Central Europe—12 percent of Poland's population was Jewish, 6 percent of Hungary's, and about 5 to 6 percent of Romania's. Furthermore, Poland and Romania were countries in which minorities constituted large sections of the population, and the Warsaw and Bucharest governments, feeling insecure, exerted strong pressure on minorities and in particular the Jewish community.

In all three countries, antisemitism was religious-nationalist rather than racialist, with the church taking a strongly anti-Jewish position in Poland. It is true that in all three countries the extreme right-wing parties for which antisemitism was a central issue increasingly developed toward fascism and racialism, and in the case of Romania and Hungary, toward an extreme form of fascism as embodied in the Romanian Iron Guard and the Hungarian Arrow Cross. In the aftermath of World War One a few riots took place in Vilna and Lvov in 1919, and there were anti-Jewish riots in Hungary following the overthrow of the Communist government of Bela Kun, during which hundreds of Jews were killed.

During the early years of the existence of the Polish republic with Joseph Pilsudski as its head, antisemitism had played a minor role. Antisemitism in Poland increased partly as a result of the world economic crisis and in particular after Pilsudski's death, when a new generation came to the fore. "Street antisemitism" was stronger in certain parts of Poland than in others; it has been noted that in western Poland, where fewer Jews lived, there was on the whole more antisemitism than in the eastern part, which had greater concentrations of Jewish communities.

The antisemitism of the church persisted—the Jews were a community of alien morality and values, hostile to Christianity, and while the church did not advocate physical violence, it favored legal measures as well as economic boycott. Some clergymen argued that baptism was not a solution: there were too many Jews and the "Talmudic soul" was too resistant. Baptism in most cases was seen as merely an attempt to break into Polish society.

There was economic antisemitism—the Jews were made responsible for the collapse of the zloty and, being middlemen, of exploiting the peasantry—underpaying the peasants for their produce and overcharging the public, and thus adding to the high cost of living.

While Jews in Poland were certainly overrepresented in the country's trade (hence the call for the Polonization of Poland's trade), they had no stranglehold. There was an "objective Jewish question" in Poland, as the Zionists maintained, in view of the social make-up of Polish Jewry, but this accounts more for the pauperization of Polish Jewry than for the growth of antisemitism. Antisemitism among the Polish peasant parties was no more pronounced than among other political parties; that antisemitism in Poland became more rabid in the late thirties than in the years before was largely due to other-than-economic causes.

The major political parties, including Pilsudski's Sanacja, developed under the rule of the colonels further toward a strong antisemitic orientation. The other big party, Roman Dmowski's National Democrats, originally pro-Russian and later pro-Mussolini, had always been strongly antisemitic. Under the rule of the colonels in the late 1930s, the economic and political situation of the Jews became critical. Legislation was passed that aimed at squeezing the Jews out of the economy and public life.

During the early years of the Polish republic, the old Russian anti-Jewish (antiminority) laws had still been in force; Jews had had to pay double taxes for certain activities, and the use of Hebrew and Yiddish in public was forbidden. These laws were eventually abolished, albeit with considerable delay, but new ones were introduced in the 1930s which, while not naming the Jews specifically, were directed against them. These laws aimed at squeezing Jews out of many trades, professions, and places of work. Mass boycotts of Jewish shops took place in Poland from 1936 to 1939. While the antisemitic propaganda of students did not succeed in keeping Jews completely out of universities, they did obtain the right to have Jews taught in separate lecture halls. Entrance to city parks was to be forbidden to Jews in some places, and maneuvers were afoot to strip most Jews of their Polish nationality.

For the antisemites, the Jews were an alien body that could not be assimilated; they were deemed essentially anti-Polish, pro-Soviet, left-wing radicals. Successive Polish governments, not only the rabidly antisemitic ones, advocated the emigration of 1.5 million Jews to Madagascar, Palestine, or whichever country was ready to have them. Isaac Gruenbaum, a prominent Zionist leader, said at the time that there were one million Jews too many in Poland. This declaration caused a great deal of resentment in certain Jewish circles—did it not play into the hands of the antisemites?—but it may have been close to the truth.

Hungary had a tradition of modern antisemitism dating back to the second half of the nineteenth century. At first the main complaint was that the Hungarian Jews were making no effort to be Magyarized, that their knowledge of the language and culture was imperfect. In fact, most of Hungarian Jewry tried hard to become assimilated, and they were second to none as Hungarian patriots. There were also a significant number of conversions, especially during the late 1930s. But Jews had also been prominently involved in the Bela Kun revolution and the Communist dictatorship of 1919, and this led to a massive anti-Jewish backlash under Admiral Miklós Horthy who, while not a rabid antisemite, was not willing to oppose a very popular mood.

The number of Jews in Hungary had rapidly grown between 1850 and the First World War mainly as the result of immigration from the East; by the turn of the century one-quarter of the inhabitants of Budapest were Jewish. At the same time, Jews had made rapid social and economic progress—about half of Hungary's lawyers and physicians were Jewish, and more than half of the leading banks and industries were in Jewish hands. The Hungarian middle class was largely Jewish or German. These demographic and social developments (very much in contrast to Poland, where most Jews were quite poor) played a significant role in the spread of antisemitism.

Antisemitism in Hungary grew in the 1930s partly under the impact of the world economic depression—as in Poland, the Jews were made responsible for the economic miseries that befell the country. The rise of Nazism in Central Europe also played an important role.

THE YEAR 1933 constituted a watershed in European politics. Until that time France and Britain had been the paramount powers and even the League of Nations mattered politically. Openly antisemitic legislation was frowned upon by Britain, France, and the United States. Furthermore, the peace treaties after World War One had provided special safeguards for minorities in Eastern Europe (because there was no confidence that these countries would treat their minorities fairly). But Hitler was showing that the Western nations could be defied with impunity; the European balance of power was changing and the Nazis did away with protection for minorities. In fact, Polish Jewry, to give just one example, had been attacked by Polish nationalists for having pressed for these laws that limited Polish state sovereignty. Ultimately these safeguards were of little help to minorities.

There were other indirect repercussions as the result of the Nazis' rise to power. Groups on the extreme Polish right became openly racialist, and some of them even declared that the main enemy to an independent Poland was neither Nazi Germany nor the Soviet Union, but the internal foe, the Jews.

The situation in Hungary was similar. When Julius Gombos, a radical antisemitic leader, came to power in 1935, a number of anti-Jewish laws were promulgated. A *numerus clausus* of 20 percent was to confine Jewish representation in various fields. This was further restricted in subsequent years under Gombos's successors since it did not satisfy the more radical antisemites. Ironically, it was revealed that one of these radicals, prime minister Bela Imredi, was of Jewish origin; this led to his resignation but not to a change in policy.

Romanian antisemitism, perhaps the most virulent in Europe during the nineteenth century, had certain common features with antisemitism in Poland and Hungary. The universities played a central part in its militancy and spread. The Iron Guard, responsible for many pogroms in later years, came into being as a students' association; many of Romania's leading intellectuals had originally belonged to it. Also as in Eastern Europe, the agrarian crisis and the global economic depression of the early 1930s had a considerable impact on the growth of social and national tensions. Unlike Poland, most of Romanian Jewry was not concentrated in the capital and other big cities; half of them lived in outlying provinces, such as Hungarian-speaking Transylvania, German-speaking Bukovina, and Russian-speaking Bessarabia.

King Carol provided some protection for the Jews, as Pilsudski did in Poland and Horthy in Hungary, but he was in no position to oppose the radicalization of domestic politics. In Vaida Voevod, Romania had a politician in power who openly called the Jews parasites and invoked the old blood libels. Octavio Goga, who became prime minister in 1938, was an important figure in a tradition of intellectual Romanian antisemitism that reached back to the previous century. While Poland never produced an influential, outright fascist party, Hungary did in the form of the Arrow Cross, which by 1940 was the second strongest party in the country. But the most radical party was the Romanian Iron Guard, originally called the Legion of Archangel Michael. This extreme antisemitic group was frequently banned by the authorities, for its social radicalism and unruly behavior (they assassinated four Romanian prime ministers) rather than its antisemitism. Although its support also came from the countryside—peasants who faced bankruptcy as the result of the agrarian crisis—its leadership was in the hands of young intellectuals. Among them were several figures who later attained world fame, such as Mircea Eliade and Emil Cioran. At the same time, antisemitism became official state policy and severe antisemitic legislation was introduced, eliminating Jews not only from public life but from various professions, a policy that was somewhat mitigated only by the corruption prevalent in the country.

All major Jewish concentrations in Eastern Europe were subject to growing antisemitism, which manifested itself not just in the general intellectual climate but, generally speaking, in attempts to get rid of the Jews by means fair and foul.

More than any other political movement, fascism shaped European political life during the 1920s and 1930s; Britain, France, and the Scandinavian countries were the only major exceptions. Antisemitism was a crucial ingredient of fascist theory and practice although it was certainly not the only one, and in the early period of some fascist parties it had been virtually nonexistent. This is true especially with regard to fascism's birth place—Italy. While Jews were very prominent in the Italian antifascist resistance from its very beginning, there were also more than a few Jewish members of the fascist party, albeit not in leading positions. The situation in Italy was to change only in 1938, mainly as the result of the ascendancy of Nazi Germany in Europe, when Italy too introduced its racial, antisemitic legislation.

Elsewhere there was no uniform pattern among fascist or profascist groups; in countries with very small Jewish communities, such as Denmark, antisemitism could not possibly be a major issue, whereas in Switzerland it was for a while a factor of some importance. Individual Jews belonged to the Mussert movement in the Netherlands. In Spain, a country virtually without Jews, the extreme right (the old Carlist party) and the profascist circles frequently invoked the *Protocols of the Elders of Zion* and, even before the outbreak of its Civil War, emphasized a conspiracy of Jews and Freemasons against Spain. But it is also true that this antisemitism by and large remained a marginal phenomenon, just as fascism, German or Italian style, never became a decisive force under the rule of General Franco.

How important was antisemitism in Nazi doctrine, to what extent was it the decisive motive that made thousands and later millions of Germans join the Nazi party? Antisemitism played a very important role in Hitler's propaganda right from the beginning, in Hitler's Munich days, and those who followed him disliked or hated Jews. But his followers had many other motivations—extreme nationalism, revanchism following the defeat in the war and the imposition of the Versailles treaty, the fear of Bolshevism, the mystic belief in the unity of the people (*Volksgemeinschaft*), and, last but not least, the Hitler cult. It is next to impossible to establish with any kind of exactitude the specific weight of antisemitism, high as it was, in this mixture of motives. It is known that among Hitler's very early followers in Munich, only about one-fifth said antisemitism was the most important single factor in their decision to join the movement. There is much reason to assume that when the Nazi party experienced its great upsurge in the late twenties and early thirties, considerations other than antisemitism—such as the impact of the world economic crisis and the failure of the Weimar republic—played the crucial role. But

Hitler's continual, relentless, and effective antisemitic propaganda fell on fertile ground.

HITLER HAD BECOME an antisemite during his early years in Vienna, where antisemitism was rampant at the time both in the mainstream of Austrian politics and as the ideology of a variety of racialist sects. Hitler was familiar with the ideas of the antisemitic sectarians and to a large extent shared them; he also understood that while antisemitism was of great potential importance in the mobilization of the masses, the traditional abstruse theories he had come to know in Vienna would be of little use in the political struggle.

Since the personality of Hitler was crucial to the rise of his party as well as to the policy of the Third Reich, it would be of great importance to know when he actually became a confirmed antisemite. But this cannot be established with any certainty; during his years in prewar Vienna some of his close associates were Jews or of Jewish extraction, and there are no indications that he was anti-Jewish at the time. In *Mein Kampf* he writes that he became an antisemite as the result of a spiritual crisis, but this is a cryptic reference and nothing is known about the specific reasons and circumstances of this crisis. All we know is that in later years his antisemitism became more and more radical. In the end, Albert Speer, who served as his adviser and minister, wrote that the hatred of the Jews was Hitler's main driving force, perhaps even the only element that moved him.

A variety of factors made antisemitism politically very attractive in Germany when Hitler appeared on the Munich political scene after the war had ended. The general upheaval after World War One had opened the door to all kinds of extreme movements on the left and the right, the economic crisis culminated in hyperinflation, and Jews had leading roles in revolutionary Communist parties. This made it possible to attack the Jews as capitalist exploiters and war profiteers, as well as agents of Germany's enemies, and as a mortal danger to all established values—family, fatherland, traditional culture. Paragraph

4 of the program of the Nazi party of 1920 stated that a Jew could not be a member of the community of the German people (*Volksgenosse*). The program also mentioned the removal of foreigners from Germany, though the details were left vague. During the fight for power in Germany, Nazi storm troopers attacked Jews in the streets, but by and large physical attacks were rare and the propaganda was limited to threats that the day of reckoning with "Juda" was near. This quickly changed after Hitler seized power in January 1933. On April 1, a general one-day boycott of Jewish shops was declared, which was accompanied by street violence; during the months that followed a series of laws made it impossible for Jewish lawyers to practice and for Jewish physicians to treat patients covered by state insurance.

According to a law of April 1933, Jews were removed from state and local administrations; there were initially a few exceptions, such as World War One veterans, but these were quickly eliminated. Yet another law removed the great majority of Jewish students from universities and other schools. On a local level, villages and small towns were declared free of Jews (*judenrein*) or, at least, access to public places was denied to Jews. Among those arrested and sent to concentration camps during the first year of Nazi rule was a high percentage of Jews, and there was a steady stream of anti-Jewish propaganda in the media, which were all controlled by the state.

The segregation of the Jews was codified in the Nuremberg laws of 1935 (the laws of the protection of the German blood and honor and the Reich Citizenship law), which tried for the first time to establish who was to be considered a Jew—although this remained a matter of some discussion and interpretation for years. Marriages between Jews and non-Jews were banned, and extramarital sexual intercourse between Jews and non-Jews became a crime punishable with heavy prison sentences. During the years that followed, pressure—often physical—was exerted to force Jews out of the German economy. Many enterprises owned by Jews had been "Aryanized" during the first year of Nazi rule; their owners were usually forced to sell their businesses at a fraction of the real value.

If during the first two years of Nazi rule there had been a certain restraint with regard to the anti-Jewish policy in view of foreign political considerations—the regime did not yet feel secure enough—such restraint disappeared as Germany reasserted its position in Europe, rearmed in contravention of the Versailles peace treaty, and left the League of Nations. The only interruption in this process of radicalization were the early months of 1936 when, in preparation for the Berlin Olympic Games, Nazi Germany tried to present to the outside world and the many visitors a face of normalcy. Almost immediately after the games, however, discussion began on ways and means to intensify the pressure on the Jews and to force Jewish emigration which, as the Nazis saw it, did not proceed fast enough. The fact that emigrants from Germany could as a rule take with them only a paltry sum of money did not help; but the Nazis were not willing to make any concessions in this respect and, on the contrary, emigrants had to pay a special high tax (*Reichsfluchtsteuer*). In 1938 every male Jew was given the additional first name of Israel, and every Jewish woman, Sarah. These names appeared on passports together with the capital letter "J"; the measure made it more difficult for Jews to obtain visas to foreign countries. According to rough estimates, Jewish assets in Germany were halved between 1933 and early 1938—from 12 billion to 6 billion reichsmarks.

By and large, anti-Jewish measures in Germany had been gradual—even in early 1938 there were still a few Jewish students in German schools and Jewish physicians treating non-Jewish patients—practices that were totally ended only in July 1938. But in Austria, occupied by the Nazis in early 1938, anti-Jewish measures were far more rapidly (and brutally) carried out, with the result that emigration of Austrian Jews in the eighteen months that remained until the outbreak of World War Two proceeded far more quickly than in Germany.

Anti-Jewish persecution quickened and became more intense with the Kristallnacht pogrom (the Night of Broken Glass) on November 10–11, 1938. A junior German diplomat had been shot by a young Jew at the German embassy in Paris; the parents of the assassin had been expelled from Germany a few weeks earlier together with thousands of other Jews of Polish nationality. Since the Poles were not willing to receive them, they were dumped in the most primitive conditions in a no man's land at the border at Neu Benschen.

The retaliatory pogrom in Germany was carried out by storm trooper units in coordination with the police and the fire brigades, which took care that the fires put to synagogues, Jewish schools, shops, and offices would not spread to non-Jewish property. Some 7,500 Jewish businesses were plundered or wrecked, and 30,000 male Jews were arrested and sent to concentration camps. In a series of further punitive laws following Kristallnacht, a collective fine of one billion marks was imposed on the German Jews (this was later increased to 1.7 billion); all Jewish commercial activities were prohibited; Jewish cultural institutions, publishing houses, and communal newspapers were closed. Taken together, these measures meant the dispossession of German Jewry and the end of communal and cultural life.

In a speech to the Reichstag on January 30, 1939, on the anniversary of his seizure of power, Hitler said that in the event of another war, the Jewish race in Europe would be exterminated. The war that Hitler unleashed was still eight months away.

THE STORY OF THE SYSTEMATIC EXTERMINATION of European Jewry has been well documented and analyzed and for the purposes of this study is retold in only the briefest outline. That Hitler wanted the physical removal of the Jews from Germany and Europe was never a secret, even though there were no detailed plans until the outbreak of the war. Forced emigration did not provide a satisfactory solution as far as Hitler was concerned, and with the conquest of Poland and the addition of two million more Jews, a number of plans were discussed and dismissed—the deportation of German Jews to Poland and, following the attack against Russia in June 1941, of Polish Jews to the Soviet Union. For a short while, the deportation of Jews to Madagascar was debated and also the establishment of a Jewish reserve in Lublin, in southern Poland. The first deportations of German and Czech Jews to the east took place in 1940, but these were on a small scale.

As Germany expanded its territory during the war, many more Jews came under Nazi rule. A variety of steps were taken to prepare and facilitate a "final solution" of the Jewish question; the term was apparently first used in March 1941 in a memorandum by Reinhard Heydrich, Heinrich Himmler's deputy. Among these steps were forcing the Jews in Central and Eastern Europe into ghettos and ordering every Jew to wear a yellow star. While hundreds, perhaps thousands, of Jews had been killed even before the invasion of the Soviet Union, and more had died as a result of disease and starvation, systematic annihilation began with the activities of the special units (*Einsatzgruppen*) that were dispatched to Russia and the Ukraine to engage in the systematic murder, usually by shooting, of Jews at the rear of the German front. But these methods were found to be wanting, as the units could not kill a sufficient number of Jews quickly enough. The mass murder was extended to territories outside Russia in August and September 1941. In a conference at Wannsee, a Berlin suburb, in January 1942, leading German officials from various ministries discussed the logistic and administrative problems connected with the "final solution."

Who had given the order to carry out the mass murder of millions of Jews? No written order has ever been found and this led some historians to believe that there had been no such order, but that there had been an automatism of sorts, that deportations and mass executions were carried out following local initiatives, and that one thing led to another—once a certain number of Jews had been killed, the annihilation of the rest seemed only a question of time. But this contradicts the nonwritten evidence—a speech by Himmler on October 4, 1943, in the city of

Poznan in which he spoke about the extermination of the Jews, and numerous postwar admissions by leading figures in the execution of the Final Solution. Orders had been given orally and often used circumlocutions ("final solution" and "transportation" instead of annihilations or killings were two of several euphemisms employed). There has been much speculation whether an oral order was given by Hitler in late summer of 1941 or only two or three months later, but the timing is hardly a matter of paramount importance, and it could well be that there never will be a conclusive answer. Evidence confirms, however, that by November 1941 a massive wave of deportations of Jews from Central and Western Europe was under way that concentrated the Jews in major ghettos such as Warsaw, Lodz, Riga, and Minsk. The number of those who died during these transports, carried out in the most primitive winter conditions with hardly any food and water provided, was considerable. Some of the deportees were employed for a while in work for the German military effort and war-related industries in labor camps, but the majority of deportees were eventually shifted to the extermination camps, which were operational by the first half of 1942. Later transports were dispatched directly to these death factories; Chelmno, not far from Lodz, was the first such center but also one of the smallest. The big death factories were Majdanek, Sobibor, Belzec, Treblinka, and, most important, Auschwitz-Birkenau, where the gas chambers used Zyklon B poison gas and the corpses were burned in giant crematoria. In most death factories, those who arrived on the transports were immediately killed; in Auschwitz, which also housed a number of factories and had over thirty smaller labor camps nearby, there was a selection at arrival: the very young, the old, and the infirm were immediately sent to be gassed; the others were sent to work. But living and working conditions were such that the chances of surviving more than a few months were very small; those no longer able to work were dispatched to the gas chambers.

Hundreds of thousands of German and Polish Jews perished during the second half of 1942; the last major Polish ghettos were destroyed in 1943 and only Lodz survived for another year. There was some armed resistance in Warsaw, Bialystok, and a few other places, but since the arsenal of the resisters consisted only of improvised explosives and light arms, the Germans put down ghetto resistance without difficulty.

About a third of the Jews living in France at the time of the German invasion were deported and killed, while the others succeeded in hiding; nearly two-thirds of Belgium's Jewish population were killed. In the Netherlands and in Greece the percentage of the Jews who perished was far higher, an estimated 75 to 85 percent. In most countries the Germans could count on the collaboration of the local administration in rounding up Jews and deporting them. Denmark and Bulgaria were the two major exceptions. Most of Danish Jewry was saved in the mass escape to Sweden in November 1943. In the case of Bulgaria, the government was willing to sacrifice the Jews living in occupied Thrace (formerly part of Greece) but not those who were Bulgarian citizens. Romania, which had a major Jewish community, was also different. Thousands were killed in pogroms inside Romania (such as at Jassy in 1941); more than two hundred thousand were deported to Transnistria, kept in camps and ghettos, where approximately two-thirds of them died from hunger and epidemic diseases.

Jews living in Italy or Italian-occupied territories were on the whole safe (with the exception of Croatia, where most Jews were killed by local fascists), until the fall of Mussolini and the German occupation of Italy in 1943. Given the late date and the relatively small number of Italian Jews who had remained in Italy (over seven thousand had emigrated by 1941), the possibilities of successfully hiding were better there than in most other European countries.

Many Russian Jews had fled with the retreating Red Army in 1941–42; as the German army advanced into Russia, the hundreds of thousands who stayed behind, unable to flee or evacuate, were murdered at mass executions (as at Babi Yar), or herded into ghettos that were later liquidated.

According to the figures published by Richard Korherr, the chief SS statistician, most of European Jewry had been liquidated by 1943. The only major Jewish community remaining was the Hungarian one, and their turn came with the German invasion of Hungary in the summer of 1944. Hundreds of thousands were transported to Auschwitz and gassed there; a much smaller number was sent to forced labor in various German camps.

The deportation of small and very distant Jewish communities continued to the very end (for instance, the Jews of Rhodes and Kos in the Eastern Mediterranean in July and August 1944). Among those employed in the execution of the final solution were locals as well as Germans; the Hungarian Arrow Cross, Romanian legionnaires, and Ukrainian personnel acted sometimes in coordination with the Nazis, sometimes on their own initiative.

As the Soviet offensive reached Poland and East Germany, the death factories were hurriedly dismantled and the Nazis attempted to obliterate the traces of the mass murder. Thousands more survivors were killed or perished during the evacuation "death marches" from concentration camps such as Auschwitz toward West Germany. As a result of starvation and epidemics in Bergen-Belsen, which had become the main absorption camp during the last months of the war, only a few thousand people who had been forced to walk all the way from the east survived the experience.

All together between five and six million Jews were killed, the great majority of continental European Jewry. Only a tiny remnant of the Jews who had lived before the war in Central and Eastern Europe remained. The fact that wholly exact figures do not exist is not surprising, given the nature of war and the secrecy imposed on the Nazi SS and Einsatzgruppen operations. Nevertheless, reliable estimates have been assembled from census figures from before the war, Nazi documents, and statistical analysis.

According to reliable estimates, the numbers of Jews killed or perished in the Holocaust were 2.7 million in Poland, 2.1 million in the territories of the Soviet Union; 559,000 Hungarian Jews, 192,000 German and Austrian Jews, 143,000 from Czechoslovakia, 120,000 from Romania, 102,000 from the Netherlands, 58,000 from Greece, 51,000 from Yugoslavia, 29,000 from Belgium, 5,500 from Italy (Wolfgang Benz in *Holocaust Encyclopedia*, 2002).

When the war ended, European Jewry had effectively ceased to exist. It was the only one of Hitler's promises he was able to keep.

What was known about the mass murder while it went on and what was the reaction of the outside world? While attempts were made to keep the killing a secret, so many people were involved one way or another that news about it reached the outside world through many channels within a short time, though the details became known only later on. Not only Jewish organizations but the Polish government in exile informed the allied governments throughout 1942, and there were protests issued in public speeches, solemn official declarations, and radio broadcasts.

Inside Germany and other European countries, the disappearance of hundreds of thousands was, of course, widely known; it was not widely known that most of the victims were gassed, but it was generally assumed that the Jews would perish and never return. Of those about to be deported, many committed suicide or tried to hide, despite the great odds of surviving in illegal circumstances. This was common knowledge even in small and isolated towns in Germany and demonstrates that there were few illusions about the fate of those deported. Initially there might have been such illusions, but news about the killing of those who left on the first transports dispelled them.

If most Jews still did not offer resistance, the reasons are obvious. The majority of those deported and gassed were elderly people, women, and little children; they had been weakened and starved and there was no hope of rescue. If millions of Soviet prisoners of war were killed without resistance, it was not surprising that Jewish civilians, with few exceptions, did not offer resistance.

The neutral countries in Europe, fearful of Nazi threats, refused to help and give shelter to those few able to cross their borders—until the tide of war had turned. The allies were in no position to extend help to the Jews during the initial phase of the war, when Hitler was victorious on all fronts. The situation changed after the siege of Stalingrad, the allied victory in North Africa, and the landing in Italy. Still, at first there was some disbelief, because the extent of the mass murder often exceeded the imagination of people living in democracies, who had only a faint understanding of Nazism and kindred movements. Frequently there were no great sympathies for the Jews and it was claimed that Jews were alarmists who exaggerated and engaged in spreading atrocity stories.

From 1943 on, much more could have been done not only by publishing the news about the Holocaust and threatening the perpetrators with post-conflict treatment as war criminals but also by interfering with the logistics of the mass murder; it ought to be recalled that the killing of Hungarian Jews and many thousands of others took place as late as 1944. The general assumption in both the West and East, however, was that the overall priority was to win the war and that no resources should be wasted for other purposes, such as helping to save civilians. With the victory over Hitler, this argument ran, European Jews too would be saved. The fact that by that time hardly anyone would be left to be saved was ignored.

In brief, the fate of the Jews, while not altogether dismissed, had low priority. It is quite possible that with only a minimal effort tens of thousands, if not more, could have been saved during the last two years of the war.

Last, there is the question of the uniqueness of the Holocaust, which continues to preoccupy experts and the general public alike up to the present day. The annals of history are full of incidents of genocide from the Old Testament and the Koran to the slaughter in Rwanda in our time. Tribes and besieged cities were annihilated; there were mass killings of heretics such as the Albigensians in South France in the thirteenth century. In modern history such abominations have become very rare in Europe and less frequent elsewhere. The behavior of the

Nazis and followers of Nazism in World War Two was a relapse into barbarism, and it is true that among the many civilians killed, the Jews were a minority.

Nevertheless, there were significant differences between the treatment of, for instance, the Armenians in World War One or the Romas and Sinti or homosexuals in World War Two. The massacre of hundreds of thousands of Armenians was limited to the eastern parts of the Ottoman empire, while those living in Constantinople and other urban centers were not affected. The Nazis did not limit the final solution to Poland and Lithuania, leaving the Jews of Paris and Berlin and Vienna in peace. Thousands of gypsies were killed as Nazi policy considered them an inferior race, but again the treatment was selective. (Django Reinhardt, the famous jazz guitarist and a *manouche* or gypsy by origin, was invited to entertain officers and soldiers of the German army; it is unthinkable that Yehudi Menuhin would have been invited.) Some countries were little affected or not at all by persecutions of gypsies. Homosexuals were detained and kept in concentration camps but only a few were killed.

The Nazi murder of the Jews was total—not selective—and it was carried out systematically, following industrial organization and techniques. It was not a series of pogroms and somewhat spontaneous massacres, nor was there an escape for Jews. Jehovah's Witnesses or Communists could gain their freedom from the concentration camps if they abjured their faith and promised to collaborate with the Nazis. As far as the Jews were concerned, their religious or political beliefs were wholly unimportant to the Nazis. The Jews were killed not because of what they did or thought but because they were Jews. In this respect the Holocaust was unique.

Chapter Seven

CONTEMPORARY ANTISEMITISM

UP TO THE END OF THE SECOND WORLD WAR, Nazi, fascist, and extreme right-wing movements were the main sponsors and carriers of antisemitism. There was little if any open antisemitism on the left; Muslim antisemitism was traditional in character and played no important role except sporadically and on a local level. This changed toward the end of the twentieth century as political movements in the Nazi and fascist tradition greatly weakened with the defeat of Nazi Germany and fascist Italy. Indeed, in many countries such movements were outlawed and, with a very few exceptions, had no major role even as the opposition. Furthermore, after the murder of millions of Jews, few Jews were left in Europe to be targets, except the communities in France and Britain.

Antisemitism did not disappear, but the particular bestiality of the mass murder made it difficult even for latter-day admirers of Hitler to explain and justify this particular aspect of Nazism. They could not argue that the mass murder had been justified, and therefore the line taken by most of them was denial—the Holocaust had never taken place, or, at most, had been greatly exaggerated.

There were other reasons for the decline of the importance of antisemitism within neofascist doctrine. One has been mentioned already—the small number of Jews who had survived made it virtually impossible to turn antisemitism into the main plank of a political movement in Europe. On the other hand, there were new social tensions caused by the postwar immigration to Europe—the arrival of millions of "guest workers," many of whom came from the Middle East, Asia, and Africa. Their numbers greatly exceeded those of the prewar Jewish communities; in contrast to the Jews, many of them had no wish to assimilate, to accept the culture and way of life of the host country. In view of their high birth rates, their presence over the years caused major demographic changes—something the Jewish presence had never done, as the Jewish birth rate had been low and declining.

True, it could not be argued with regard to these newcomers (as it had been said of the Jews during an earlier period) that they dominated the economic and cultural life of their host countries. These new arrivals dominated the street, public housing, public transport, and public services; some of them displayed open hostility toward the way of life of the host country and in some cases engaged in terrorism. Although xenophobia did not disappear, its advocates were compelled to look for different targets if they wanted to have political impact. One example: Ten percent of the French expressed strong anti-Jewish feelings in a public opinion poll in 2002, but the antagonism toward Muslims was considerably stronger, almost three times as frequently expressed. In Britain, Germany, Russia, and other European countries, unfavorable views vis-à-vis Muslims were twice as frequently expressed than negative views vis-à-vis Jews. Events in the Middle East certainly affected the image of Israel in the media, yet this was not reflected in popular attitudes toward Jews; in fact, such attitudes were slightly more favorable in 2002 than they had been in 1991.

Uncontrolled immigration rather than the Jewish presence provided the basis for neofascism beginning in the 1970s. While neofascism was still strongly nationalist and xenophobic in outlook, there was a new element, an orientation toward Europe or, perhaps more accurately, toward a fortress Europe, simply because the political weight of the various countries that had once been great powers had greatly declined over the years. It is not much of an exaggeration to define neofascism as defensive in nature—not of its own volition but because of its weakness, in contrast to the aggressive character of the traditional fascism.

In some instances there was even a genuine retreat from antisemitism, such as in Italy where neofascism had been a force to reckon with after the end of World War Two. Gianfranco Fini, head of the National Alliance and later a minister in the Silvio Berlusconi government dissociated himself and his party from racism and antisemitism as did the other major right-wing party, the Northern League. To the extent that there were antisemitic publications or activities in Italy, they came from very small segments of the extreme right that consist of a few hundred members only, from the extreme conservative wing of the Catholic Church, and from the far left—one of whose ideologists wrote that Jews were "practically nonassimilable germs," a statement that was defended by the radical Manifesto group.

The Italian Jewish community consists of 30,000, the French of 600,000, most of them refugees or descendants of refugees from North Africa. Jews are far more prominent in the economic, cultural, and political life of France than of Italy. Antisemitism has been rampant in France since the 1970s and Jean-Marie Le Pen's far-right-wing National Front has polled close to 20 percent in some elections. Its voting reservoir comes mainly from the old blue-collar working class and its leaders have never made a secret of their anti-Jewish feelings. Le Pen has more than once declared that the Holocaust was no more than a footnote to twentieth-century history and not a very important one at that. In his party's political activities and propaganda, however, the main issue has been immigration from Africa (5 million Muslims now live in France). There was a marked increase in antisemitic incidents in France beginning in the 1990s, manifested in graffiti, threats, arson, and physical attacks, but to the extent that the perpetrators could be identified, relatively few came from groups like the National Front; many incidents were attributed to young Muslims. Antisemitic activities in Britain and Germany have been sponsored by smaller and more radical right-wing groups, and in these countries too, the influx of millions of foreigners, rather than Jewish conspiracies, had become the main political issue. Public opinion polls showed that not-too-friendly attitudes toward Jews extended well beyond these extremist groups; substantial sections of the population in most European countries expressed the opinion that Jews had too much influence, that their loyalty to the country of residence could not be taken for granted, that they were harping too loudly and for too long on the mass murder of their coreligionists during World War Two.

In Germany a substantial part of the population was critical of the financial restitution that was made to Jews for property stolen under the Nazis and for other damage suffered. Opinion polls in Germany in 2004 showed that only about one-third of the population was opposed to antisemitism; between 6 and 8 percent firmly believed in antisemitism, and the majority of the population held views somewhere in between. Similar polls in Russia showed that 42 percent believed that Jews had too much influence and 28 percent suggested restoration of a Pale of Settlement (such as had existed in czarist times) to which Jews should be confined. These feelings, however, did not necessarily translate into political action.

There seems to have been no obvious (or at least no consistent) correlation between antisemitism in postwar Europe and the size of the Jewish communities. Hungary is the only country in Eastern Europe with a sizable Jewish community, whereas Romania has only about 1,500 Jews; as far as the extent and intensity of antisemitism is concerned, there was hardly any difference between the two countries. The number of Jews in Spain and in Greece is now minuscule (20,000 and 1,500 respectively); however, public opinion polls showed a higher degree of anti-Jewish feelings than in, for instance, France and Britain, which have much larger Jewish communities. But such antisemitism was latent, subacute rather than manifest. It showed itself in popular aversion to Jews rather than in any specific political or social activities.

The case of Greece is of interest; it once had a sizable Jewish community, most of which was deported and murdered during the war. Antisemitism today is found mainly among some radical church circles and among the left—including the left-wing intelligentsia (Mikis Theodorakis included) and terrorist groups—hardly among conservative and center parties. Groups belonging to the extreme right in Belgium and Holland, to give another example, have gone out of their way to stress that they had nothing to do with fascism, old or new. Nor did the ideologues of the New Right (or neofascism)—such as Italy's Giulio Evola, France's Alain de Benoist, or Belgium's Jean François Thiriart—show any pronounced interest in antisemitism. They were preoccupied with the establishment of a European front— political as well as cultural, opposing the United States. Some of them expressed ecological concerns, others favored a third way, combining ideological elements of the far right with those of the extreme left, something like the National Bolshevism of the 1920s brought up to date. Above all, there is antiglobalism and anti-Americanism as the doctrinal glue; according to de Benoist, "America is the most evil rogue state and thus our greatest enemy." From this passionate anti-Americanism it is only one step to the allegation that everything in America belongs to the Jews and that they have a decisive impact on its policy. De Benoist may be too cautious to make this step, but leading German sectarians such as Horst Mahler, once a leading left-wing terrorist, had no such hesitations.

If extreme right-wing groups have had electoral successes, it has been based almost entirely on the fear of the rising number of immigrants, the apparent impotence of the political establishment to limit immigration, and the emergence of expanding local ghettos. However, in the 1990s, and especially after September 11, 2001, such concerns were no longer limited to the extreme right; they were voiced equally from the center and the left. On the other hand, violent opposition against immigrants from the Middle East and Africa would go hand in hand with sympathies for such figures as Saddam Hussein (for instance, in the case of Le Pen in France or Jörg Haider in Austria), and in some instances even for Osama bin Laden and al-Qaeda.

If in the political and ideological arsenal of neofascism and the extreme right in Europe, antisemitism suffered a steady decline, the question arises: who was behind the continuing anti-Jewish threats and attacks? Certain radical sects and individuals ought to be mentioned, who owing to recent techniques in the field of communication (the Internet and blogging) have found it easier than ever before to spread their gospel. Such sects continue to exist in virtually every country and there are individuals who have their followers among them. The names of two should be mentioned here. Horst Mahler, one of the cofounders of the Baader-Meinhof terrorist gang, over the years has become a leading ideologist of the German neo-Nazis and their fellow travelers. According to Mahler, the hatred of Jews is natural, and the Auschwitz lie was invented by the Jews to keep the German people in perpetual servitude. In France, Roger Garaudy, former member of the Politburo of the Communist party, has gone through a similar shift from extreme left to extreme right views. For these two men— and they are by no means the only ones—antisemitism was certainly a basic ingredient of their new ideology. Jacques Verges, a well-known lawyer, had been a prominent Maoist sympathizer, but he moved on to defend Klaus Barbie, one of the leading figures in the execution of the final solution in wartime France. "Carlos the Jackal," the infamous terrorist of the 1970s and 1980s and the most radical left-winger of them all, converted to Islamism and his political opinions developed accordingly.

In addition to these figures, youth groups such as the skinheads have emerged; some are well organized on a nationwide and even international basis, others who have developed their own subcultures pop up sporadically. Some are ideologically motivated at least in part; others are criminal or semicriminal. With their own uniforms, music styles, football violence, and their thirst for militant action, they certainly have been strongly affected by antisemitism even though their immediate targets are usually other groups deemed hostile simply because they are more easily identifiable.

Antiracialist legislation concerning both incitement and discrimination in France, Germany, and other European countries has compelled antisemites to use circumlocutions to describe their purposes. The laws are not too difficult to circumvent by using coded terms for Jewish people ("East Coast" or "New York"), just as Soviet Communists had done during Stalin's last years. Furthermore, such legislation has had unexpected repercussions: statistics concerning antisemitic activities in Western Europe were showing that many were carried out not by the foot soldiers of the extreme right or of the far left but by young Muslims. However, to state this baldly could be interpreted as "Islamophobia," for even if true, it singles out one specific ethnic group as particularly prone to engage in anti-Jewish activities. It could be argued that even the publication of statistics on antisemitism is racialist in character and should be discontinued. Since there are many more Muslims than Jews in postwar Europe, their sensitivities had to be taken into account in order not to poison relations between the communities. Thus, it came as no surprise that a major study on the subject, Manifestations of Antisemitism in the EU 2002–2003, undertaken by the European Union communities through the European Monitoring Centre on Racism and Xenophobia, had to be substantially rewritten because it had called a spade a spade and not an agricultural implement.

WHAT HAS BEEN SAID with regard to Western Europe and the prominent part of young radical Muslims in antisemitic activities is certainly not true with regard to Eastern Europe and Russia, which experienced a considerable upsurge in antisemitism after the breakup of the Soviet empire. This upsurge did not come as a complete surprise; everywhere in this part of the world ethnic tensions that had been suppressed under the dictatorships came to the fore once the pressure from above disappeared.

Antisemitism in Russia had deep roots; to a certain extent it had been official state policy particularly during Stalin's last years and to a lesser extent under his successors. Unofficial discrimination against Jews continued in many fields. While Jews could be frequently found as deputies in many organizations in industry or in academe, the top jobs were virtually barred to them. They could not serve in the army except perhaps in the medical corps or in some scientific capacity, could not join the foreign ministry or the security services. A low level of antisemitic literature, both fiction and nonfiction, continued to appear. During the last years of Soviet rule, unofficial antisemitic groups (such as Pamyat) made their appearance. Jews were attacked by the nationalists for being responsible for Bolshevism and by the Communists for having undermined the Soviet state and society and having brought about its downfall; there had been, after all, a fairly large number of Jews among the dissidents.

These accusations found many believers among the many who suffered under the Communist regime—and from the consequences of its breakdown. Old antisemitic themes and motifs reappeared: those described in the *Protocols*; the Jews had always intended to harm Mother Russia; one of Lenin's grandparents had been a Jew who had been baptized. Influential circles within the Orthodox Church contributed their part to the campaign. The fact that Jews had been among the main victims of the Soviet regime especially during the last decades of its existence did not help much, nor did the fact that the majority of Russian and Ukrainian Jews had left the country after the breakup of the Soviet Union. It could always be argued that individual Jews were among the main benefactors of perestroika and the privatization of the economy. Within a few years, many of the oligarchs who had amassed billions found themselves exiled or in prison, and although this might have helped the politicians who were responsible for their ouster, it did not soften opinions about the Jews.

How to explain the survival of antisemitism in Russia? That these feelings were deeply rooted in the country, and that considerable numbers of Jews had been instrumental in supporting and representing an unpopular regime did not help. Still, this explanation is not altogether satisfactory: Stalinist Russia in its time enjoyed a reasonable amount of popular support from its citizens, and antisemitism had been rampant in Russia well before 1917. In addition, Jews had virtually disappeared from the party leadership after World War Two. But anti-Jewish sentiments, even if suppressed, survived, and once they could be vented more freely than before, they reappeared.

Russia after the breakdown of Communism was a country in economic and social crisis and full of national resentment—not unlike Germany after the First World War; similar also was the resulting search for those responsible for the downfall of the mighty empire. True, it was not easy to put all the blame on the Jews, because in recent years those who have challenged Soviet power were not the Jews but the ungrateful non-Russian nationalities in the Baltic, the Ukraine, the Caucasus, and Central Asia. Nor did the Jews blow up Russian theaters, schools, and housing complexes. This made it difficult, if not impossible, for nationalists and former Communists to elevate antisemitism to the main plank of their political program; even the most simple-minded could not be persuaded that Jewish terrorists were ambushing Russian soldiers in Chechnya. But even if it was not the most important single issue in the programs of the nationalists and the Communists, the Jewish problem did survive as a factor in Russia's political life.

The Jews in all of Eastern Europe today probably number no more than 100,000 and about three-quarters of these live in Hungary. Neofascist parties appeared after 1989 in all these countries; the impetus for their emergence was in most cases social, such as unemployment, but traditional extreme nationalism did play a role in Romania and Hungary. These neofascist movements differ considerably from their prewar predecessors—there is no strict organization, no cult of the leader; the parties are predominantly populist in orientation, aiming for representation in parliament (as in Poland, Hungary, and Romania) rather than dominating the street.

What role does antisemitism play at present in the political life of these countries? A relatively small one, in view of the tiny number of Jews surviving—which is, moreover, rapidly shrinking through emigration, mixed marriage, and a low birth rate. The antisemitic propaganda is often rabid, but the Jewish issue is simply not important enough to serve the cause of these parties. For East European ruling parties and governments, antisemitism of this kind is an embarrassment in view of their desire to become integrated in a united Europe.

There is an inclination (for instance, in Romania and the Baltic countries) to play down the involvement of these countries in the massacre of the Jews during the Second World War. The fact that Jews were prominently represented in the post-1945 Communist leadership is dwelt upon; the fact that Jews were purged from the party—for instance, in the Slansky trial of 1952 in Prague—is seldom mentioned, and neither are the waves of expulsion of Jews from Poland in 1958 and 1968.

It is argued that more Poles than Jews were killed under the Nazis and the Communists, and in Romania there was a strong trend to rehabilitate Marshal Ion Antonescu and the other pro-Nazi leaders from the Second World War. At the same time, it ought to be mentioned that individuals of Jewish extraction have represented their countries in leading positions—Bronislav Geremek and after him Adam Rotfeld as Polish foreign minister, Petre Roman as Romanian prime minister. Muslim antisemitism has appeared in Chechnya and occasionally in the Central Asian republics, mainly as an importation, but it has been of little political consequence, and in some Muslim republics it has not appeared at all.

TRADITIONAL ACCUSATIONS against Jews remained part and parcel of antisemitic doctrine after 1945, but there was one major new element— Holocaust denial. As seen from an antisemitic point of view, the murder of millions of Jews in Europe was a major embarrassment and political obstacle. The unspeakable barbarism of Auschwitz and the other death camps antagonized decent people irrespective of their politics and ostracized the antisemites: if these were the consequences of antisemitism, who would want to be part of a movement of this kind? Hence, the necessity to show that there had been no Auschwitz, or that it had been greatly exaggerated, or that the Nazi leadership had not known about it.

The Nazi leadership had taken great care to obliterate all traces of the death camps. Orders had been given to destroy all gas chambers and that no survivor of the camps was to fall alive into the hands of the Russians and the Western Allies. However, the leadership could not erase their earlier public pronouncements of their intentions. Hitler had announced in his 1939 anniversary speech to the Reichstag, even before unleashing the war, that the war would lead not to "the Bolshevization of the world" but to "the annihilation of the Jewish race," and Heinrich Himmler in a famous speech to SS leaders in Poznan in October 1943 had mentioned a "very grave matter . . . about which we will never speak publicly . . . I mean the extermination of the Jewish race." Though many Germans knew that the Jews had been deported and would not return, few had an overall picture of the extent of the mass murder—the details were suppressed at the time—the way it was organized and carried out. Many German soldiers after the war said that they had never witnessed anything of this kind—especially if they had served in the navy, the air force, or in North Africa, they were no doubt sincere and truthful.

The first well-known case of Holocaust denial occurred in France soon after the war. A socialist parliamentary deputy named Paul Rassinier argued that since he had been a prisoner at the Nazi camp of Buchenwald in 1943 and had never seen a gas chamber, the Holocaust must have been a lie. The murder of six million Jews was simply a myth. But why should anyone wish to launch or perpetrate such an infamous lie? According to Rassinier and many who followed in his steps, it must have been an Allies-Jewish intrigue, part of a scheme to blackmail Germany to indemnify the so-called victims, and perhaps also to mobilize support for the establishment of the state of Israel.

There is little doubt that Rassinier, whose evidence strongly influenced other early "revisionists" such as David Hoggan, who developed his ideas on the subject in a Harvard dissertation, was sincerely convinced of the essential truth of his arguments. But his evidence was based wholly on his own experience, and he had been detained in a German concentration camp that housed mainly political prisoners, common criminals, homosexuals, Christian pacifists—Buchenwald and Dachau were the most notorious of these but they were never meant to be death factories with gas chambers for the annihilation of Jews. The death camps, including Auschwitz, Maidanek, and Sobibor, were all located outside of Germany in the occupied territories.

Following the pioneering work of Rassinier, Holocaust denial (also called revisionism or negationism) spread to many countries. Among its most prominent representatives were Robert Faurisson, a literature professor in France; David Irving and "Richard Harwood" in Britain; Fred Leuchter and Ernst Zuendel in Canada; Arthur R. Butz in the United States. Institutions and periodicals were founded with the sole aim of refuting the "Auschwitz lie," such as the *Journal of Historical Review* and the *Annales d'histoire revisioniste* in the United States and France respectively. None of these experts had any specialized knowledge of the subject or had been in Eastern Europe during the war. That their findings were found false in a number of trials (against Irving, Zuendel, and Faurisson) has made no difference; the revisionists regarded themselves as fighters for historical truth against the overwhelming forces of world Jewry.

Politically, the Holocaust deniers hailed from a variety of camps even though a majority belonged to the far right, but there are also members of the French extreme left (*La vieille taupe*) among them. A few were professional nay-sayers who can be found in every historical debate; even while Napoleon was still alive, books were published demonstrating that he had never existed. A subsequent generation of revisionists, some of them Jewish by origin, and mainly from the extreme left, would not deny that Jews had been killed or maintain that the mass murder was a hoax. Instead, they claimed that it had been based on the collaboration between Nazis and Zionists, and that the sole purpose of the great publicity given to the Holocaust decades after the event was to provide political help to the state of Israel and its right-wing, semifascist policies.

Some of the revisionists argued that no Jews had been killed at all, though some tens of thousands might have died as a result of diseases or the harsh living conditions in Eastern Europe during the war. Others claimed that the Nazi leaders were perfectly justified in taking extreme measures against the Jews since they had declared war on Germany. Yet others pointed to the fact that no written order by Hitler to engage in the extermination had ever been found; the idea that orders to carry out mass murder are seldom if ever given in writing had not occurred to them.

What of the admission by Nazis who had taken a leading part in the "final solution" and openly admitted it—such as Rudolf Hoess, the first commandant of Auschwitz; or Adolf Eichmann, in charge of "Emigration and Evacuation" (Nazi euphemisms for expulsion and deportation), who organized and managed the transportation of Jews to the death camps; or Kurt Gerstein, who had tried to alert the Allies to the use of poison gas for killing the Jews? This was not serious evidence, it is argued; these people had obviously been tortured.

Some revisionists focus on technical questions. They claim that gas chambers had not been found, and when confronted with evidence to the contrary, they would claim that the structures had served other purposes, such as disinfection. They argue that it would have been technically impossible to kill so many people in so short a time. Still others concentrate on statistics; they claim that the number of Jews living in Eastern Europe had been exaggerated, and the number of survivors artificially inflated. This still leaves millions unaccounted for—where had they disappeared? Perhaps, the revisionists speculate, they had emigrated to America or some other countries during the war.

It is perfectly true that wholly exact population figures did not exist (even though during the war the SS produced statistical progress reports about the number of Jews liquidated). To be precise, it is known how many Jews had lived and were deported from countries such as Germany, Czechoslovakia, and Holland, but there are no exact figures about, for instance, the Soviet Union. It is true, furthermore, that the number of Jews killed in Auschwitz was initially exaggerated, but the number of those who died on the way to the death camps was understated. Estimates by serious historians of the total number of those killed vary between 5.1 and 5.9 million.

Such discrepancies are not something extraordinary; there are no exact figures about the losses of other peoples—military and civilians— in both World War One and Two, even as far as Germany is concerned, a country with a nearly perfect statistical tradition. This is true particularly with regard to the later phases of World War Two, when the Nazi administration had broken down, when confusion reigned, when many were buried without the customary registration. There were also cases of exaggeration of the losses, such as in the bombing of Dresden toward the very end of the war: many historians assumed until fairly recently that between 100,000 and 200,000 had been killed, whereas exact investigation eventually showed that the number of victims was about 35,000. But about the magnitude of the disaster that had befallen European Jewry there can be no disagreement—before the war there had been major communities on the continent; after the war they existed no longer.

Lastly, there has emerged a more moderate trend of revisionism in the form of "the relativists." The relativists argue that while a few million Jews had probably been killed, this should be seen in historical perspective. A great many people perished during that war—and on other occasions throughout history. In other words, while the Holocaust was sad and reprehensible, it was by no means unique in the annals of history. This was the official line in the Soviet Union and the Communist countries of Eastern Europe. The Jews had suffered, but not more than other people, and it is wrong to single out their suffering or to set up special memorials. Nor is it clear that the Nazis had intended all along to kill European Jewry, they argue: is it not true that up to the outbreak of the war their policy had been to force the Jews to emigrate? What happened after 1939 is not clear, they claim—perhaps some local leaders had been overzealous in carrying out what they thought was Hitler's desire; perhaps such local initiatives had developed a momentum of their own with one thing leading to another.

A great deal of energy has been invested by Jewish experts and others to refute the revisionist arguments. This has not been too difficult because the evidence concerning the organization and execution of the mass murder is overwhelming. Refutation is a necessary exercise, but it can never be wholly successful because Holocaust revisionism is more often than not politically motivated and thus impervious to rational refutation. As quickly as one set of revisionist arguments is refuted beyond any shadow of doubt, the negationists will bring up another set of arguments, however spurious.

ARAB AND MUSLIM ATTITUDES toward the Holocaust are of particular interest. During the first two decades after the end of World War Two, this was not an issue of great interest to Arab governments, the media, the intellectuals, or the men and women in the street. This began to change only in the 1970s, and there was a crescendo during the subsequent years with a flood of movies, television documentaries, books, articles, conferences, and other events arguing at one and the same time that the Holocaust had been justified and that it had never taken place.

The arguments used were more or less the same as those used by European classical antisemitism; but since there were no laws against racialist incitement as in Europe, Arab media could be far more outspoken than the European antisemites. It was maintained that the Jews were the enemies of all mankind, were seditious bloodsuckers; if they had been persecuted at all times in all countries, it was simply their own fault. Jews, it was claimed, were essentially evil and wanted to dominate not just Germany but the whole world. For the most part, the field of accusations against the Jews had been exhausted by European antisemites and there were only a few innovations emanating from the Middle East. The traditional blood libel (that Jews were killing Christian children for ritual purposes on Passover) did not make much sense in the Muslim world. Instead, it was claimed that Jews were abducting and slaughtering Arab children in order use their body organs for transplantation to their own. The Jews were, an Iranian professor declared on Tehran television, the source of all corrupt traits in humanity; Hitler had therefore been perfectly justified gassing and burning them; if anything, he should be blamed for letting some of them survive. But soon after, the president of Iran made it known that the Holocaust had never taken place. Again, it was not made quite clear why the Jews, eager to dominate the world, had made a start in Palestine; a small country without any natural resources would seem the worst possible base for global expansion.

This kind of argument is shared by the Islamists, the secular nationalists, and also parts of the Arab left. However popular among the less-educated sections of society, it proved sometimes an embarrassment to governments and also to a minority of intellectuals, largely because of the impression it created in the West but also because of the intellectual company statements like these attracted. Lastly, there were some who were not enthusiastic about this line of propaganda because they knew that it was largely nonsense.

Denial of the Holocaust has been official Arab policy for a long time. In the early 1950s Charles Malik, Lebanese foreign minister and a Christian, had declared that the murder of the Jews in Europe had been mere Zionist propaganda, and Egypt's Gamal Abdel Nasser, the hero of pan-Arab nationalism in the 1960s, put it even more strongly: "no person, not even the most simple one takes seriously the lie of the six million Jews who were killed." This thesis was subsequently taken up by the Islamists and their intellectual supporters, who viewed the Holocaust as the founding myth of the state of Israel. Leading Western rejectionists, such as Roger Garaudy, toured the Middle East and were given enormous publicity.

As for the specific arguments concerning the "Auschwitz lie," they had all been advanced by European and American revisionists: there had not been that many Jews in Europe in the first place; they had not been deported; death camps had not existed; it would have been physically impossible to murder so many people in such short a period; the admissions by leading executioners such as Rudolf Hoess and Adolf Eichmann had been extracted by means of torture. And if indeed a few thousand Jews had perished, this had happened following an agreement between Zionists and Nazis according to which assimilated Jews should be liquidated whereas Zionist Jews should be permitted to survive.

On a somewhat more sophisticated level it was argued that many Jews indeed might have been killed during World War Two, but this had nothing to do with Palestinians or the Arabs, and why should the Palestinians suffer and pay the price for crimes committed in Europe? And in any case, the crimes subsequently committed by the Jews in Palestine and elsewhere were infinitely greater than those of the Nazis. Arab purveyors of Holocaust denial faced certain obstacles. Whereas the accusation against the Zionists of having collaborated with the Nazis was a very serious and (if true) damaging accusation in Europe, this was not so in the Middle East, where Hitler and his party had enjoyed wide sympathies at the time.

This, in briefest outline, was the Arab and Muslim reaction to the Holocaust sixty years after the event. There are no reliable polls showing to what extent these versions were truly believed, but according to all evidence they were accepted by the majority, probably the great majority, of Arabs and stated with great emotional intensity.

No MENTION HAS BEEN MADE so far of antisemitism in the United States. Few Jews lived in America before the middle of the nineteenth century, although the United States was a country of various groups of immigrants. The founding fathers envisaged the republic as Christian-Protestant in character but also stressed religious freedom. There had been from the very beginning prejudice and discrimination against Jews, but there were no ghettos in America, no pogroms, no systematic persecution. As Leonard Dinerstein, the historian of antisemitism in America, wrote in 1994, "They were not as victimized and as exploited as Irish Catholics, they were not pushed out of society as the Indians and they were not enslaved like the Africans."

Antisemitism such as it was in the United States was religious in motivation; it came out of both Protestant and Catholic churches. In many places Jews were not considered socially acceptable, even if wealthy and well connected. A leading Jewish banker was barred by a judge from registering in a Saratoga Springs hotel in 1877. If high society and churchgoers rejected the Jews, so did the Populists (and later the Progressives) of the late nineteenth century. For them, the Jews were parasites; they had arrived as peddlers and within a few decades had become major merchants and bankers. Many of the ills of American farmers and artisans were attributed to the machinations of Jewish international finance capital as embodied by the Rothschilds. But the Rothschilds were not American, nor did they have a major presence in the United States.

Antisemitism manifested itself largely in keeping Jews out of certain professions, elite universities, and social and athletic clubs, but not as a major political issue. There was considerable opposition to Jewish immigration during the last decades of the nineteenth century and the years before World War One, but there was also opposition to

Irish and Chinese immigrations. Still, immigrants were needed for the economic development of the country. Eventually unlimited immigration was stopped and schedules established to reduce the influx of newcomers. Antisemitism increased during the interwar period, mainly, no doubt, as the result of political and social tensions and the great economic depression. American Jews experienced some restrictions; they were generally not employed by leading corporations; they could not live in certain restricted communities, and they were sparsely represented in the professions. Henry Ford, one of the best known and most admired Americans, was also a rabid antisemite who engaged in anti-Jewish propaganda such as the promotion and distribution of the *Protocols* and other antisemitic material; he did, however, change his mind toward the end of his life.

Anti-Jewish accusations made in America followed more or less the same lines as in Europe. Jews were thought to be revolutionaries who were undermining traditional Christian and patriotic values; at the same time, they were condemned for being too eager and successful in the pursuit of mammon, of becoming too quickly the apostles and practitioners of capitalism. Fears were expressed that Jews had obtained too much economic and political power, even though few were among the leading bankers and none among the industrialists prior to World War Two. As for Jewish political influence, it was nearly nonexistent or, at best, insufficient to help open the gates of America a little wider for refugees from Nazism in the 1930s. By that time, Jews had attained leading positions in the print media, publishing, and the entertainment industry, especially in Hollywood, but out of fear of antisemitism they leaned over backward not to promote any specific Jewish concerns. To give but two examples: the *New York Times*, which was in Jewish hands, had very little to report about the mass murder of European Jewry during World War Two, and Hollywood moguls were equally silent.

During the 1930s, in the wake of the Great Depression, antisemitic organizations emerged that had a considerable outreach. Two of the most influential were headed by churchmen: Father Coughlin, a Catholic, and Gerald Smith, a Protestant. They bitterly attacked Roosevelt's "Jew Deal" (and the Jews involved in his administration), claiming that the Jews were warmongers. Most of the elements of their sermons came from Nazi sources, although as fundamentalist Christians they could not share the basically pagan views of the Nazis. It was the misfortune of these movements that they coincided with Nazi attacks against America—both on the political and the military level, and that support for Hitler and all he stood for came to be considered unpatriotic and even treasonable. The Reverend William Dudley Pelley, another antisemitic leader, was charged with sedition and given a 15-year jail sentence.

This antisemitic tradition did not entirely disappear in the postwar period but found successors and imitators in a variety of sects and militias too numerous to mention. Some engaged in political propaganda, others prepared for terrorist actions such as the one in Oklahoma City in 1995. They all belonged to the extreme right, believed in the existence of a Zionist Occupation Government (ZOG, meaning the existing Washington administration) and all kinds of weird conspiracy theories concerning UFOs, Jews, international organizations, and virtually all racial and ethnic minorities. Some groups were fanatically religious, others pagan in orientation. They stood for social justice as they understood it, for states' rights, against international finance. Some of the most outspoken of them believed that America could be saved from certain doom only as the result of the physical extermination of blacks, Latinos, Jews, and virtually all non-Nordic nationalities. The *Turner Diaries*, a fictional account glorifying extreme violence in graphic detail and the source of the ZOG phrase, sold more than 250,000 copies even though it was neither reviewed in the media nor sold in regular bookshops.

The very extremism of these sects puts them outside the pale, and they could not prevent the advance of the minorities (including the

Jews) in the postwar period after the ban on all kinds of discrimination. If Jews were still excluded from certain clubs or professions, these were unimportant; to be Jewish or of Jewish extraction no longer constituted a hindrance in almost any field of human endeavor. If there was a renewal of antisemitism (or at least a feeling of a second coming), this came from altogether different quarters than in the past. Black militants from the Nation of Islam and other such groups were in the front rank of attacks against the Jews. This came as a shock to Jewish communities; the majority of American Jews have been liberal in outlook and still are. No other group has been as active in the struggle for the civil rights of the blacks, and some had been killed as a result. While there had never been a formal Jewish-Black alliance, relations on the communal level had been seemingly normal, at times even warm and cordial. Martin Luther King, for example, and Adam Clayton Powell, the leading black politician of the Roosevelt era, had expressed friendly views vis-à-vis the Jews. How then to explain the sudden turn?

There had been in fact a fairly strong antisemitic element in the black mental makeup early on, probably under the impact of the southern Christian influence ("the Jews have killed our savior"). In later years, black migrants to the north met Jews in the big cities as landlords and shopkeepers who, they came to believe, exploited them. There were small-scale anti-Jewish riots in Harlem, New York, and in Chicago in the 1920s and 1930s. While the NAACP, one of the leading black organizations, opposed Nazism from the beginning, there were considerable sympathies for Hitler among the blacks at the time, including his policy toward the Jews. These sympathizers were quite oblivious of the fact that the Nazis regarded the blacks as an inferior race; the feeling in black neighborhoods was that even if the position of Jews in Nazi Germany might have been bad, it was not half as bad as that of the black in the United States. Above all there was the feeling, as Ralph Bunche put it (one of the first blacks to rise to a major position in the Department of State and formerly a political scientist at Howard University), "it was safe to scorn the Jew"; it was less safe to scorn the white majority.

Over the years, black resentment of the Jews may have grown because they were once a despised minority outside the mainstream of American society and had gradually succeeded, becoming wealthier, acquiring a good education, and rising in the social scale, while the situation in the black ghettos remained extremely bad for a long time. Seen from this perspective, the fact that Jews were so prominent in the struggle for equal rights was of little importance. Perhaps it was the bad conscience of the Jews that impelled them to make amends? Some historians discovered that Portuguese Jews had been involved in the slave trade. This allegation was correct, but true mainly with regard to Brazil and Curacao, and the role of the Jews in these unsavory dealings had certainly been of much less consequence than that of the Arab slave traders, let alone the black tribal leaders in Africa, who had sold without compunction their fellow citizens. A leading black historian estimated that the Jews involved in the American slave trade had been perhaps 2 percent.

All this rationalizes to some degree why the antisemitic wave of the 1980s and of Louis Farrakhan and his followers in the next decade should not have come as a total surprise. But it offers no full explanation because the source of black grievances and complaints about the Jews, real or perceived, had largely disappeared—the Jewish shopkeepers and landlords in the ghettos had moved out long ago, their place taken by Koreans, Latinos, and blacks. There were no longer many places where black and Jewish interests clashed, where indeed they met. It was still true that, as Bunche had put it many years before, it was safer to scorn the Jews than the white majority; it was also true that Jews were more sensitive and, instead of ignoring attacks, felt greatly aggrieved and reacted in almost every case. However, the importance of black antisemitism should not be overrated; it was never an issue of paramount political importance. For certain black leaders the issue was a convenient one to gain applause in meetings, but it was of no major relevance to the real concerns of the black community. It was not at the top of the agenda of Jewish communities either.

THE ISSUE OF CONTEMPORARY LEFT-WING ANTISEMITISM has been and continues to be a major bone of contention. Just as Arabs have argued for a long time that they cannot possibly be anti-Jewish (in contradistinction to being anti-Zionist) because they too are Semites, left-wing spokesmen have maintained that allegations of this kind are base calumnies; the left, standing for peace, progress, and equal rights for all, cannot possibly be motivated by antisemitism. This is true if the yardstick is the religious antisemitism of the churches or the Koran or the racialist antisemitism of the Nazis. Seen from this perspective, even the extreme left cannot possibly be defined as antisemitic—they do not want to exterminate the Jews, they simply want them to disappear as Jews, as Jean-Paul Sartre noted many years ago. In fact, not a few people of Jewish origin can be found in their ranks.

But this is only part of the story, for both the left and antisemitism have changed their character over time. Nor is it true that anti-Jewish attacks emanating from the extreme left are invariably connected with the policies of the state of Israel and its close alliance with imperialist America. One group of the German terrorist left, headed by Dieter Kunzelmann, planned to blow up a meeting of the leadership of the Berlin Jewish community in 1969, killing as many as possible. This was a meeting to commemorate Kristallnacht 1938, the largest Nazi prewar pogrom; it had nothing to do with the state of Israel and Zionism.

It is one of the fundamental tenets of belief of the extreme left that while other nations have the right to have their own state, the Jews have not. They did live after all for two millennia without a state, and any attempt to turn back the wheels of history is essentially reactionary. It is bound to conflict with the vital interests of other people and dispossess them. Hence, the extreme left concludes that Arab and Muslim enemies of Israel are progressive because they are anti-American and anticapitalist, however illiberal their ideology in other respects; that they should be supported, whereas Israel and those affirming its right of existence are a priori enemies of progress and peace.

This thinking leads to a rapprochement between the extreme left and the extreme Islamists on both the doctrinal and the political level, as in Britain. On the fringes of their anti-Zionist demonstrations, there have been calls to "kill the Jews" and physical attacks, but the extreme left argues that they cannot be made responsible for such regrettable excesses of zeal on the part of their partners. It is a well known fact, they further argue, that progressive movements in backward countries are still afflicted with antiquated ideological elements. Still, with all this, they are basically progressive, and the illiberal ideological remnants of the past are bound to disappear over time; they are less important, the far left claims, than the "objective" progressive role of these movements. If they do not make fine distinctions between Zionists, Israelis, and Jews, the extreme left says, this is regrettable but forgivable. The inhabitants of Israel are after all mostly Jews, and the Arabs' hatred is therefore bound to be directed against all Jews, just as in the Second World War "German" became a synonym for Nazi.

The case of the extreme left against Israel and the collaboration of the extreme left with antisemitic groups can be more easily justified on pragmatic than doctrinal grounds. It has provoked ideological differences among the left in Europe as well as in America. However, the turn of the extreme left against the Jews is by no means limited to the misdeeds of the state of Israel and its close collaboration with the United States. Historically, it goes back to well before the American-Israeli alliance came into being in the 1970s and it extends to a great variety of issues. Antiglobalists regard the Jews as an enemy because of their alleged support of international capitalism; radical feminists are very critical of the Jews because five thousand years ago they were instrumental in replacing the matriarchy with the patriarchy. In Europe, left-wing internationalists regard Jews as a conflict-causing element—at a time when national borders are disappearing in Europe, why do the Jews need a state of their own? (According to a public opinion poll in 2003, 59 percent of Europeans believed that Israel was the country most dangerous to the preservation of world peace.) It seemed to follow that but for these nationalist, indeed atavistic, aspirations, there would be peace and harmony between the third world and Europe, and the danger of terrorism as well as other such threats would be much reduced.

Some writers of the left, including some Jews, have argued that the importance of the Holocaust has been exaggerated, if not deliberately exploited. One Jewish academic of this persuasion, a Canadian professor named Michael Neumann, has argued that antisemitism hardly exists and where it exists, it ought to be treated as a huge joke. Mikis Theodorakis, famed Greek musician and composer and a hero of the European left, said in an interview that the Jews were the root of all evil, that they controlled not only world finance but all orchestras that would not perform his works. He also noted that there was really no antisemitism and that Jews were simply masochists who liked the role of victims. Similar voices have not been infrequent on the left.

When the British Labor party launched antisemitic attacks against two Conservative leaders (Michael Howard and Oliver Lettwin) who were of Jewish extraction, this had nothing to do with Zionism and Israel since these political figures were in no way involved in pro-Israel activities (or indeed in Jewish life), but simply with the fact that as Jews they were vulnerable. (About half of the British electorate indicated that it would not want a Jew as prime minister.) It could well be that those who launched these attacks were motivated merely by "practical" considerations. The influence of Muslim communities in Western Europe is growing and they might well be decisive in dozens of electoral constituencies. Why not appease these communities by propaganda that caters to their popular moods such as antisemitism? This is true not only for Britain but also for France and other European countries, and such activities are likely to increase in the years to come.

Old-style Communists in Russia and its nationalist allies—the differences between these two groups are now barely visible to the naked eye—accused Jews of ritual murder and demanded the ban of all Jewish organizations in January 2005. But this had nothing to do with Zionism and Israel, and it would not be difficult to adduce other such examples.

It would be an exaggeration to maintain that contemporary antisemitism is exclusively or predominantly left wing in character, just as in previous ages it would have been an exaggeration to apportion all the responsibility for antisemitism to conservatives. But it is true that for a variety of reasons the extreme left (or, to be precise, what now goes by that name) has in recent years adopted an anti-Jewish stance which in part can be explained with reference to opposition to Israel, but which also has components quite unconnected with Zionism and Israel.

According to research in Western Europe in 2002, 63 percent of those surveyed in Spain believed Jews had too much power in the business world (44 percent in Belgium, 42 percent in France, 40 percent in Austria, 37 percent in Switzerland, 32 percent in Germany, and 21 percent in the United Kingdom). Perhaps more significantly, 58 percent in Germany thought that Jews were talking too much about the Holocaust (57 percent in Spain, 56 percent in Austria, 52 percent in Switzerland, 46 percent in France, 43 percent in Italy). It can be argued that such figures may be meaningless since the figures for those who had never even heard of the Holocaust were almost as high (and even higher among the younger generation). But as so often happens, it was the perception that mattered, not the facts. In brief, while the conflict between Israel and the Arabs has provided much fuel for the spread of anti-Jewish feeling in the Muslim world, it cannot explain antisemitism among blacks in the United States any more than it can among groups in Russia, Eastern Europe, and elsewhere.

Chapter Eight

ASSIMILATION AND ITS DISCONTENTS

THE SIMPLEST EXPLANATION OF ANTISEMITISM has come, not surprisingly, from the antisemites: antisemitism is the inevitable reaction of non-Jews to the misdeeds of the Jews. The Jews did reject the message of Jesus Christ and Muhammad. They kept apart from other people, lived by their own law, and did not mingle with others. They believed themselves superior, having been selected to have a special covenant with God.

It is difficult to think of minorities anywhere in the world that have been popular throughout history, but on top of the frequent antagonism against minorities, the "usual xenophobia," Jews have been on the receiving end of special animosity and hatred. And it is also true that antisemitism did not disappear when Jews tried to escape the stigma of being Jews by conversion, whether it was in sixteenth-century Spain or in the age of assimilation in Germany and France.

That Jews stuck together even in the pre-Christian period seems evident and that they were a stiff-necked people even the Bible says. With the rise of Christianity, the accusations of deicide followed and, in the Middle Ages, the charge that Jews in their secret books were ridiculing Jesus as well as Mary. Generally speaking, it was argued that the Jews believed that the Talmud and the other commentaries to the Old Testament were more important and binding than the Bible. The Talmud was said to be full of blasphemous (from a Christian point of view) and immoral commandments; the non-Jew could be defrauded, robbed, even killed with impunity; his life was worth no more than that of an animal.

For several centuries, Jewish religious spokesmen have tried without much success to explain that most of the allegations were either exaggerated or totally false. But not all accusations were groundless. Being a compilation of the comments of generations of commentators, much of the time contradicting each other, the Talmud did indeed contain nonsensical and even immoral sayings, but no more so than the writings of other religions of that period. It was true, for instance, that the Talmud contained anti-Christian statements; this proved very embarrassing, so for a time the rabbis claimed that the Jesus mentioned in the Talmud referred to someone else and that the "gentiles" who appeared were really pagans. This caused new problems because according to the Talmud—which had been in part composed when most Jews did not yet live in the diaspora—it was forbidden for Jews to do business with gentiles, which was hardly a practical proposition in subsequent centuries. Eventually, the anti-Christian references were censored and deleted.

With all the Talmud's strange and contradictory commandments and taboos, however, decisive in the final analysis was the principle of *dina di malkuta dina*—the law of the land (in which the Jews lived) was supreme and overruled all other interpretations and comments. Another circumstance seldom remembered was that as time passed, fewer and fewer Jews were familiar with the Talmud, and by the nineteenth century, it had become a virtually forgotten book (or rather a series of books encompassing many thousands of pages), accessible only to a few experts if only because of the variety of obscure languages in which it was written. It is an irony of history that not only the antisemites but also the great majority of the Jews who have written about antisemitism have had only the faintest knowledge of the Talmud. Nevertheless, the Talmud remained up to the Nazi era the cudgel with which the enemies of the Jews could beat their victims

In the course of time other accusations followed, the most prominent of which was the so-called blood libel—that the Jews had to kill Christians (preferably children) around Passover because they needed the blood of Christians for their ritual ceremonies. This and other accusations continued sporadically until the early twentieth century. That on various occasions the churches and even the pope had declared these charges unfounded was not of much help in changing attitudes.

The situation in Muslim countries was different inasmuch as neither the Talmud nor the blood libel figured in the persecution of the Jews. The Jews had not killed the prophet, they had only schemed against him, and because they had rejected his message, they were to be considered an inferior group. This charge of rejection was, of course, correct, and it theologically resulted in the inferior status of the Jews in the Islamic world.

Motivations for Jew-hatred other than theological ones appeared in the Middle Ages, and they became more frequent and more prominent as the influence of religion waned in the nineteenth century. One of the main accusations from early history concerned usury—money lending on the basis of excessive profit. Both Christianity and Islam banned usury, yet economic progress, and even normal economic activity, was impossible without the investment of capital—kings and poor peasants and everyone in between frequently needed money, and it was in this connection that the Jews came to fulfill an important function in society. Though the Old Testament also forbids usury, this ban was interpreted as a ban only on lending money to other Jews. Hence, money lending emerged as a predominantly Jewish occupation during several centuries in various European countries.

Money lending is a necessary and even vital institution but not a popular one in society; it made those doing it vulnerable to charges of being "bloodsuckers" and "parasites." When Shakespeare created the figure of Shylock Jews had been expelled from England for just over three hundred years, but the figure of the usurer out to get his pound of flesh was engraved in public consciousness. The issue at stake was not really whether money lending was necessary but whether the Jews had entered it out of greed (as antisemites claimed) or because most other professions were barred to them. Seen in historical perspective, it would appear that in most of Christian Europe their choice of professions was indeed extremely restricted; they could engage in trade (but not all forms of trade) and money lending. In countries where other professions were open to them, such as Muslim Spain and the Ottoman empire, one finds more Jewish blacksmiths than Jewish money lenders. The high tide of Jewish usury was before the fifteenth century; as cities grew in power and affluence, the Jews were squeezed out from money lending with the development of banking. Following centuries of church condemnation of Jewish usury, the Jews were expelled from many countries and regions, their communities were impoverished, and very few individuals had the necessary capital to engage in money lending. Money lending continued, of course, and the Lombards took 250 percent interest (this, however, did not cause a wave of anti-Lombardism).

Few Jews were found in occupations of primary production such as agriculture or mining. As long as they were permitted to own land, there were Jewish landowners in countries such as Spain and France; the most famous commentator of the Bible, Rashi, owned vineyards in France. Elsewhere, Jews could in principle own land but they could not employ non-Jews as laborers. In many countries, they could not work as artisans except for the small Jewish market because the urban guilds feared their competition.

It is also true that agriculture, being primitive, afforded only a minimal existence, the lowest of all living standards, and throughout the Middle Ages, people fled from the countryside in many countries (*Landflucht*). In the circumstances, farming had little if any attraction. However, the Jewish exodus from the countryside began even earlier, and economic historians have given us various explanations for why this happened.

First, literacy was a religious commandment for Jews, and it was, of course, far easier to comply with this obligation in an urban surrounding than in the isolation of the countryside. There is much reason to believe that many Jews did stay in agriculture but eventually became Christians or Muslims; this could explain the fact that the number of Jews remained static throughout the Middle Ages while the general population doubled or trebled. Finally, there was the temptation of a higher living standard in the cities, even though the prospects of finding congenial and rewarding work there were limited. Jews could and did own land in the Muslim world throughout the Middle Ages and also, in certain circumstances, in Poland. But more often, Jews worked as agents of the big landowners, usually from the nobility, as middlemen, or in agricultural trade.

What about the accusations of Jewish money lenders taking excessive rates of interest, the main charge on the part of the churches? Leading economists from Adam Smith to John Maynard Keynes have favored imposing a ceiling on interest rates, and there are national laws to this effect to this day. The rates of interest taken in the Middle Ages were very high, certainly excessive by modern standards. But the risks at the time were enormous and there was little security in a feudal society. When Jewish usurers loaned money to kings or noblemen, there was always the danger that they would never see their money again, be arrested or expelled, or have their money confiscated. They had no power, and the laws were only sporadically observed. There was no protection in this profession and no one was more exposed and vulnerable than the Jews.

In early modern history Jews were no longer prominent in money lending, and in the nineteenth century, with their gradual emancipation, attacks against the Jews changed in character. As Jews left the ghettos and streamed into professions that had been barred to them earlier, and as their material position improved, with some becoming rich and influential, the main charge against them was the allegation that Jews aspired to world domination. Jews, it was claimed, had pushed themselves into the front ranks of the political establishment, especially the left-wing and liberal parties. There were exceptions— the one prominent British politician of Jewish descent, Benjamin Disraeli, was hardly a man of the left, nor was the chief ideologue of the nineteenth-century German Conservatives, Friedrich Stahl. But by and large the charges were correct; there were not many Jews among the parties of the right or in the confessional-religious parties because these groups did not want them as members.

Did Jews in politics pursue any specific Jewish agenda? The answer is obvious. The Jewish communities were small in number; they could not constitute a power basis for any aspiring politician. Jews in European politics did not appear as representatives of any specific Jewish interests. On the contrary, Jewish politicians often tried to distance themselves as much as possible from their coreligionists; Rosa Luxemburg's letter to a Jewish friend—in which she said, essentially, do not come to me with your specific Jewish complaints—was an extreme case but not altogether untypical. It was genuine, not opportunistic. She must have felt self-conscious with her Polish Jewish background, but even more decisive was the fact that she seems to have felt closer to the wretched, persecuted Indians in Putamayo, Colombia, according to her own writings, than to the East European Jews who perished in the pogroms.

Many Jewish politicians were in the vanguard of progress, human freedom, and internationalism. This invited attacks on the part of those who did not share their enthusiasm, who thought that these revolutionary Jews had no respect for the traditional values of a nation, were not good patriots, and were, in general, a ferment of decomposition. Their bona fides were questioned: they did not really care about the exploited and oppressed masses they claimed to represent but were really out to gain power for themselves and their cliques, many of them also of Jewish provenance. The fact that these Jews had not only distanced themselves from their community but often turned against it was ignored—perhaps, the accusers speculated, it was a mere stratagem to mislead the non-Jews.

It was argued that Jews had amassed great riches—and thus enormous power—not through honest labor but by speculation and the exploitation of the toiling non-Jews. Jews were successful entrepreneurs and able to adapt more quickly to the changing economic and financial climate precisely because their status had been marginal in the days of the ghetto and because they had not been permitted to grow deep roots. This was coupled with the accusation that the Jews were corrupting society, that mammon was their idol, as the young Marx put it.

The enormously wealthy Rothschilds were often in the European public eyes, because there were five Rothschild sons who presided over financial establishments in Frankfurt, London, Vienna, Paris, and Naples in the early nineteenth century. In contrast, the great majority of European Jews were small traders and peddlers, although they worked very hard and their sons often became professionals, lawyers, and physicians. More than any other stratum of society, Jews were upwardly mobile. About half of the doctors in Vienna and more than half in Warsaw in the early twentieth century were of Jewish origins. The social and economic rise of the Jews was bound to generate amazement and envy; the Jews, as one antisemitic French author wrote, had become the kings of our time. Consequently, it was claimed that European antisemitism was directly connected with their rise; a correct conclusion albeit a trite one: had the Jews remained poor like the Dalets (Untouchables) in India, they would hardly have inspired fear and envy.

Jews became prominent in the cultural life of their native countries. They were among the leading publishers of books and newspapers, the dominant art dealers and musical impresarios. They were among the literary and musical critics; they set the tone, they could make and unmake the careers of writers and artists. This, too, was bound to provoke opposition and resistance—who had invited them, who had given them that much power? Was it not a fact that Jews lacked true creativity? Was it not true that they failed to understand the spirit and deeper emotions of the culture of their country? According to their critics, the Jews were a negative, destructive force and true genius escaped them. They were sarcastic, but true humor remained alien to them. And there were warning voices even from among the Jews that they had arrogated to themselves the role of managers of the culture of other nations.

Such general accusations quite apart, there were constant complaints about negative features of the "Jewish character" that, the critics of the Jews claimed, made true integration difficult or impossible, hard as the Jews might have tried. Jews were said to be greedy, arrogant, and aggressive; they had to push themselves always to the top of the line; dignity, modesty, and altruism were qualities alien to them. They were by nature dishonest and disloyal. They were cold rationalists, incapable of deeper feeling; true spiritual life, the realm of the soul, was outside their ken. They took care of each other but remained always critical or hostile to non-Jews. They were overly ambitious and competitive, quite incapable of team spirit or team effort, always devious, never straightforward.

There was a great deal of fear and suspicion of the Jews because of their alleged unbridled sexuality. It was said that they were fatally attracted to Aryan women and were out to violate and defile them. They were allegedly behind the white slave trade, especially in Eastern Europe (at one time after World War One, 17 percent of Warsaw's prostitutes were said to be Jewish—a regrettable figure, but not unusual given that the percentage of Jews among the general population was almost twice as high). Jews were accused of being behind much of organized crime, perhaps in view of their international ties and connections.

Lastly, critics cited the physical appearance of the Jews as inferior to other races. Swarthy, with hooked noses, blubbery lips, and round shoulders, they were fat and flatfooted, could not properly walk or stand straight; it was claimed that their body language was excessive and ostentatious. Often dirty and smelly (of onion and garlic), loud in their behavior, they were said to be physical cowards, generally wishing to escape a fair fight. Walther Rathenau, the German foreign minister killed by antisemites in 1922, once wrote: "All of us wish we would look like Germans."

This then was the picture (or the caricature) of the Jew depicted in many novels and cartoons in many countries. Repulsive, he clearly belonged to another, inferior race. This physical image or stereotype of the Jew was for obvious reasons far more often used by antisemites in northern countries, where an Aryan race was believed to prevail and physical differences easier to recognize. Farther south in Europe, where one more frequently encountered the "Mediterranean type" (and the consumption of onion and garlic), there was less emphasis on the exterior characteristics of the Jews, and more stress was placed by antisemites on the Jews' supposed devious mentality and hidden negative characteristics.

Antisemites prided themselves on being able to recognize a Jew even at a great distance; however, in practice this was often not easy. Some leading antisemites looked like Jews and vice versa. In such cases, the deceptive character of the Jew could be blamed. Even the Nazis were willing to concede that there had been a handful of decent Jews, and some of the most violent attacks against the Jews had been made by fellow Jews: Otto Weininger, for instance, author of a classic antisemitic book, committed suicide at age twenty-two (in the very room in which Beethoven had died)—no doubt, according to Nazi thinking, because of despair at having been born a Jew and therefore unable ever to overcome this ineradicable stigma.

But even if there were a few decent Jews, it was clear that there should be no mixing with this race. Antisemites were firm believers in the purity of race; if the great countries and civilizations in history had declined and disappeared, this had happened because the healthy, positive racial kernel had shrunk owing to inferior racial influences. Hence, the inference was made that the mixture of races was the greatest misfortune that could affect a people.

When the state of Israel was established, new accusations emerged against the Jews living in the diaspora. Jews were made responsible for the policies of the Israeli government. Generally speaking, a high percentage of Europeans believed that Jews were more loyal to Israel than to their home country (according to a survey in 2002, 72 percent in Spain, 58 percent in Italy, 55 percent in Germany and Austria, 50 percent in Belgium. In no European country save the United Kingdom was the percentage less than 40 percent). Were charges of this kind unjustified? Parallel investigations showed that the majority of Jews outside Israel felt a special relationship toward that country. There was only one step from establishing this undoubted fact to allegations of greater loyalty and to "the Jew cannot be trusted."

AMONG THE JEWISH PEOPLE, the idea of defense against antisemitism originated centuries ago. Medieval rabbis and communal leaders had tried to persuade kings, nobles, and Christian leaders that the accusations against them were unjustified, that antisemitic texts rested on forgeries. If some Jews had become miserable creatures, this was more often than not because they had to live in inhuman conditions, they argued; given a fair chance, they would prove themselves as decent, as productive, and as honest as other citizens. Sometimes these attempts of persuasion were successful, but more often they were not.

The condition of the Jews eased in the late eighteenth century with the spread of the Enlightenment, which led to the emancipation of the Jews. Invoking the ideals of the Enlightenment, Jews could not only demand equal rights but also protest against persecution and defamation. Attacks against a minority were not in line with the spirit of progress and were often in violation of the law of the land. In 1840 the Alliance Israelite Universelle was founded in Paris, in 1871 the Anglo Jewish Association in London, in 1873 the Israelitische Allianz in Vienna, in 1893 the Centralverein in Berlin. In the United States the American Jewish Committee was established in 1906 and the Anti-Defamation League of B'nai B'rith (the ADL) in 1913. All these organizations, but particularly the Centralverein and the ADL, were meant to defend Jews against antisemitic attacks. The Abwehrverein (Association for the Defense Against Antisemitism) had been created in Germany in 1890, to which leading non-Jewish intellectuals belonged. However, the activities of the Abwehrverein were limited to occasional appeals whereas the day-to-day work was done by the Centralverein, a purely Jewish organization.

How could such a defense be organized? The Centralverein was quite emphatic: it stressed that "we are not German Jews but Germans of Jewish faith." To be a Jew did not mean to belong to another people or nation or race but simply to be a member of another religion. In other words, the Jews were first and foremost loyal and patriotic citizens of the country in which they lived, and any attempt to undermine or doubt their status was tantamount to defamation.

In what ways could Jews be defended against antisemitic attack? The Centralverein published a periodical called *Abwehr* (defense) *Blaetter* in which it tried to draw attention to particularly glaring cases of defamation and discrimination. Some Jews realized early on that a dialogue with the antisemites was unlikely to be productive; if antisemitism was based on prejudice, it could not be eradicated by facts and rational arguments. Furthermore, some of the facts adduced by the antisemites could not be refuted—certain Jews had indeed become very rich, and Jews were represented in some professions in numbers well beyond their part of the population by the late nineteenth century. If Jews emphasized their patriotism, this was denounced as tactless obtrusion. Why could Jews not understand that their company was not wanted? Another problem for the defenders was the steady immigration of Jews from Eastern Europe—one of the standard objections of the antisemites was their fear of being flooded by undesirable elements from the East—even if these migrants in their majority had no wish to remain in Europe and wished instead to continue on their way to America and South Africa.

The aim of mounting a defense was to reach the large number of the uncommitted non-Jews, those who had no strong feelings about antisemitism. The Jewish defenders would stress the positive achievements of the Jews, from which Germany had benefited in its economy, culture, and reputation in the world. If the number of Jewish lawyers was out of proportion, so was the number of Jewish Nobel Prize winners. Jews had served in the armed forces of their country in the war of 1870–71 as well as in the First World War. The first (and only) member of the German parliament who had been killed during the very first days of the war, Ludwig Frank, had been a Jewish volunteer, age 40. Alfred and Gustav Flatow, German Jews, had won gold medals at the first Olympic Games in 1896, as had a number of American Jews. (Both Flatows perished in the Holocaust.)

Whether all this had much impact is more than doubtful. For every Jewish Nobel Prize winner the antisemites would refer to a Jewish litterateur who had ridiculed hallowed German traditions and values, or a Jewish businessman who had engaged in speculation and failed or had been involved in corruption and had been apprehended. There were many such failures and corrupt practices and the great majority of these concerned non-Jews. But the Jewish culprits were singled out and there was nothing the defenders could do about it. Much depended on circumstances and the political situation. The fact that the Flatow cousins had won medals in the Olympic Games hardly registered in Germany, but the fact that two Jewish pugilists, Daniel Mendoza and Samuel ("Dutch Sam") Elias, were the leading boxers of their time undoubtedly had a certain influence on the image of the Jews among the broad English public in the early nineteenth century. There were few Jews in England then and the role of sports in British public life was greater than in Germany and Austria, the sense of fair play more pronounced. The fact that Jews played a leading role in American boxing in the 1920s and 1930s, with Benny Leonard and

Barney Ross, Kid Berg and Maxie Rosenblum, probably influenced some attitudes in the United States. But America was a country of immigrants, and antisemitism could not have the same political impact as in Europe.

During the late nineteenth and early twentieth centuries, the Jewish defense organizations would admonish fellow Jewish citizens to make a greater contribution to their countries in order to disprove the antisemitic allegations. They would condemn those whose behavior was detrimental to the Jewish community at large, urge them not to attract unwelcome attention and not to provide grist for the antisemitic mills. In addition to the propagandistic work, the defense organizations would take legal action against the defamation of individuals and groups wherever possible.

Differences in circumstances should again be noted. While some of the more farsighted Jewish observers in Germany and Austria were quite pessimistic about the chances of success of this kind of "defense" against antisemitism, there was more optimism in Britain and France. The activities of the Central European Jewish defense organizations may seem futile in the light of subsequent events, but the historical context ought to be remembered; before the First World War the belief in progress was still strong and there was the widespread assumption that antisemitism, a remnant of medieval obscurantism, was bound to disappear, even though there were bound to be relapses from time to time.

Only when antisemitic movements had greatly expanded and the majority of society had been infected did the defensive struggle become quite hopeless. This was the situation in countries in which an "objective Jewish question," as the Zionists put it, existed. Czarist Russia was one such country, as were Poland and Romania; and the situation also became critical in Germany and Hungary in the late 1920s. In brief, the smaller and less visible the Jewish community was in a country, the better were the prospects for defense against antisemitism. America was different because it was a country of immigrants, even though the functioning of the melting pot remained sometimes problematic.

Was there an "objective Jewish question" in Germany and Austria? There is no easy answer to this question: in contrast to Poland, the answer would certainly be no, since German Jewry was less than one percent of the total population. But there was a strong tradition of antisemitism in these German-speaking countries, and the rise of the Jews certainly contributed to the growth and violence of antisemitism. We also know from many individual recollections that many of the Jews growing up in the nineteenth and early twentieth centuries were barely aware of antisemitism on the personal level; for them it was not a major threat. Conditions varied from place to place and sometimes according to the sensitivity of the individual. Paul Ree, a friend of Nietzsche, fainted when Lou Andreas Salome, a lady accompanying them, mentioned Jews in his presence. Not everyone was that sensitive.

If antisemitism in the nineteenth century generated among European Jews an eagerness to defend themselves, there was also the wish to escape the stigma and the burden once and for all. Many thousands left the Jewish community; those who abandoned Judaism came especially from among the wealthier and the more assimilated circles, and mostly lived in the big cities rather than in the smaller communities. German Jewry lost most of its establishment in the nineteenth century through mixed marriages and conversion. Many of those who did not convert did consider taking this step at one stage or another in their lives, including several leading figures in the field of Jewish studies, such as Leopold Zunz and in the following century Franz Rosenzweig; leading thinkers, such as Sigmund Freud; and even the father of modern political Zionism, Theodor Herzl, who played with the idea of advocating mass baptism a few years before he began fighting for the creation of a Jewish state.

Once the walls of the ghettos had been breached and the hold of Jewish religion had waned, what was there to keep the community together other than piety vis-à-vis parents and ancestors? There was, of course, also the feeling that it was somehow indecent, perhaps even cowardly, to leave a community under attack, especially if one did not particularly care about Christianity; few Jews converted out of deep religious conviction.

To be a Jew was for many a burden, a source of frequent embarrassment, except for the firm religious believers. Most Jews believed that they had certain things in common with fellow Jews, but how deep was the affinity, how to define it? Were they a thousand-year-old family of affliction, in the words of Heinrich Heine? They were certainly no longer a nation, having lived for so long in the diaspora, and the differences between various branches of Jewry were so great that most of them no longer believed that they were a people anymore.

Although the social life of assimilated Jews was predominantly with other assimilated Jews, there was a vague feeling of solidarity when Jews in other countries were attacked. This made it difficult, perhaps impossible, to define the peculiar form of cohesion that still existed among them—perhaps a shared mentality, or the fact that the outside world usually regarded them as Jews irrespective of how they defined themselves. But there was really little specifically Jewish about assimilated Jews, and the glue that bound them to other Jews was not very strong. While the attraction of religion in general had declined in most parts of the world throughout the nineteenth and twentieth centuries, the Jewish religion, despite efforts to modernize and reform it, was probably even less attractive than other religions for those who were not deep traditional believers. In brief, as far as many assimilated Jews were concerned, the burden of being Jewish outweighed the positive elements. Why hang on to traditions that had become meaningless?

The problems of assimilation and its discontents are of interest in the present context where they impinge on Jewish self-hatred and Jewish manifestations of antisemitism. Much has been made of this fascinating phenomenon of Jewish self-hatred, but it ought to be remembered that it was not frequent in Germany and Austria except among some intellectual and literary circles, and outside these countries it was even rarer. Those who drifted away from Judaism in Europe and North America did so not because of acute hatred but because being categorized as a Jew had become meaningless, or worse, an embarrassment. And even if they were antagonistic toward Judaism and their fellow Jews, it was hardly wise to engage in public attacks against Jews because this would only attract attention to their own Jewish extraction. Freud called them "badly baptized" (*schlecht getauft*). In its extreme manifestations, when the self-loathing turned to militant antisemitism among individuals such as Arthur Trebitsch, an early Jewish Nazi, or Otto Weininger or Maurice Sachs in France, it was a problem more for individual psychopathology than for historical or cultural analysis and generalization.

Jewish self-hatred is a problem that has been insufficiently investigated; some literary critics and historians have attributed to Jews a specific propensity toward self-hatred, but this is far from certain. Few people live at total peace with themselves and the saying *Le moi est haissable* was coined not by a Jew but by Blaise Pascal. True, Jews uprooted from their heritage and yet not accepted by their surroundings were likely to be affected more than others; and internationalist feelings were for sound reasons more widely found among Jews than Jewish patriotism. But in principle, the phenomenon was not a specific Jewish one.

ALTHOUGH SOME HIGHLY ASSIMILATED JEWS in the nineteenth and early twentieth centuries accepted part of the antisemitic critique of Judaism as lacking in spirituality, the same critique could be said about early Zionism. Political Zionism was rooted less in the deep spiritual longing of Jews in Eastern Europe to return to their ancient homeland than in the recognition of the anomaly of Jewish existence. This anomaly was cultural and psychological as well as socioeconomic, and its historical roots were obvious. Jews had lived in segregation for many centuries and it would have been miraculous if persecution and isolation had not left traumatic scars. The desire to survive in adverse circumstances had shaped the behavior of European Jews and had often brought out negative features. It had a crippling effect not so much on the intellect as on the character and the physical development of this persecuted minority. In order to survive, all kinds of compromises, some morally questionable, had to be made. Such a situation was not a good school for virtue, let alone for heroism as Nietzsche, the intellectual idol of that period, would have wanted it. It was conducive to deep suspicion toward the outside world, not toward good citizenship. In Eastern Europe, in view of their numbers many Jews had become *luftmenschen*, people living off of air, a term that had been coined to characterize their precarious social situation on the margins of society. They were not fulfilling any useful, let alone necessary, role in society, had no obvious, visible source of income.

Zionism arose out of deep dissatisfaction with this state of affairs and the fear that the anomaly of Jewish existence was not just bound to generate antisemitism but that it could lead to the physical destruction of Jewish communities. The Zionist answer was simple: there was no future for many, perhaps most Jews in Eastern Europe. The social structure of the Jewish communities in these countries could not be changed by reforms carried out locally; the Jews would not willingly become peasants in Poland or Hungary or Russia—quite apart from the fact that the native peasants would hardly have welcomed this. The only realistic way to solve this enormous problem was mass emigration to Palestine.

The Jewish question could only be solved through return to their ancient homeland, where they would establish a new society with a normal and healthy social structure. There would be a Jewish culture, part of Europe (with the official language perhaps German) but certainly different in character from the culture of the descendants of Teuton and Arminius the Cheruscan. Particular emphasis was put by some early Zionists on the return to the land, for the divorce of the Jews from the land and from nature had been, as they saw it, in many ways the root of the evil in the diaspora. Only with the emergence of a Jewish peasantry would the organic tie be reestablished and would a healthy society develop. Zionist leaders such as Max Nordau emphasized the importance of improving the Jewish physique and physical improvement; hence, the stress on physical fitness— *Muskeljudentum.*

ZIONISM EMERGED as a reaction against the cultural and spiritual tradition of the ghetto and the *shtetl,* and the one-sided education of the *heder* (the religious school). It aimed at the restoration of self-respect among the Jews. The absence of a Jewish defense at the time of the pogroms in the 1880s and again at the time of the Kishinev pogrom (1903) had been a deep shock. This dissociation from the East European *shtetl* extended to the rejection of the (bastard) language (Yiddish) spoken there and the revival of Hebrew.

At the same time, Zionism turned against Jewish assimilationists, those unwilling to acknowledge that they belonged to a nation apart, unwilling to identify as Jews even though they were such in the eyes of others. These opponents of Zionism from among the assimilationists were opposed to a national revival because they felt that they had not that much in common with their coreligionists. They were fearful that this would endanger their status and expose them to charges of disloyalty to their native country.

Young Jews could try to show that they were as good as others in fields traditionally considered un-Jewish, for instance, by establishing their own dueling associations at universities. Still, in the final analysis, it was the majority in the society in which they lived that decided who belonged and who did not. Jews might do their best for the country in which they had been born and grown up, but even if they had influential positions in the academic and cultural life, they would still remain outsiders in the society if the majority did not want them.

In retrospect, the analysis of antisemitism by Zionism was closer to the mark than that by other Jewish circles from the left or the right. Zionists were willing to concede that there were serious anomalies in the Jewish existence in many European countries. They did not argue that assimilation could never work, but they thought it would not solve the Jewish question in time in the countries with the most numerous Jewish communities, where the problem was most acute. Within the Zionist movement were voices claiming that Zionism had gone perhaps too far in its "negation of the diaspora," and that sometimes it had come dangerously close to accepting the arguments of the antisemites. But this was not the decisive weakness of the Zionist movement. Its real weakness was the fact that it could offer an alternative and escape to only relatively few. Palestine was not in Jewish hands and free emigration was impossible. The age of nationalism had dawned. Zionism had appeared too late on the political scene to make a decisive contribution to the solution of the Jewish question— but again, for historical reasons, it could not have appeared much earlier. This was the historical tragedy of the Zionist idea.

Since Zionism came so late, the establishment of a Jewish state was bound to provoke resistance. The Arabs were many and the Jews were few; Zionist aspirations collided with the claims of others and this was bound to lead to a renewal of hostility. According to Herzl, the aim of a Jewish state was the restoration of dignity to the Jews and the chance for a life in peace. But there was to be no peace.

Chapter Nine

ANTISEMITISM AND THE LEFT

MODERN ANTISEMITISM as it emerged in the early nineteenth century was nationalist, racialist, and right wing-populist in inspiration. This was the age of nationalism and of the *Volk*. The Jews, as the antisemites saw it, didn't just belong to another religion; their character and mentality were essentially different, alien to the values and traditions of the French, Germans, Poles, Russians, and other European peoples. They were destructive elements, parasites who made no positive contribution to society; their main occupation was accumulating wealth and, through their money, political and cultural influence. The antisemites claimed that the Jews wanted to conspire and dominate, and constituted a major, perhaps mortal, danger to the normal development of other nations. There were many more suspicions and accusations and they all amounted to the demand to expose and combat Jewish influence, if it was not possible physically to remove them. This then was the predominant strain of antisemitism throughout the nineteenth and early twentieth century.

The left, on the other hand, was the heir of the Enlightenment and its ideals were those of the French Revolution, not only of liberty and equality but also of fraternity. The left wing stood for the liberation of the oppressed. In view of its basic ideological orientation, the left wing as a group could not possibly be antisemitic.

Furthermore, the "Jewish question" was not a central one for the left, which was preoccupied with the worldwide struggle between oppressors and oppressed, exploiters and exploited. In this global confrontation, the Jews were a small and not very important factor. No wonder that in this global confrontation Jews were prominently involved in the left-wing camp that promised the Jews at long last full emancipation and liberation. "Left wing" was a synonym for progress and freedom, just as "right wing" was tantamount to the old order in which the Jews had been among the main victims.

Thus, the left, the protagonist of freedom, was the great hope of many Jews, except perhaps the very orthodox among them who preferred conservativism to liberal, let alone revolutionary, ideas. The very orthodox feared that the new freedom would bring about the disintegration of traditional Judaism. But it is also true that among the leftists there was an anti-Jewish element from the very beginning. This appeared in the writings of the early utopian socialists for whom the Jews were the prominent representatives of the new capitalism (as personified by the Rothschilds) that was the main enemy. The young Marx wrote a long essay replete with anti-Jewish stereotypes, and the not-so-young Ferdinand Lassalle, the great popular leader of the early German working-class movement, wrote in a love letter that he hated the Jews.

It could be argued with some justification that these and other anti-Jewish utterances were rooted in psychological resentment rather than deep ideological conviction. The state of European Jewry after the fall of the ghetto, following centuries of oppression and a miserable existence, was deplorable. The young Jewish revolutionaries imbued with the modern ideas were anything but proud of their Jewish ancestry. They had nothing but scorn for the antiquated religious practices of traditional Judaism, the lack of culture among a community to which they felt no ties and from which they wanted to dissociate themselves as quickly and as a radically as possible. There was considerable embarrassment and even physical repulsion—Marx, whose outward appearance was not "Nordic," called Lassalle a "Jewish Nigger."

Jewish leftists saw themselves as citizens of their countries, patriots of the world, not members of an anachronistic sect. Among leading European Jewish socialists in the nineteenth and early twentieth centuries, it is difficult to find many who had any sympathies for their poor and downtrodden brethren in Eastern Europe. On the other hand, however often they stressed that they should not be approached with complaints of specific Jewish sufferings (as had Rosa Luxemburg), however often they stressed that they were not Jews in any meaningful sense (as had Leon Trotsky), however great their expressed disinterest in things Jewish, for their enemies Jews remained despicable and dangerous.

This was their personal predicament; the Social Democrat and early Communist parties did not want to have any truck with antisemitism, which was the "socialism of fools" (Engelbert Pernersdorter). It would not be difficult to find incidents of antisemitism in the history of left-wing parties beginning with the socialist revolutionaries (the People's Will) in Russia in the 1870s. But these were isolated incidents, in no way typical for the socialist and Communist movements in general. It is true that Marxist ideologists from Lenin to Karl Kautsky bitterly opposed Jewish national movements—in the case of Lenin, not just Zionism but also the anti-Zionist Bund; still, this too cannot possibly be interpreted as manifestations of antisemitism, attacks against Jews as such.

Socialist and Communist parties prior to World War Two were careful not to go out of their way in their defense of Jewish communities against antisemitic attacks; this was done out of political opportunism and tactical considerations rather than from deep conviction. Populist antisemitism was quite popular and it was politically unwise even for a left-wing party to engage in a direct confrontation with such widespread public sentiments.

In the 1950s, however, a new left-wing doctrinal attitude, sometimes sponsored by Jewish radicals, developed; its roots can be traced back to an earlier period. Abram Leon, a young Belgian Trotskyite and former Zionist, published during the Second World War a little book on the Jewish question "from the point of view of historical materialism" that contained antisemitic motifs. He argued, for instance, that historically the Jews had chosen usury as their main occupation not because other professions were barred to them but out of an inner, essential inclination. No one had prevented them from becoming peasants or workers or choosing some other productive job; they had opted for usury; those who did not admit this were fools or liars. Neither Trotsky nor Lenin had ever argued on these lines and professional historians of the Marxist persuasion (such as Maxime Rodinson) rejected this kind of argument as ignorant. Leon perished in the Holocaust, and although his writings could be rejected as the aberrations of a semieducated young man, his little book became in the following decades something like a cult book in certain circles of the extreme left. It was translated and often reprinted, and it can be seen as a forerunner of the new antisemitism of the last third of the twentieth century.

Trotskyism, however, was a fringe movement at the time, while Stalinism after the Second World War was the dominating force in the Soviet Union and Eastern Europe, and it too turned openly antisemitic during the early 1950s. This was manifest in a variety of declarations and actions. Jews with very rare exceptions were removed from leading positions in the state, party, armed forces, economy, and public life in general. Jewish Communists who had adopted Russian names to hide their ethnic origins were identified in the media as aliens by mentioning their original names. (Stalin, Molotov, and others had also changed their names, but this was different.) The remnants of Jewish culture, theater, and publications were destroyed; Jewish organizations such as the Anti-Fascist Committee, founded during the war, were dissolved; its members were arrested and some were executed. A major anti-Jewish propaganda campaign was undertaken that claimed that the Jews were enemies of Russia and Communism; it culminated in the arrest of leading Jewish doctors who were accused of having poisoned Communist leaders. Stalin planned to deport Soviet Jewry to distant parts of the country, and only his sudden death in March 1953 seems to have intervened.

While antisemitic stereotypes were constantly used, it would have been politically inopportune to attack Jews as Jews following the mass murder committed by the Nazis during the war—the parallels with Nazi Germany would have been too striking. Thus, Jews were usually termed "Zionists" or "rootless cosmopolitans." However, there was not a single Zionist among the victims of the anti-Jewish purges; they were fervent anti-Zionists, faithful sons and daughters of the Communist party and the Soviet fatherland. Their crime was being Jews, not engaging in any ideological deviation, let alone treason.

This antisemitic campaign was not limited to the Soviet Union and had strong repercussions in other East European countries. An intense anti-Jewish propaganda campaign was launched in these countries from 1949 to 1952, sometimes in connection with the anti-Tito campaign (the Yugoslav leader had distanced himself from the Communist camp in 1947–1948). The anti-Jewish character of the purges and trials was perhaps most obvious in Prague in the 1952 Slansky trial; the accused were all former leading members of the Communist party, and if two or three non-Jews were included among them, this was no doubt done for propagandistic reasons. The interrogators called the Jewish accused "Jewish swine" and enemies of the people, who had wormed their way into the party and state to cause maximum harm to the cause of Communism and progressive mankind.

Similar trials were carried out or prepared in other so-called People's Democracies, with slight differences in timing. In East Germany, Paul Merker, a non-Jew (who had spent the war years in Mexico, not in the Soviet Union), was designated the main culprit. He was accused of having overemphasized the role and the suffering of the

Jews among the Nazi victims, and he had even suggested that Jews should be compensated to a certain extent for the property that had been robbed by the Nazis. According to the party line in the Soviet bloc, the fact that Jews had been systematically killed by the Nazis in contrast to all other groups or nationalities was played down: the Jews had been mere "passive victims," not active antifascists; they had been persecuted but they were second- or third-level victims. Merker was saved because the investigations against him lingered on, and after Stalin's death they had to be discontinued. However, he was never fully rehabilitated, and a number of other leading Jewish cadres had been meanwhile sentenced to long prison terms; others had died under interrogation or were driven to suicide. Most Jewish Communists in East Germany were demoted or excluded from the party, but many were reinstated after 1955.

In Hungary, where the percentage of Jews in the supreme leadership was higher than in all other Communist countries, Matias Rakosi, the party leader and a Jew, had foreseen the coming of the antisemitic campaign and early on warned the Soviet security organs about the infiltration of hostile (Jewish) elements in the party. In Romania leading Jewish Communists were squeezed out and some (such as Ana Pauker) sentenced to lengthy prison terms. In Poland too, Jews were heavily represented in the upper echelons of leadership (Jakub Berman, Hilari Minc, Roman Zambrowski), but opposition to Communism was so great and the absence of reliable Polish cadres—reliable from Moscow's point of view—so obvious that the removal of the Jews occurred only after Stalin's death, in 1956 and 1968. Ultimately, as in the other People's Democracies, Jews were totally eliminated from leading positions in the Polish state and party.

The elimination of Jews from government office and the antisemitic public climate affected not just Jewish Communist party members but also the remainder of erstwhile substantial Jewish communities, and it resulted in the emigration of many of them, principally from

Romania, Hungary, and Poland. In the Soviet Union there was initially great reluctance to let the Jews go; the desire to get rid of them collided with the ideological claim of having solved the national problem once and forever.

What were the motives of Communist antisemitism and how did it differ from that preached and practiced by the Nazis? The persecutions of the early 1950s can be explained in part with reference to the personal attitudes of Josef Stalin and his paranoia, which became more obsessive with old age. Among the many other factors was the anti-Jewish feeling shared by other Soviet leaders and rooted in the population at large. Although by 1950 few Jews were left in leading positions in the Soviet Union, this was certainly not the case in the People's Democracies, and their replacement sooner or later by native cadres was inevitable—that it should proceed in this particular gruesome and mendacious form was another issue.

Communist antisemitism under Stalin had in common with Nazi and fascist antisemitism the belief in a Jewish world conspiracy. This was an essential part of Communist doctrine; the role allegedly played by Kuhn, Loeb, and other Wall Street banks in the struggle against the Soviet Union in the early 1920s still echoed in the Communist memory. Soviet Jews were not the only ethnic group with coreligionists living abroad. But in the case of the Armenians, for example, the concentration of their people and the center of their religion were inside the Soviet Union, while in the case of the Jews, most were located abroad and, of course, the state of Israel acted as a magnet.

The deep belief in plots and conspiracies preceded the Cold War—it was at the bottom of the great purges of the 1930s, the allegations that leading Communists had sold out to the Gestapo, to the Japanese secret service, to British and French imperialism. With the outbreak of the Cold War, the United States became the main enemy, and since the American Jewish community was sizable and influential, Jews everywhere became a priori suspect. This remained the case, albeit not in such an extreme form, after Stalin's death, even though there were no leading Jewish cadres left to be purged. Nevertheless, the anti-Jewish propaganda machine continued its work. Soviet foreign policy, which had initially been neutral in the Arab-Israeli conflict, sharply turned against Israel after 1967, and Russia broke off diplomatic relations. But as far as Jews in the Soviet bloc were concerned, the propaganda campaign was preoccupied only to a limited extent with the misdeeds of the state of Israel; it followed classical antisemitic lines. According to the books and pamphlets by various official writers, issued by the propaganda department of the Communist party or Soviet army intelligence (there was no certainty about the identity of the sponsors), the teachings of Judaism inspired inhuman deeds, provided the chauvinistic idea of the Jews as the chosen people, and led to their notion of ruling over other people of the world. These teachings were an unsurpassed textbook of bloodthirstiness and hypocrisy, treason, perfidy, and vile licentiousness. Jews had been Hitler's fifth column, the propagandists claimed; they had financed the Nazis and they were instrumental in trying to overthrow the Soviet order. These antisemitic texts were accompanied by cartoons that resembled and in some cases reproduced Nazi propaganda.

The crudeness of these publications caused negative reactions and embarrassment among Communist party members outside the Soviet Union. From time to time this propaganda was tuned down, but it basically continued up to the last years of the Soviet Union. After the fall of the Soviet Union, it was taken up and intensified by both former Communists and the extreme right, and also by sections of the Russian Orthodox church, which could now claim that their dire prophecies about the Jewish cabal had come true.

There were certain differences in the attitudes toward Jews in the People's Democracies. In East Germany for the obvious historical reasons—recollections of Nazi ideology and propaganda—there were fewer instances of openly antisemitic attacks, and few if any attacks against the Old Testament and the teachings of Judaism. Jews were denounced as the "class enemy" and the term Zionist was usually preferred when denouncing Jews. Unlike in the Soviet Union, positions in the state and party leadership, except for the brief period noted above, were not barred to Communists of Jewish origin. Furthermore, as East Germany tried to normalize relations with the United States in the 1980s, the anti-Jewish attacks became far more infrequent. The same is true, to a lesser extent, with regard to the other Eastern European countries. The decline in openly antisemitic incidents had more to do with the lessening of the intensity of the Cold War rather than with any profound ideological change.

Seen in retrospect, there were, of course, other significant differences between Nazi-style antisemitism and Communist antisemitism. Above all, Communism would emphatically deny that its repression of Jews as communities or individuals or its anti-Jewish political indoctrination had anything to do with antisemitism. It would argue that the Communist system treated all ethnic groups equally and that ethnic belonging was of no significance—if individuals were attacked or repressed, this was because they were enemies of peace, or agents of capitalism or of imperialism, not because they were Jews.

In view of its ideological tenets, Marxism-Leninism, even in its Stalinist phase, could not be openly racialist; the Soviet Union, furthermore, was a multinational empire and a few Jews were always left unmolested even at the worst of times. Marxism, after all, was the heir of the Enlightenment and the ideals of the French Revolution, and the concept of a superior master race was unthinkable—even though Soviet ideology had gone a long way from the early internationalist days to something akin to National Socialism. Marx had been born a Jew and many other Jews of an earlier period had been Communists—this history could not be rewritten.

Even in the days of Marx and Engels, however, not all people had been considered equal—Poles and Hungarians, for instance, were considered progressive whereas Russians were a reactionary force in world history, and the South Slavs, unimportant. Later, there was an official Marxist-Leninist doctrine of absolute equality, but there was an unwritten party line according to which some groups were more progressive than others and Jews were considered reactionary. The very least that was demanded of Jews in order to be accepted as equals was to dissociate themselves totally from Judaism, not only from the Jewish religion or sympathies with Zionism but from any identification with other Jews, and to actively struggle against all national Jewish feelings. Only on these conditions could these non-Jewish Jews—to use the expression coined by one of them, Isaac Deutscher—hope to be treated as comrades in the fight for justice and progress. Even in these circumstances, a residue of suspicion and hostility remained.

Communist anti-Judaism is also of interest because of the interchangeable use of the terms "Zionism" and "Judaism." The Bolsheviks had opposed Zionism even before the revolution of 1917 (as had leading Social Democrats such as Kautsky), but the use of the term "Zionism" as a synonym for Judaism and Jew had been unthinkable. Among the Jews left in the Soviet empire after the Second World War were no more than perhaps a handful of Zionists, because the true Zionists had used the opportunities at the end of the war to emigrate to Palestine. Those attacked as Zionists under Stalin and his successors were anything but Zionists; most of them knew little and cared less about the Jewish state that had come into being in 1948. Hence, it is legitimate to define the Communist attitude toward Jews during much of the postwar period as anti-Jewish even though this antisemitism differed in character from previous religious or racialist manifestations.

The influence of the Communist parties and of Communism greatly declined with the disintegration of the Soviet Union, but the New Left remained an influential player on the political scene in many countries. It was among these groups and especially among the most radical of them that antisemitic views emerged. Again, as in the case of the Communists, there were emphatic denials on the part of those charged with antisemitism: this was a base calumny spread by right-wing nationalist

Jews; many of the leading figures of the New Left, of the Trotskyites, and other leftist groups were Jews, and the charges of antisemitism were merely an attempt to silence critics of right-wing, aggressive, and reactionary policies followed by the state of Israel.

The occupation of the West Bank following the Six-Day War of 1967, the struggle against terrorism, and the policies of the right-wing Likud in general generated anti-Israeli feelings among leftist groups (and others) in both Europe and America, as it did among Arabs and Muslims. However, as indicated earlier, there had been hostility toward Israel even before 1967; Israeli policies after that date are not sufficient to explain the anti-Jewish attitudes that developed on the political left. At least some of the other motivating forces involved ought to be mentioned.

While Jews continued to be prominently involved with the radical left in the West, especially with the Trotskyites and similar groups, these were "non-Jewish Jews." On the other hand, Jews were at least equally prominently involved in the anti-Stalinist and anti-Communist camps during the Cold War, and this, the far left was not willing to forget and to forgive, especially when their assessment of the Soviet Union and Communism was borne out by the collapse of the Soviet empire in the late 1980s.

Furthermore, as the result of social and economic developments, increasing numbers of Jews had moved from the left to the center; for sentimental reasons most American Jews would still vote for the Democrats although they could equally support the Republicans. Although in years past, there had been no room for Jews in conservative parties, this was no longer the case; there were no longer significant antisemitic sentiments in these circles. Among radical populists of the left in Europe as well as in America, attacks—sometimes veiled, sometimes outspoken—were launched against the Jews. If the right was no longer what it had once been, the character of the left had also changed. Once there had been a democratic left and a Marxist or anarchist left, but as time went by, populist elements became much stronger among them.

This populism with equal ease could turn to the right or to the left, and could cooperate with reactionary, antisemitic groups.

AS FAR AS ISRAEL IS CONCERNED, it is useful to recall once again that a majority of the radical left (except, for a short time, the Communist parties following the Soviet lead) had been against the creation of the state of Israel, which, as they saw it, was at best an anachronism, a relapse into bourgeois nationalism at a time when the whole world was moving toward internationalism. Thus, the radical left wing considered Zionism and the establishment of Israel a retrograde, reactionary development, while the Arabs were seen as progressive fighters for national liberation.

From this perspective, the fact that there was a strong labor and left-wing movement among the Israelis was of little consequence, as was the fact that there was no significant Arab left, even though anti-imperialist, quasi-Leninist phraseology was adopted in certain Arab circles during the 1960s and 1970s. Later on, extreme nationalism and religious fundamentalism took over in the Arab left. As far as the radical left was concerned, "objectively" the Arab opponents of Israel were a progressive force and had to be supported. Even the classics of Marxism and Leninism had taught that the struggle for national and social liberation in backward countries could assume strange and antiquated forms. On the other hand, Israeli left wingers, whatever their political doctrines, were "objectively" reactionary and pro-imperialist.

Thus, even in the 1950s and early 1960s, there was an identification in Western radical left-wing circles with Palestinian insurgents, which manifested itself in ideological writings as well as the wearing of the kaffiyeh and the dispatch of Western terrorists ("Carlos the Jackal" and members of the Baader-Meinhof gang) to training camps in Arab countries. Eventually, members of these terrorist groups made common cause with Arab terrorist organizations in aircraft hijackings and other operations. The Baader-Meinhof group welcomed the killing of Israeli athletes at the Munich Olympics as yet another step in the struggle of national liberation. They took part in attacks against Israelis and European Jews. As they saw it, the Jews living in what had earlier been Palestine had no right to a state of their own; they should and would have to emigrate or find their place in an Arab country and society.

Such declarations and demands in an extreme form were by no means shared by all segments of the left, and it is debatable whether the very radical, terrorist, or proterrorist leftist groups could still be considered "left wing" in any meaningful sense. They defined themselves as being of the left, but early fascism, after all, had also proclaimed itself anticapitalist, anti-imperialist, and against plutocracy. This new left-wing doctrine probably had more to do with third-world romanticism than with ideas of the traditional left. Whether ideologically legitimate or not, the anti-Jewish character of this propaganda emerged clearly well before 1967 when, as the result of the Six-Day War, Israel occupied the West Bank and Gaza. It showed itself also in aspects that had nothing to do with Israel—such as Holocaust denial or denigration.

This school of thought found more than a few adherents, mainly among neo-Nazis and their sympathizers. It was also adopted by groups of the extreme left such as *La vieille taupe* (the Old Mole) in France as well as former leading Communists such as Roger Garaudy, who had moved from the Politburo of the French Communist party to the extreme right. Others had adopted what they called a "third position." *La vieille taupe* was attacked for its advocacy of Holocaust denial, as was Robert Faurisson, the French author of the standard text and manifesto detailing the allegations. But Faurisson's book had a preface by Noam Chomsky, the most famous spokesman of the American left, and this caused a minor scandal.

The Baader-Meinhof gang and allied groups, which claimed its anti-Nazism was second to none, argued nevertheless that Germany had somehow to overcome the incubus of Auschwitz. As Horst Mahler, the lawyer of the group at the time, later put it, the "Auschwitz lie" had been "fabricated by our enemies to destroy us and eventually the whole German people." As far as the Jews were concerned, to these groups yesterday's victims had become the killers of today ("ZioNazis") who wanted to exterminate the Palestinians, and Moshe Dayan was the Himmler of Israel. The case of "Carlos the Jackal" was not untypical. The most prominent terrorist of the 1960s and 1970s, this Venezuelan gunman had moved from ultraleftist positions that rejected Soviet policies as not sufficiently revolutionary to identification with the struggle waged by Osama bin Laden. Whether to define such a position as Communist or fascist might be a moot point; the anti-Jewish element was obvious and the denial of the Holocaust was part of his new ideology.

Holocaust denial also became part of the ideological arsenal of Arab propaganda against Israel and the Jews. Seen from an Arab point of view, this was not a rational and logical argument, for had it not been for the mass murder of the Jews by the Nazis, the state of Israel would, in all probability, never have come into being. But it was an illustration of how emotional factors got the better of clear thinking.

In their extreme form, the Holocaust deniers of the left were not many, but there was a considerably larger group of people who expressed similar theses in a watered-down version or fought for the right of the Holocaust deniers to express their views. Yet others claimed that while the Holocaust had indeed taken place, it had been exploited and instrumentalized by chauvinist Jews to gain international sympathy, to extort money from the international community in compensation for the funds robbed by the Nazis, and also to justify Israeli politics.

Individual Jews of the far left played a leading part in the "deconstruction" of the history of the Holocaust: this campaign was quite successful because it coincided with the emergence of a widespread reaction against being reminded of the Holocaust. Was it not true that too much had been made of the murder of the Jews for too long, and was it not correct that other cases of mass murder were taking place in the contemporary world? Why should the Jews insist on preferential treatment and stress the exclusive character of the Holocaust? Above all, would this emphasis on the Holocaust not be of help to Israel?

Two other considerations—one of practical politics, the other ideological-psychological—played an important role in the emergence of anti-Jewish feelings among the European left. (Practical politics and ideological considerations were also in play in America, where left wing radicals would find excuses, if not justifications, for the likes of Louis Farrakhan's Nation of Islam, Al Sharpton, and others who claimed that Jews had been the leading slave traders among their other crimes.)

There had been a time when the industrial working class had been considered the natural ally of Social Democrat and Communist parties, but over recent decades this segment of society had shrunk and its ethnic composition had changed. Following the great immigration wave into Europe in the 1960s and 1970s, a strong Muslim element emerged in what remained of the European industrial working class. The rapid population increase among these newcomers from Turkey, North Africa, and the Arab world made them a factor of political importance. Socialist and Social Democrat politicians as well as the Greens in Germany and other political parties had to take into account the mood and the demands of these new voters whose numbers could be decisive in dozens of constituencies, and it was no secret that anti-Jewish feeling ran high in these circles.

If this applied to moderate socialists and their electoral calculations, the more radical left wing, such as various Trotskyite and New Left groups, went still further, were more outspoken, and felt fewer restraints. Small and isolated, they had been searching for decades for allies, as they tried to work through established political parties and unions in a policy termed "entryism"; this however had proved unsuccessful. For them, this new "proletariat" seemed yet another opportunity to strengthen their influence and to create a mass base.

Although traditional Trotskyite ideology is in no way close to radical Islamic teachings and the shariah, since the radical Islamists also subscribed to anticapitalism, antiglobalism, and anti-Americanism, there seemed to be sufficient common ground for an alliance. Thus, the militants of the far left began to march side by side with the radical Islamists in demonstrations, denouncing American aggression and Israeli crimes. In Britain a new political party named Respect was established, uniting Trotskyites, Stalinists, Muslim Brotherhood militants, and similar groups. And it was only natural that in protest demonstrations militants from the far right would join in, antisemitic banners would be displayed, anti-Jewish literature such as the *Protocols* would be sold. One could not reasonably expect the politically unsophisticated to make the fine distinctions between Zionism and Judaism. On occasion shouts such as "death to the Jews," "death to gays," or "down with women's rights," or the advocacy of suicide terrorism would embarrass left-wing militants, but it was a small price to pay for gaining powerful allies.

Similar alliances of various, more inchoate groups—anarchists, ATTAC (Association for a Taxation of Financial Transaction and for Assistance to Citizens, an international antiglobalization organization), and other "autonomous" organizations who appeared under the general umbrella of antiglobalism—were forged for public demonstrations. Individually, most of them were not antisemites, or at least not more antisemitic than members of other parties, and they would angrily reject any such imputation. But opinion polls established that as far as they were concerned, the enemy was not just Ariel Sharon; they were convinced that Jews were far too influential in world politics in general, that Israel (not the proliferation of nuclear weapons, not al-Qaeda, not even America) was the greatest danger to world peace. And since the majority of the inhabitants of Israel were Jews, since many Jews outside Israel had family there, and many Jews sympathized with the state of Israel albeit disagreeing with its government, it would follow that Jews in general were responsible for Israel (unless they would actually fight it), that the world would certainly be a safer place if Israel did not exist. It was clear to what conclusions such reasoning would ultimately lead.

Seen in this mirror, Jews were the new Nazis. They were systematically exterminating the innocent Palestinians, enclosing them in ghettos. But Israeli misdeeds quite apart, Jews had been responsible for international crime in the past, from the black slave trade to the white slave trade (prostitution), corruption, and many other crimes. Although these denunciations were often rejected by the more responsible leaders of antiglobalism and the left, they persisted nevertheless. It is also true that the charges of Nazism and Nazification did not always mean what they seemed to mean, especially when emanating from Arab sources. Nazism in the Arab world had never been the worst of crimes; on the contrary, Hitler and his regime have retained considerable popularity to this day on the basis that the enemy of one's enemy must be a friend.

There was a belief on the left that Jews were the main force behind globalism and this together with the rise of anti-Americanism (and the conviction that Jews were running American policy one way or another) was the doctrinal source of anti-Jewish feeling on the left. Great powers have never been popular in history, and anti-Americanism was nothing new except that in the nineteenth through the mid-twentieth centuries it had been far more widespread on the right in Europe than on the left. Attacks against "plutocratic America" under the warmonger President Franklin Rosenfeld (Roosevelt) had been frequent in the age of the Nazis.

As the Cold War ended, America had emerged as the sole superpower, and this created an entirely new situation. Many on the radical left could not accept that the wrong side had prevailed in the Cold War, and they came to regard aggressive American imperialism as the enemy of all peoples. This was true under Bill Clinton's administration and especially under President George W. Bush, who followed an aggressive foreign policy in Afghanistan and Iraq. America, and in particular the Republican administration, became the great menace to be combated and in the struggle against it, all allies were welcome. Where did the inspiration for American policy originate? From the neoconservatives and Leo Strauss. Leo Strauss (1899–1973), a political philosopher of German Jewish origin, came to America in the 1930s and taught for many years at the University of Chicago. He had written about Xenophon and Plato, about Spinoza and Hobbes and Maimonides, but in reality (according to the New Left version) he was a cryptofascist; the insidious message of his work had been to establish American global hegemony and American world empire by means of deception. Strauss, it was maintained, had established a cabal of mainly Jewish students, the so-called neoconservative school, and his disciples attained positions of immense influence under the Bush administration in the late 1990s. It would be difficult to show that the president or the vice president of the United States, the secretaries of defense and state, or the head of the Central Intelligence Agency had ever heard of Strauss, but so powerful and insidious was Strauss's ideological legacy that almost imperceptibly it had shaped American foreign policy, culminating in the invasion of Afghanistan, Iraq, and the war against terror, through the machinations of his Jewish acolytes, ardent supporters of right-wing Zionism acting in unison and with great determination.

The foregoing, in briefest outline, was the quasi-academic New Left explanation of much or all that had gone wrong with American policy; in a simplified form through the mass media, it reached a far wider public. In the case of the *Protocols of the Elders of Zion,* those pulling the strings had been rabbis and bankers; the leading figures in this new conspiracy were professors of philosophy. As in the case of Communism in its Stalinist and post-Stalinist phases, the New Left and the antiglobalists faced some barriers to openly proclaiming racial antisemitism, the idea of superior and inferior races. Code words were used but, nonetheless, the radical left and antiglobalism certainly had what some observers called a "Jewish problem." Jews were regarded with distrust unless they made it abundantly clear that they actively participated in the struggle against capitalism, imperialism, globalism, and, in some cases, the existence of a Jewish state.

Whether to call these suspicions of Jewish intrigues, the imputation of double loyalties, and the denunciation of excessive Jewish influence antisemitic or to use other terms is a question of semantic interest that could be endlessly discussed. The New Left attitude toward the Jews certainly resembled more that of the medieval church than that of the age of racialism; there was salvation through conversion. Some of the similarities with earlier forms of hostility toward Jews as a group or individuals were certainly more than superficial, and they were part of what has been called, for want of a more accurate—and less offensive—term, the new antisemitism.

Chapter Ten

ANTISEMITISM AND THE MUSLIM WORLD

THE APPEARANCE OF POLITICAL ANTISEMITISM in the Arab and Muslim world is of relatively recent date. Antisemitism was believed to be an exclusively European phenomenon; Arab and Muslim spokesmen often argued that by definition they could not be antisemites because they were Semites themselves. But the terms "Semite" and "semitic" refer to a group of languages, and the fact that Jews at one time spoke a language (Hebrew) related to Arabic no more ruled out conflicts between these two peoples than, say, conflicts between Russians and Germans, or French and British were eliminated because all of them spoke languages belonging to the Indo-European family.

The Koran and its interpreters had a great many conflicting things to say about the Jews, and these writings have been of importance in shaping Arab and Muslim attitudes to this day—especially in ages when fundamentalist religion figured prominently. At the time of the prophet Muhammad, Jewish tribes lived in the Arab peninsula, particularly in Medina and its vicinity. Muhammad tried without much success to convert them to his new religion. They refused to accept his message; eventually he fought them, defeated them, and most of them were killed.

But the Koran also says that Muhammad had Jewish friends and there is even a verse that can be interpreted as saying that Allah promised Jerusalem to the Jews. Verses preaching tolerance can be found: there should be no coercion in matters of religion (Sura 2:256); both Moses and Jesus were genuine prophets; Jews and Christians are referred to as *ahl al-kitab* (the People of the Book) and they should be better treated in Muslim societies than pagans.

It is equally easy, however, to find quotations stating that *jihad* (holy war) is the sacred duty of every Muslim believer, that Jews and Christians should be killed, and that this fight should continue until only the Muslim religion is left (Sura 8:39). As al Baqara, the second sura of the Koran, says about the Jews, slay them (the sons of apes and pigs) wherever you catch them. Or, as one of the two chief interpreters of Muhammad, Buhari, says, the last hour will not come until the Muslims fight against the Jews, until a Jew will hide himself behind a stone or a tree, and the stone or the tree will say, "Oh Muslim, there is a Jew hiding behind me. Come and kill him" (Sahih, 4:52.176). This has been quoted countless times to this day, and it even appears in the constitution of Hamas, the Palestinian Islamist organization. Jews are said to be treacherous and hypocritical and could never be friends of the Muslim. The fact that the holy writings of Islam contained many anti-Jewish declarations should not perhaps be regarded as something in the nature of exclusive, unprecedented hostility; similar hostile remarks can be found concerning Christians, all non-Muslims, and in particular pagans.

How did the Jews fare under Muslim rule? By and large, considerably better than in Christian Europe up to the eighteenth century, and there was no holocaust in the Muslim world. On the contrary, there were times and places in which the Jews prospered, materially and culturally. This is true above all with regard to Spain in the early and high Middle Ages; this period has entered Jewish history as the golden age of Andalusia.

Jewish historians of the nineteenth century have somewhat exaggerated the degree of freedom and well-being Jews in Spain and Portugal enjoyed. Certainly the Jews in these countries fared better than under the Visigoths who preceded the Muslim invaders, and better than under the Christian rulers who followed them. The exaggeration, deliberate or unconscious, probably came about to put the suffering of the Jews in Christian Europe into even starker relief. But it is also true that the Jews in Muslim countries were, as the Koran puts it, in a state of wretchedness because they had rejected Muhammad's message. Jews were much of the time in daily practice and in principle regarded with contempt, cowardly and treacherous, and an element of corruption.

In Baghdad and elsewhere, Jews had to wear a yellow badge or headgear to distinguish them. There were major pogroms in Granada (1066) and Fez (1465) in which thousands were killed, and these were not the only attacks. Some North African Jewish communities were forcibly converted; in Yemen and Baghdad at various times many synagogues were destroyed. There was a new wave of pogroms in the late eighteenth and the early nineteenth centuries, mainly in North Africa. In the Ottoman empire the authorities did not, on the whole, tolerate massacres of this kind.

The legal status of Jews in the Muslim world was that of *dhimma;* they enjoyed protection as second-class citizens (*dhimmis*). They were permitted to practice their religion (but not too loudly or ostentatiously), had to pay a special poll-tax (*jizya*), and were subject to a great variety of restrictions. They could not bear arms or be public servants (although Jews during certain periods did serve as administrators and even ministers). They were not permitted to ride horses or camels. In the street they had to give Muslims the right of way; they were not permitted to give evidence in court in their own defense. Muslims could marry Jewish women, but Jewish men were forbidden to have intercourse with Muslim women or to marry them.

Muslim empires stretched from North Africa to South and Central Asia, and the treatment of Jews was by no means uniform. Hence, it is difficult to make sweeping generalizations. It could be argued that second-class citizen status was preferable to not having any rights at all. Jews were tolerated as long as they accepted their inferior status. Muslims did not hate and fear the Jews so much—they were not accused, after all, of having killed the founder of their religion (only of having tried to do so); they were not considered a dangerous element, only a weak and miserable one. This they had inflicted on themselves.

Muslims were always superior to the Jews, who had forfeited their erstwhile status as a chosen people by rejecting Muhammad. This, by and large, was the rationale for their status in law as in the conduct of daily life. If attacks against Jews and riots took place, this had to do mainly with the character of the rulers and also with suspicion and envy on the part of the general population, and because individual Jews had somehow attained positions of political influence and affluence. At times there was antisemitism from above, at other times from below, and sometimes little or none. If Jews prospered in a Muslim society, they were well advised to refrain from showing it. All this refers to the Middle Ages and the early modern age; there was a slow improvement in the position of the Jews during the last two centuries of the Ottoman empire.

IN ITS MODERN FORM, Muslim antisemitism appeared only in the nineteenth century, largely through the influence of Christian Arab communities. Accusing the Jews of ritual murder had been virtually unknown in the Muslim world, but with the Damascus affair in 1840, this European importation showed itself in the Near East. Pater Tomaso, a Capuchin monk in Damascus, suddenly disappeared. His fellow monks falsely accused the local Jews of ritual murder; heads of the community were arrested, tortured, and confessed; some died as the result of the torture. A local French diplomatic agent was the main force behind these accusations; the affair was publicized widely throughout Europe and provoked widespread protest until the Ottoman authorities admitted that the accusations had been wholly wrong.

However, it was not to be the last attempt to charge individual Jews and Jewish communities with ritual murder; similar accusations were made in many cities in the Ottoman empire in the nineteenth century—some as late as 1897–98 in Algeria and 1901–02 in Cairo. In all these cases, the charges originated with Orthodox and Catholic Christian communities, frequently with the support of European consular agents who were usually French or Greek. In parts of the Ottoman empire where Christian communities did not exist, such incidents did not occur. In the case of French involvement, there was probably a connection with the Dreyfus affair; many members of the French diplomatic and consular corps were anti-Dreyfusards as was true also of the French colonial administration in North Africa. A British ambassador to Constantinople, Sir Gerald Lowther, also played an important role in the propagation of antisemitic texts, and some of the European antisemitic literature was translated into Arabic before the turn of the century—for instance, August Rohling's *The Talmud Jew*.

The Jewish colonization of Palestine (at that time part of Damascus district) began in the 1880s, but it was on a very small scale and provoked little interest outside Palestine. Nor did the Zionist congresses (the first took place in Basel in 1897) generate much attention. Najib Nasser, a Christian Arab, published in Haifa a periodical entitled *Al Karmel* that was anti-Zionist, and a Lebanese Christian, Najib Azouri, located in Paris and writing in French, went beyond anti-Zionism in a book, published in 1905, that echoed anti-Jewish allegations that had probably originated with the French right. However, these publications did not reach wide audiences. It was only with the First World War, the Balfour declaration, and the establishment of a Jewish homeland that anti-Zionism became a major issue for the Palestinian Arabs and, to a lesser degree, for the neighboring Arab countries, which had attained independence after the breakup of the Ottoman empire.

While Palestinian and Arab spokesmen had long asserted that their opposition to Zionism had nothing to do with their attitude toward

Jews in general, who were their cousins if not their brothers and had always lived in peace in their midst, anti-Zionism turned increasingly into hostility against all Jews. This manifested itself early on in physical attacks—for instance, the massacre of the old non-Zionist Hebron Jewish community in 1929; the Baghdad-Farhud pogrom of June 1941 in which hundreds were killed; attacks in Constantine, Algeria, in 1934; and the Tripoli, Libya, massacres in 1945 and 1948 in which many scores perished. It manifested itself even more clearly on the ideological level. The Zionists, after all, were Jews and they enjoyed the support of fellow Jews around the world. Under these conditions, to make fine distinctions between good Jews and bad Zionists seemed unnecessary and, from a political viewpoint, counterproductive. The Iranian leadership not only wants to destroy Israel, it also maintains that the Holocaust never happened.

There were significant differences between European and Arab antisemitism. European antisemitism was rooted in a variety of theological and later racialist motives that did not apply, or applied to a lesser degree, in the Arab world. Nor did psychological, economic, and social factors that were relevant in European antisemitism necessarily operate in the Middle East and the Muslim world. Arab and Muslim antisemitism initially had nothing to do with economic crises and the rise of capitalism, and very little to do with the spread of globalization.

As Yehoshafat Harkabi pointed out many years ago, Arab and Muslim antisemitism was the result of, not the reason for, the hostile Arab attitude toward Israel; it gradually became a "means of deepening, justifying and institutionalizing this hostility among Arabs" and subsequently also among fellow Muslims. But it was not the only reason. Although in Europe the stereotype of the Jew was that of the parasite, in the Arab world, on the contrary, it was—especially after 1948—that of an aggressor, assassin, and warmonger. This was doubly unacceptable—that the Palestinian homeland was stolen was bad enough, but that the perpetrators were Jews, always considered weak and cowardly, was altogether unacceptable. Because Islam had been traditionally a warring, expansionist religion, the defeats of 1948 and 1967 by an enemy whom no one had ever taken seriously represented a great trauma for Islam's adherents.

Arab antisemitism has changed its emphasis over time. Between the two world wars the emphasis had been on the revolutionary, Communist, atheist, and thus subversive character of the Jews. This also figured in the various declarations of the grand mufti of Jerusalem who found shelter in Nazi Germany. The fight against Bolshevism and world Jewry was more or less the same battle, and Bosnian volunteer units, established with the help of the mufti, took part in the murder of Yugoslav Jewry. Anti-Communism was the fashionable attitude at the time, but after World War Two this changed as the Soviet Union became a political ally of the Arab world. The emphasis thereafter was on the capitalist, imperialist, pro-American character of world Jewry.

The early European inspiration of Arab antisemitism has been stressed, and in later years too certain aspects of European antisemitism (including Holocaust denial and justification of Nazi crimes) continued to find a warm reception and many imitators in the Arab and Muslim world. This is true particularly with regard to the alleged conspiratorial character of world Jewry; the *Protocols of the Elders of Zion* and similar literature including Hitler's *Mein Kampf* found nowhere more enthusiastic readers and adapters than in the Arab and Muslim world. A Beirut edition of the *Protocols* figured on various best-seller lists. Rohling's *The Talmud Jew* generated no less than twenty-two books in Arabic on the same subject. While in earlier years—up to the late 1960s—the "Jewish issue" had still been a minor one, in the late 1960s it became a central topic in Arab discourse. The miserable and despised Jew turned into a superhuman, demonic, almost omnipotent figure—a danger to the whole world, the instigator of a new world war. Belief in plots and conspiracies had a hallowed tradition in the Arab world and no further European encouragement was needed in this respect.

Another important feature of Arab antisemitism in recent decades has been its Islamization. Increasingly use was made of selective

anti-Jewish quotations from the Koran, the fact that the Jews were perfidious, selfish, avaricious, obstinate, fraudulent, domineering, and
bloodsucking. This kind of propaganda, which was also reflected in
Arab belles lettres and cartoons, was bound to raise occasional doubts
and contradictions—if the Jews were all cowardly pimps and degener-
ate prostitutes, how to explain that they had defeated the Arab armies?

This Islamization of antisemitism was clearly connected with the
rise of Islamic fundamentalism and the Muslim Brotherhood (especially Hamas in Palestine). The basic texts of the Muslim Brotherhood
and allied movements contain openly anti-Jewish rather than anti-
Zionist propaganda. It was in many ways a natural phenomenon
considering the *Zeitgeist* in this part of the world, and it helped to
maintain solidarity between Palestinians and Muslims elsewhere. Texts
such as the books of Sayyid Qutb—often called the father of radical
militant jihad, who was executed in Egypt in the days of Gamal Abdel
Nasser—targeted Judaism. According to these texts, Zionism was, of
course, inimical to the Arabs and Muslims, but the Jews were responsible too for such other catastrophes as the breakdown of the caliphate
in the early 1920s (they had allegedly unleashed World War One for
this specific purpose), for the spread of atheism and materialism, the
destruction of family ties, and the promotion of pornography.

The anti-Jewish component in Islamist doctrine is by no means
restricted to Palestinian Arabs and the neighboring countries. It appeared prominently in Iran after the Khomeini revolution, when the
Protocols were given wide publicity; among other accusations, the
Jews were made responsible for homosexuality and lesbianism. The
Jews, the Khomeinists argued, were in the forefront of anti-Islamic
propaganda. And in a country not noted for Islamist leanings and even
farther distant from Israel than Iran, Mahathir Mohamad, then prime
minister of Malaysia, in a speech in 2003 which attracted worldwide
attention, said that the Europeans killed six out of twelve million Jews
"but today the Jews rule the world by proxy." Further, he said that
they survived two thousand years of pogroms not by hitting back but

by thinking. They invented and successfully promoted Socialism, Communism, human rights, and democracy, so that persecuting them would appear to be wrong, and that they may enjoy equal rights with others. The speech was widely applauded by the many Arab and Muslim statesmen present.

Anti-Jewish statements by prominent Muslim clerics are heard by Arab-speakers throughout the world. Sheikh Youssef el Qaradhawi, who because of his weekly program on Al Jazeera is perhaps the most influential of these—he's also known as the mufti of television—said that "there is no dialogue between us and the Jews except for the sword and the rifle." In his appearances in Europe, this aspect of his teachings was always played down or even denied, but in this and countless other instances reference was made not to Zionists and Israelis but simply to Jews. Muhammad Sayyed Tantawi—possibly more respected than Qaradhawi due to his position as Sheikh Al Azhar, the head of the Cairo religious seminary, the most famous and authoritative in the Muslim world—in his 1966 dissertation discussed the dark history of the Jews with particular emphasis on their crimes, atrocities, and their deceptive practices. Quoting the Koran, he called the Jews "pigs and apes," but in a subsequent change of mind, caused perhaps by the intervention of Egyptian leaders, he later declared that this should not be done.

As these Muslim preachers saw it, the whole world was hostile toward Islam, and the Jews were even more hostile than others. The Jews were the chief agents of imperialism and democracy (a movement unacceptable to Islam because it places the sovereignty of the people and individual human rights above Allah). According to these clerics, America, the great Satan, was more powerful, but Israel and the Jews, albeit the weaker little Satan, were more virulent and dangerous; the Jews were racists and had to be destroyed before the kingdom of Allah could be established on earth.

ISLAMIST ANTISEMITES have collaborated with European antisemites of the left and with the neofascist antisemites in convening various conferences, protest meetings, demonstrations, and declarations. The main ideological contribution of Islamism has been in the field of conspiracy theory. These theories have a long history in Europe, dating back in their modern form to the French Revolution and perhaps even earlier. Although indigenous conspiracy theories had long existed in the Middle East and the Muslim world, the willingness to believe them was probably greater there than anywhere else.

After World War Two the neo-Nazis, the Trotskyites, and especially the Arab media claimed that the Zionists had entered a conspiracy with Hitler to kill millions of Jews and, on the wave of pro-Jewish sympathy after 1945, to establish a Jewish state. After September 11, 2001, the production of conspiracy theories went into high gear. Among the theories: the attacks in Manhattan and Washington had been planned and carried out by the Jews, particularly by the Mossad; was it not true that the Jews working in the World Trade Center had been warned not to go to work on that day?

Other non-Islamist conspiracy theorists argued that the attacks had been launched by al-Qaeda but that Osama bin Laden was an agent of the Mossad whose real name was Ben Landau. Muslim spiritual and political leaders argued at one and the same time that the attacks could not possibly have been carried out by their coreligionists because they lacked the needed sophistication and that they were proud that such a deadly blow had been administered to the hated Americans. According to public opinion polls, a majority of Arabs believed that the attacks of September 11 had been carried out by the Jews—even though bin Laden had said that his supporters had done it.

Still other conspiracy theories maintained that Israel was deliberately supporting the radical Palestinian resistance so that it could hold on to the occupied territories and perhaps kill or expel all Palestinians if violence further escalated or at a time of war. From this perspective, the American president was seen as a puppet of the Israelis who could easily blackmail him because they knew compromising details about his family. In earlier years, conspiracy theorists from the extreme right had argued that the Jews had been able to blackmail Bill Clinton through the Monica Lewinsky affair—at a decisive stage in the war against terror, the argument went, the president was preoccupied with his own intimate problems.

For the left wing and Islamist believers in conspiracy theories, events in the Middle East were only a small part of a giant global plot in which the neoconservatives (most of them Jews) played a decisive role. The philosophical writings of Leo Strauss on Plato, Spinoza, and Hobbes became the new *Protocols of the Elders of Zion*. The possibilities of developing new conspiracy theories in this crowded field are endless. They have become an important component of the new antisemitism, but its motives and its great attraction for people from various parts of the political spectrum have as yet been insufficiently studied.

The new Judeophobia is not limited to propaganda; there have been violent attacks against Jewish institutions in Argentina (probably organized by the Iranian government) in which scores of people were killed, against Jewish restaurants in Paris, and against individual Jews in many European countries. Daniel Pearl, an American journalist, and Nicholas Berg, another American civilian, were murdered (and their murders were televised) in a particularly gruesome way because they were Jews, not Zionists. There have been many such cases, and though contemporary Islamists have also killed many non-Jews in Pakistan, Iraq, Egypt, and elsewhere, the question arises: why were Jews singled out? Why did antisemitism become perhaps the most important single factor in the new Muslim ideology, not only in North Africa, the Middle East, and parts of Asia, but perhaps even more prominently among the strong and growing Muslim diaspora in Europe? Why the prevalence of "kill the Jews" slogans that had not been heard in the streets of Europe since the days of Adolf Hitler?

This new antisemitism had more than one motive. The Muslim immigrants in Europe came from countries in which latent antisemitism had been endemic, and it was therefore easy for radical preachers to

whip up anti-Jewish feelings based on traditional religious and cultural motives. These Muslims, especially the younger ones among
them, had a great many complaints against European societies which,
they claimed, did not treat them as equals and, however permissive,
often did not permit them to transfer their traditional customs to
Western Europe if these conflicted with the laws of Western societies. In addition, there was a great deal of free-floating aggression
among these young, often unemployed, Muslim males that needed
an outlet.

A culture of violence came into being and European Jews, a small
minority, were an obvious target in these circumstances; it was obviously less risky to attack Jews than members of the majority ethnic
groups, even though such confrontations also took place frequently.
There was envy: the Jews, many of them relatively recent immigrants,
had been successful; many of them were well-to-do, had influential
positions in the political, economic, and cultural spheres. Why were
the Muslim immigrants less successful? It could only be the consequence of a conspiracy of deliberate discrimination.

Then there was Israel. The Jews had stolen Arab land, had expelled the original inhabitants, and were cruelly oppressing those under
their rule. They had driven the Palestinians to utter despair; Arab television was showing daily the effects of occupation and the martyrs
giving their lives in the struggle against the enemies of Allah. Was it
not the duty of every believer to show solidarity with his brethren
under attack?

The incitement of the preachers in the mosques played an important role, but the anti-Jewish attacks might have happened even without
the Islamic religious component, as other examples show. In the United
States, for instance, the black-Jewish alliance of past decades had
broken down and antisemitism in segments of the black population
had became prevalent, but this had little to do with what the Koran
and its interpreters were saying about the Jews. Furthermore, the Palestinian cause was not that close to the heart of the American blacks.

As far as the Muslim communities in the Middle East, North Africa, and Asia are concerned, there can be little doubt that the recent major wave of antisemitism was exacerbated as the result of the existence of the state of Israel. Antisemitism would have been rampant among these immigrants even if Israel had not existed, but Israel gave them a cause for which support could be rallied outside their community—and it gave them an effective slogan. The anti-Jewish propaganda of Al Jazeera, Al Manar, and other television channels gave them an enormous outreach in the Middle East as well as in Western Europe, an outreach far larger and more intensive than antisemitic movements had enjoyed in the past.

What could Zionism and Israel have done to defuse this development? The main raison d'être of Herzlian Zionism had been to find a secure homeland for the Jews and to solve the Jewish question in Europe by evacuating them to a country where they could live a normal life. The Zionists were accused of settling in a country with which the Jews had a close historical connection but ignoring the fact that this country, Palestine, was not empty.

This accusation is only half true; while Palestine was not empty, its total Arab population was at the time (in 1900) about one-quarter that of Vienna, where Herzl made his home. In other words, it was not exactly overpopulated. But, it is argued, was it not a sacred country for Muslims all over the world? Yes and no: it contained important Muslim religious shrines but it was not sacred to the extent that the Arab peninsula was, an area in which, the Koran says, no non-Muslim should reside. Palestine was not empty in 1900, but it is also true that there had been a Jewish presence in the country throughout history— there was a Jewish majority in Jerusalem in the nineteenth century, well before Zionism appeared on the scene.

In retrospect, it is doubtful that a conflict between Jews and Palestinians could have been prevented. As the Palestinian Arabs (whose number was growing faster than that of the Jews prior to 1948) saw it, they had been reduced to a minority in their homeland. If the Jews needed a home, why should they, the Palestinians, suffer the consequences of European antisemitism? So they went to war against the partition of Palestine in 1948 with the help of the neighboring Arab countries—and lost.

Millions of people were expelled from their homes after World War Two in Europe as well as in Asia, but eventually they were resettled and the situation was normalized within a generation or two. If the Jews in Palestine had numbered a hundred or at least fifty million, this normalization would probably have happened in the Near East too. Muslims and Arabs have accepted throughout history their expulsion from countries that had once been in their power—from Spain to the Balkans to India. But they could not possibly accept that the Jews, that small and despised minority, should want to take over Palestine. Hence, they refused to resettle the refugees and wanted to continue the attacks against the Jews in the hope that over time the many would prevail over the few.

Prior to the Six-Day War, there was no room for a compromise settlement with the Palestinians, who rejected the very existence of Israel as a matter of holy principle. But after 1967 Israel could and should have made an effort to find a modus vivendi with a neighboring Palestinian state. Instead, they waited for an Arab initiative that never came. They were hanging on to the occupied territories and they solemnly declared that an undivided Jerusalem was theirs and would never again be divided.

While radicalism and religious fundamentalism swept the Muslim world, there was a religious-nationalist wave in Israel also. Although it affected a smaller part of the population, it was a vociferous and politically influential minority. Oblivious of political and demographic realities, it followed a political line that was bound to provoke not only Palestinians but Muslims everywhere. This greatly contributed to the spread of antisemitism in the Muslim world and to the international isolation of Israel. Those unwilling to give up the occupied territories with an Arab majority claimed that Arabs were unappeasable, would not be satisfied with Israeli compromises, and wanted Israel to disappear from the map.

This may well have been true for the extremist groups, and it is probably correct that the great majority of Palestinian Arabs would not have been saddened by the demise of Israel. But it is also true that the Arab extremists were not in a position to achieve their eventual aim nor, had they achieved some of their goals, would they have had the all-out support of the Muslim world to pursue their maximum, ultimate aims.

There was a reasonable chance that a provisional compromise solution could have been reached, and nothing endures like the temporary. It was probably this fear of losing wider Muslim support once a provisional solution had been achieved that made the Palestinian radicals and leaders such as Yasser Arafat refuse to accept a partial solution. But if so, Israel should have acted unilaterally, which it did not; hence the steady aggravation of the situation.

Of particular importance in this context was the status of Jerusalem. Up to 1967 virtually all Israeli politicians were aware of the stake that the major religions had in this city. But the victory in 1967 and the occupation of Temple Mount had an intoxicating collective effect, something not dissimilar to the "Jerusalem syndrome" affecting individuals. This led to the various declarations and resolutions never to divide the city again and not to share sovereignty, and this, in turn, facilitated the Islamization of antisemitism.

It is not easy to define and categorize Islamic antisemitism according to Western lines. It is not racist; Islam, being a religion that extends over various continents and many countries and includes white and black people, cannot possibly subscribe to a theory believing in superior and inferior races—at least not on the abstract level.

In some ways the Muslim attitude toward Jews resembles the Communist attitude toward Jews in Stalin's days. In principle, Communism was opposed to any form of ethnic or racial discrimination, but in reality some peoples were considered more equal than others. In a similar way, the original Muslims (the Arabs) are considered superior to those who embraced Islam only later in history. Nor can the world of Islam accept Jews and other non-Muslims as equal citizens in a society based on shariah; the strong emphasis on conspiracy theories also puts it into a category apart. Although Christianity too had such total, seemingly boundless ambitions, engaged in crusades, established the inquisition, and burned witches, this was many centuries ago; like other religions, it has outgrown its role as a militant church while radical Islam has not. In the twenty-first century it has become the central force in the attacks against Jews.

It is absurd to argue that contemporary Muslim antisemitism is wholly unconnected with the existence of Israel and the policy of Israeli governments. But it is also true that this antisemitism is acting as a lightning rod used both by governments and Islamists; were it not for Israel and the occupied territories, the underlying aggression would find other outlets. It would, in all probability, turn even more against Arab and Muslim governments that have disappointed the hopes of broad segments of their societies. The aggression would not lessen as far as anti-Americanism and anti-Westernism are concerned. Instead of shouting "death to the Jews," the radical young Muslims demonstrating in the streets of Europe would find another cause to embrace and another address for their attacks, as the riots in France in 2005 have shown. This function of antisemitism as a lightning rod in Europe as well as in the Arab and Muslim world is often underrated.

Chapter Eleven

IN PLACE OF A CONCLUSION

ANTISEMITISM IS A HISTORICAL TOPIC, but because it has not yet ended, it is not solely of historical interest. The time to write its epitaph has not yet come.

There can be no dispute that the character of antisemitism has changed in recent centuries. Up to the Second World War most Jews lived in Europe, including the Soviet Union. Today almost half the world's Jews live in Israel, with the United States as the second largest community. As the result of the Holocaust, the demographic distribution has radically changed. While in principle there can be antisemitism even in the absence of Jews—Pakistan is just one example—it is unlikely that in such circumstances antisemitism can be a decisive political issue. The weakness of neo-Nazism, a traditional pillar of antisemitism, and the emergence of major Muslim communities in Europe are other factors that will probably have a decisive impact on the character of antisemitism in the twenty-first century.

The difficulty in differentiating between antisemitism and anti-Zionism has been stressed more than once in these pages. But here again the question arises whether traditional terms explain more than they obfuscate. The hostility of sections of the contemporary left is postracialist; it has little to do with the antisemitism of the Nazi era. Nor has the left today much in common with the traditional left of the nineteenth and the early twentieth centuries; although often populist and anticapitalist in character, it can with equal ease turn left or right. Anti-Zionism is another outdated term, for Zionism, the movement aimed at the ingathering of the exiles and the establishment of a Jewish state, no longer exists as a significant political factor. The state has come into being, and substantial numbers of immigrants can no longer be expected. The history since 1948, in any case, is that of the state of Israel, not of Zionism. The ideology of that state includes Zionist elements but also many others. In the contemporary era, antisemitism is no longer as clear as it was, and it is used simply for want of another, more satisfactory term. But whatever the semantics, hostility toward Jews as individuals and/or a collective still exists and is unlikely to cease any time soon.

There are other factors that make a discussion of the future of this phenomenon of antisemitism highly speculative. The assimilation of Jews outside Israel continues and the birth rate (with the important exception of the Orthodox) is low; the Jewish communities in Europe and the Americas do not sustain their numbers into the next generation. It is not clear how many Jews identifying themselves as such will remain outside of Israel in the year 2050, let alone by the end of this century. An orthodox religious remnant will continue to exist, and in this sense the belief in the eternity of Israel (*nezah israel lo yeshaker*) will be justified; but this applies more to the spiritual than the real world. And it could be that in these circumstances global antisemitism might disappear or at least decline in importance. The critical mass needed for a movement such as antisemitism may no longer exist. Still, these are speculations, and they do not take into account the future of the state of Israel and the attitudes toward it.

At the present time antisemitism, by whatever name, is still much more than a mere historical memory.

BIBLIOGRAPHY

THE FIRST HISTORICAL BIBLIOGRAPHIES on antisemitism were those published by the Wiener Library in London (Helen Kehr, Janet Langmaid, Ilse R.Wolff, eds.), including *Prejudice* (London, 1971). The most up-to-date is the Felix Posen bibliography at the Vidal Sassoon Center at Hebrew University, Jerusalem, which covers so far 40,000 mainly contemporary items.

The list of books below provides no more than a guide to further reading.

General Works

S. Almog, ed. *Antisemitism through the Ages.* Oxford, 1988.

S. W. Baron. *A Social and Religious History of the Jews.* 19 vols. New York, 1952–1983.

A. Bein. *The Jewish Question.* Rutherford, NJ, 1989.

H. H. Ben Sasson, ed. *A History of the Jewish People.* 12th ed. Cambridge, Mass., 2002.

J. A. Chanes. *Antisemitism—A Reference Handbook.* Santa Barbara, Calif., 2004.

S. L. Gilman and S. T. Katz. *Antisemitism in Times of Crisis*. New York, 1991.

G. I. Langmuir. *History, Religion and Antisemitism*. Berkeley, 1990.

L. Poliakov. *A History of Antisemitism*. 4 vols. New York, 1965–1986.

R. Wistrich. *Antisemitism: The Longest Hatred*. New York, 1991.

The Ancient World

L. H. Feldman. *Josephus and Modern Scholarship*. Berlin, 1984.

J. G. Gager. *The Origins of Anti-Semitism*. New York, 1985.

M. Hengel. *Judaism and Hellenism*. Philadelphia, 1981.

J. Isaac. *Genese de l'antisemitisme*. Paris, 1956.

G. L. Langmuir. *Towards a Definition of Antisemitism*. Oxford, 1990.

R. Ruether. *Faith and Fratricide*. Minneapolis, 1974.

P. Schaefer. *Judaeophobia*. Cambridge, Mass., 1998.

J. N. Sevenster. *The Roots of Antisemitism in the Pagan World*. Leiden, 1975.

M. Stern. *Greek and Latin Authors on Jews and Judaism*. 3 vols. Jerusalem, 1974.

V. Tcherikover. *Hellenistic Civilization and the Jews*. New York, 1979.

Z. Yavetz. *Judenfeindschaft in der Antike*. Munich, 1997.

Christianity

G. Baum. *The Jews and the Gospel*. London, 1961.

O. Chadwick. *A History of Christianity*. New York, 1998.

A. Davies, ed. *Antisemitism and the Foundations of Christianity*. NewYork, 1979.

W. Horbury. *Jews and Christians in Contact and Controversy*. Edinburgh, 1998.

K. Latourette. *A History of Christianity*. Vol. 1. San Francisco, 1975.

J. Parkes. *The Conflict between the Church and the Synagogue*. London, 1934.

S. Sandmel. *Anti-Semitism in the New Testament*. Philadelphia, 1978.

M. Simon. *Verus Israel*. Paris, 1964.

K. Stendahl. *Paul Among Jews and Gentiles*. Philadelphia, 1976.

A. L. Williams. *Adversus Judaeos*. Cambridge, U.K., 1935.

The Middle Ages

Y. F. Baer. *A History of the Jews in Christian Spain*. 2 vols. Philadelphia, 1961–1966.

R. Chazan. *European Jewry and the First Crusade*. Berkeley, 1987.

R. Chazan. *Medieval Stereotypes and Modern Antisemitism*. Berkeley, 1997.

A. Dundes. *The Blood Libel Legend*. Madison, Wis., 1991.

J. Edwards. *The Jews in Christian Europe, 1400–1700*. London, 1987.

S. Eidelberg. *The Jews and the Crusades*. Madison, Wis., 1945.

D. Kertzer. *The Popes Against the Jews*. New York, 2001.

G. Kisch. *The Jews in Medieval Germany*. Chicago, 1949.

J. R. Marcus. *The Jew in the Medieval World*. New York, 1972.

H. A. Obermann. *The Roots of Antisemitism in the Age of Renaissance and Reformation*. Philadelphia, 1981.

C. Roth. *The History of the Jews in Italy*. Philadelphia, 1946.

C. Roth. *A History of the Marranos*. New York, 1974.

J. Trachtenberg. *The Devil and the Jews*. New Haven, 1943.

The Enlightenment and After

J. Frankel. *Prophecy and Politics*. Cambridge, U.K., 1981.

L. Greenberg. *The Jews in Russia*. 2 vols. New Haven, 1944.

A. Hertzberg. *The French Enlightenment and the Jews*. New York, 1968.

J. I. Israel. *European Jewry in the Age of Mercantilism*. Oxford, 1986.

J. Katz. *Out of the Ghetto*. Cambridge, Mass., 1973.

J. Katz. *From Prejudice to Destruction*. Cambridge, Mass., 1980.

H. Levine. *Economic Origins of Antisemitism*. New Haven, 1991.

M. Marrus. *The Politics of Emancipation*. Oxford, 1971.

R. Ruerup. *Emanzipation und Antisemitismus*. Goettingen, 1975.

S. Stern. *The Court Jew*. Philadelphia, 1950.

Z. Szajkovski. *Jews and the French Revolution*. New York, 1970.

Racialist Antisemitism

S. Almog. *Nationalism and Antisemitism in Modern Europe*. New York, 1990.

P. Birnbaum. *Le Moment antisemitique*. Paris, 1995.

R. F. Byrnes. *Antisemitism in Modern France*. Bloomington, Ind., 1950.

N. Cohn. *Warrant for Genocide*. New York, 1966.

C. De Michelis. *The Non-Existent Manuscript*. Lincoln, Neb., 2004.

J. D. Klier and S. Lambroza. *Pogroms: Anti-Jewish Violence in Modern Russian History*. Cambridge, Mass., 1992.

W. Laqueur and J. Baumel, eds. *Holocaust Encyclopedia*. New York, 2002.

R. S. Levy. *Antisemitism in the Modern World*. Lexington, Ky., 1991.

H. D. Loewe. *Antisemitismus und reaktionaere Utopie*. Hamburg, 1978.

H. D. Loewe. *The Tsars and the Jews*. New York, 1993.

P. Massing. *Rehearsal for Destruction*. New York, 1949.

E. Mendelssohn. *The Jews of East Central Europe between the Two World Wars*. Bloomington, Ind., 1983.

B. F. Pauley. *From Prejudice to Persecution: A History of Austrian Antisemitism*. Chapel Hill, 1992.

P. Pulzer. *The Rise of Political Antisemitism*. Cambridge, Mass., 1988.

J. Reinharz, ed. *Living with Antisemitism*. Boston, 1987.

H. Rollin. *L'Apocalypse de notre temps*. Paris, 1991.

P. L. Rose. *German Question/Jewish Question*. Princeton, 1992.

I. Schorsch. *Jewish Reactions to German Antisemitism, 1870–1914*. Philadelphia, 1972.

H. A. Strauss, ed. *Hostages of Modernization*. 2 vols. Berlin, 1993.

S. Volkov. *Juedisches Leben und Antisemitismus im 19. Jahrhundert*. Munich, 1990.

M. F. Zumbini. *Die Wurzeln des Boesen*. Frankfurt, 2003.

Antisemitism and the Left

E. Haberer. *Jews and Revolution in Nineteenth-Century Russia.* Cambridge, Mass., 1995.

T. Haury. *Antisemitismus von Links.* Hamburg, 2002.

B. Lazare. *Antisemitism, Its History and Causes.* Lincoln, Neb., 1995.

A. Leon. *The Jewish Question.* Mexico City, 1950.

E. Mendelsohn. *Essential Papers on Jews and the Left.* New York, 1997.

E. Silberner. *Sozialisten zur Judenfrage.* Berlin, 1962.

Z. Szajkovski. *Jews, War and Communism.* 2 vols. New York, 1972, 1974.

A. Vaksberg. *Stalin Against the Jews.* New York, 1994.

R. Wistrich. *The Left Against Zion.* London, 1979.

R. Wistrich. *Socialism and the Jews.* New York, 1985.

Jews and Muslims; Antisemitism in the Muslim World

Bat Ye'or. *Eurabia.* New York, 2005.

M. Cohen. *Under Crescent and Cross.* New York, 1995.

S. D. Goitein. *Jews and Arabs.* New York, 1974.

Y. Harkabi. *Arab Attitudes to Israel.* New York, 1974.

M. Kuentzel. *Jihad und Judenhass.* Freiburg, 2003.

B. Lewis. *Semites and Antisemites.* New York, 1999.

B. Lewis. *The Jews of Islam.* New York, 1987.

N. Stillman. *Jews of Arab Lands.* Philadelphia, 1975.

N. Stillman. *The Jews of Arab Lands in Modern Times.* Philadelphia, 1991.

Contemporary Antisemitism

W. Benz. *Antisemitismus in Deutschland.* Munich, 1995.

J. Brent and V. Naumov. *Killers in White Gowns.* New York, 2004.

L. Dinerstein. *Antisemitism in America.* New York, 1995.

S. Friedländer. *Nazi Germany and the Jews*. Vol. 1. New York, 1997.

Z. Gitelman. *A Century of Ambivalence*. New York, 1988.

H. Graml. *Antisemitism in the Third Reich*. Oxford, 1988.

P. Iganski and B. Kosmin, eds. *The New Antisemitism*. London, 2003.

A. Lindemann. *Esau's Tears*. New York, 2000.

D. Rabinovici, U.Speck, N. Sznaider. *Neuer Antisemitismus?* Frankfurt, 2004.

V. Rossman. *Russian Intellectual Antisemitism*. Lincoln, Neb., 2002.

G. Schoenfeld. *The Return of Anti-Semitism*. San Francisco, 2004.

P. A.Taguieff. *Les Protocoles des Sages de Sion*. Paris, 2004.

P. A. Taguieff. *Precheurs de Haine*. Paris, 2004.

Interpretations

H. Arendt. *The Origins of Totalitarianism*. New York, 1951.

F. Bernstein. *Jew-Hate as a Sociological Phenomenon*. New York, 1950.

E. Cramer. *Hitler's Antisemitismus und die Frankfurter Schule*. Dusseldorf, 1979.

G. Erner. *Expliquer l'antisemitisme*. Paris, 2005.

H. Fein, ed. *The Persisting Question*. Berlin, 1987.

A. Finkielkraut. *Au nom de l'autre*. Paris, 2003.

S. Gilman. *Jewish Self-Hatred*. Baltimore, 1986.

E. Reichmann. *Hostages of Civilization*. London, 1950.

J. P. Sartre. *Antisemite and Jew*. New York, 1995.

E. Simmel. *Antisemitism: A Social Disease*. Boston, 1946.

S. Volkov. *Antisemitismus als kultureller Code*. Munich, 2000.

INDEX

Abraham (Ibrahim), 14, 74
Abwehr Blaetter
    (periodical), 161
Abwehrverein (Associa-
    tion for the Defense
    Against Antisemit-
    ism), 161
Action Française, 87
Acts, book of, 46
Adorno, Theodor, 31
Afghanistan, 188
Africa, 126, 127, 130
African Americans, 145–
    47, 150, 202
Agimet, 60
Agobard of Lyons, 51
agriculture, 154–55
Ahasuerus, 39
ahl al-kitab (People of the
    Book), 68, 192
AIDS, 62
Akkadian language, 21
alcohol, 80
Alexander II, 54, 82, 83
Alexandria, 41, 44
Algeria, 195, 196
Alliance Israelite
    Universelle, 97, 160

Almohads, 68
al-Qaeda, 130, 200
Amalekites, 59
Ambrosius, 50
American Jewish
    Committee, 161
anarchists, 186
Anglo Jewish Association,
    160
*Annales d'histoire
    revisioniste*, 136
anomie of society, 35
anti-Americanism, 14, 17,
    129, 187–88
Antichrist, 47, 55
Anti-Defamation League
    of B'nai B'rith, 161
Anti-Fascist Committee,
    174–75
antiglobalism, 186
Antisemitism (Samuel), 34
antisemitism (term), 21–
    22, 93
*Antisemitism: Its History
    and Causes* (Lazare),
    27, 28
anti-Zionism
    and anti-Americanism,
    17

    and antisemitism, 7, 9,
        18, 20, 207–8
    controversy, 5–6
    generalized to all Jews,
        195–96
Antonescu, Ion, 134
Apion, 41
Apolonius, Molon, 41–42
appearance of Jews, 43,
    54, 80–81, 158–59,
    168, 193
appeasement policies, 12,
    16
Arabs and Arab societies
    anti-Zionism, 195–96,
        198
    Arab-Israeli conflict, 178
    conspiracy theories, 20,
        197, 200–201, 206
    and critics of Jews, 148
    expulsions of Jews, 68
    in France, 13
    fundamentalism, 182
    and Holocaust, 139–42,
        184
    and Israel, 196–97, 202,
        206
    and Nazism, 187

Arabs and Arab societies
    (*continued*)
  political influence, 185
  propaganda, 198, 203
  and references to Jews,
    6, 148
  relationships with Jews,
    18, 147
  and Russia, 16
  slave trade, 146
  sources of antisemitism,
    5, 196–97
  and Soviet Union, 197
Arafat, Yasser, 205
Arendt, Hannah, 32–33
Argentina, 201
Armenians, 124, 177
Arrow Cross of Hungary,
    107, 112, 121
Aryanism, 92, 93
Ashkenazi Jews, 72
Asia, 126, 134, 203
Assembly from Alsace
    Lorraine, 72–73
assimilation
  in ancient Rome, 44
  and character traits of
    Jews, 158
  Clermont-Tonnerre on,
    72–73
  continuation of, 210
  difficulty of, 2, 91, 165–
    66
  in France, 151
  German philosophers
    on, 74
  in Germany, 151
  Holbach on, 72
  in Hungary, 110
  of non-Jew minorities,
    126
  in Poland, 80–81, 109
  and Zionism, 169
Association for a Taxation
    of Financial Transac-
    tion and for Assistance
    to Citizens (ATTAC),
    186
athletes, Jews as, 162–63
Auschwitz-Birkenau
    extermination camp
  death toll, 138

and denials of
    Holocaust, 130, 141,
    184
  gas chambers, 119, 121
  location, 136
  public reaction, 135
Austria
  attitudes toward Jews,
    150, 160
  and defenses against
    antisemitism, 163
  demographics, 78
  emigration, 116–17
  and Holocaust, 122
  and Jewish identity, 166
  Jewish population, 36
"Autoemancipation"
    (Pinsker), 26–27
Azouri, Najib, 195

Baader-Meinhof terrorist
    gang, 130, 182–83
Babi Yar mass execution,
    120
Baghdad, Iraq, 193, 196
Bahai in Iran, 8
Balfour Declaration, 195
Ballin, Albert, 93–94
Baltic countries, 134
Banu Qurayza tribe, 67
barbarism, 34
Barbie, Klaus, 130
Beilis trial (1911), 89
Belgium
  attacks on Jews, 57
  attitudes toward Jews,
    129, 150, 160
  expulsions of Jews, 54
  and Holocaust, 120, 122
  political parties, 11
Belzec extermination
    camp, 119
Benoist, Alain de, 129
Benz, Wolfgang, 122
Berg, Kid, 163
Berg, Nicholas, 201
Berlin, Germany, 36–37
Berlin Olympic Games,
    116
Berlusconi, Silvio, 127
Berman, Jakub, 176

Bernard of Clairvaux, 53
Besarabets (newspaper),
    85
Bialik, Haim Nahman, 85
Bialystok ghetto, 120
Biarritz (Retcliffe), 96
Bin Laden, Osama, 130,
    184, 200
Biro Bidzhan (Soviet
    district), 30
Black Death, 38, 54, 60–
    62, 67
Black Hundreds, 84, 87–
    89
blacks, 145–47, 150, 202
blogging, 130
blood libel, 55–57
  accusations, 66, 80, 153
  Beilis trial, 89
  Damascus trial, 56, 194
  Hugh of Lincoln, 56
  Luther on, 64
  Muslim version, 140
  in Romania, 112
  St. William of Norwich,
    55–56
Bloody Sunday in St.
    Petersburg, 88
Boer War, 103
Bohemia, 65
Bolshevism
  and Nazism, 113
  participation of Jews in,
    83, 104, 105, 132
  and spread of antisemit-
    ism, 30
  and Zionism, 180
Bomberg, Daniel, 59
bourgeois society, 31
boycotts of Jewish shops,
    109, 115
Brafman, Iakov, 82
Britain
  antisemitic activity, 128
  attitudes toward Jews,
    65, 149, 150, 160
  and defenses against
    antisemitism, 163
  demographics, 11
  expulsions of Jews, 36
  ghettos, 71

immigration, 95
imperialism, 33, 177
Jewish population, 66,
125
legislation, antisemitic,
110
and Livingstone, 13
Muslim population, 126,
148
political parties, 186
British Mandate in
Palestine, 30
Browe, Peter, 31
Buchenwald camp, 135–
36
Bulgaria, 120
Bunche, Ralph, 145–46
Bush, George W., 187–88
Butz, Arthur R., 136

Cairo, Egypt, 195
Caligula, 41
Calvinism, 64
Capistrano, 54–55, 56–57
capitalism
and Communism, 179
Friedrich on, 34
Jews associated with,
114, 143, 148, 172
Marxists on, 31
and socialism, 28, 79,
172
Sombart's study of, 25–
26
caricatures of Jews, 159
Carlist party, 113
Carlos the Jackal, 9, 130,
182, 184
Carol II, King of
Romania, 111
Catherine II, 79
Catholic Church
attacks on Jews, 80
and Dreyfus case, 102
and emancipation of
Jews, 78
and establishment of
ghettos, 62–63
and Italian antisemitism,
127
popes, 53, 54, 56–57, 61

Central Europe. *See also*
specific countries
and defenses against
antisemitism, 163
and Holocaust, 118, 119
Jewish population, 107
regional variations in
antisemitism, 69
status of Jews, 71
Centralverein, 161
Chamberlain, Houston
Stewart, 93, 94
character traits of Jews,
158–59, 167
Chechens and Chechnya,
7, 133, 134, 204
Chelmno extermination
camp, 119
China, 204
Chmielnicki, Bohdan, 66
Chmielnicki massacre, 69
Chomsky, Noam, viii, 183
Christianity. *See also*
Catholic Church
and Black Death, 61–62
blood libel cases, 55–57,
153, 195
charity for Jews, 75–76
and conversion of Jews,
54, 108
Crusades, 38, 51, 52–53
desecration of Host, 57
Fourth Lateran Council,
54, 57
Inquisition, 62–63, 70
and Islam, 19, 52, 67–
68, 192
and Judaism, 3, 45–52,
53–55, 62–64, 66, 142
Judaism's rejection of,
1, 36, 151
and Judaizers, 48
militancy, 206
and Nazism, 144
persecution, 45, 52
political influence, 10
in Russia, 132
theologians, 31
threat of Jews to, 80, 143
in United States, 142
Cicero, 42

Cioran, Emil, 112
circumcision rite, 41, 43,
44
citizenship rights, 41
Civilta Cattolica, 57
class enemies, Jews as,
179
Claudius, 41
Clement VI, 54, 61
Clermont-Tonnerre,
Stanislas, comte de,
72–73
Clinton, Bill, 187, 201
Cold War, 179, 181, 187
Cologne, Germany, 52
Communism
avoidance of
antisemitism, 173
breakdown, 133
equality emphasis, 206
and fall of Soviet Union,
180
and Holocaust, 124
and "Jewish question,"
30
motives behind
antisemitism, 177
participation of Jews,
14, 114, 132, 133,
174, 176
and Polish population,
134
propaganda, 105, 175
and references to
Zionism and Judaism,
180
repression of Jews, 179
and revolutions, 30, 99
in Russia, 150
and working class, 184
and Zionism, 180
competition, Jews as, 77,
80, 95, 143, 154
concentration camps, 115,
117, 119, 121
Congress of Vienna, 76
conscription, 81, 82, 86
conspiracy theories
in Arab world, 20, 197,
200–201, 206
and Biarritz, 96

conspiracy theories
(*continued*)
and Communism, 177–
78
and *Protocols of the
Elders of Zion*, 29, 82,
96–102
on revolutionary
ambitions, 30, 156
in United States, 144
Constantine, 49, 50
conversion of Jews
church on, 54, 108
and German Jewry, 164–
65
German philosophers
on, 74
and Inquisition, 70
and issues of equality, 91
and military conscrip-
tion, 81
motivations, 165
Pobedonostsev on, 84
and prevalence of
antisemitism, 151
conversion to Judaism, 54
Copts in Egypt, 8
Coughlin, Charles
Edward, 144
countryside, flight from,
154–55
court Jews (*Hofjuden*), 65
Croatia, 120
Cromwell, Oliver, 64
Crusades, 38, 51, 52–53
Czechoslovakia, 118, 122,
138

Dachau camp, 136
Dalets (Untouchables) in
India, 8, 157
Damascus trial of 1840,
56, 194
David (biblical), 97
Dayan, Moshe, 184
death camps, 119, 121,
135, 136, 141
defenses against
antisemitism, 160,
163–64, 168
democracy, 24, 199

democrats, 34, 181
demographics, 78
demonopathy, 26
Denikin, Anton, 104
Denmark, 113, 120
department stores, 95
depictions of Jews, 159
deportations. *See*
expulsions of Jews
Deutscher, Isaac, 180
Devil, 55, 199
diaspora, 39
Diodorus, Siculus, 41
disease in Jewish
population, 40
Disraeli, Benjamin, 14,
156
Dmowski, Roman, 109
"doctor's plot" in Soviet
Union, 62
Donin, Nikolas, 58
Dresden bombing, 138
Dreyfus case, 27, 29, 73,
101–2, 195
Drumont, Edouard, 102
Dubrovin, Alexander, 87
Duehring, Eugen, 22, 93
Durkheim, Emile, 35

East Germany, 175, 178–
79
Eastern Europe. *See also
specific countries*
antisemitic activity,
131–32, 134
attitudes toward Jews,
167
Freemasons, 73
Holocaust, 118, 119,
123, 139
Jewish population, 16–
17, 107, 128, 133, 138
minorities, 110
pogroms, 78
propaganda, 175
regional variations in
antisemitism, 66, 69
slave trade, 158
socioeconomics, 79
Stalinism, 174
status of Jews, 167

transition to modern
antisemitism, 5
Eastern Orthodox Church,
80, 132, 178, 195
economic sources of
antisemitism, 36, 38
competitors, Jews as, 77,
95, 143, 154
in Germany, 114
in Hungary, 110
in Poland, 108
prosperity of Jews, 62,
143–44, 157
education
in Germany, 115, 116
lack of secular
education, 72, 80
literacy of Jews, 155
restrictions on Jews, 82,
109
in Romania, 111
Edward, Prince of Wales,
103
Efraim the Syrian, 48
Egypt, ancient
attitude toward Jews, 43
destruction of Elephan-
tine temple, 40
exodus from, 40, 42, 44
xenophobia, 2
Egypt, modern, 11
Eichmann, Adolf, 137, 141
Eisenmenger (professor),
58, 82
Elephantine temple, 39–40
Eliade, Mircea, 112
Elias, Samuel "Dutch
Sam," 162
emancipation
advocates, 71
and Enlightenment era,
160
in France, 29
German philosophers
on, 74–75
and nature of
antisemitism, 155–56
opposition, 54, 65, 73–
77, 80–81
Petlyura on, 104
Pinsker on, 26
in Russia, 29

emek ha'bacha (the valley of tears), 61
emigration and immigration
    from Africa, 127
    from Austria, 116
    from Central Europe, 61
    and demographic shifts, 11, 12
    from Eastern Europe, 66, 134, 161–62
    from Germany, 95, 116
    Hitler on, 117
    from Hungary, 176
    during Middle Ages, 53
    of Muslims, 201–2
    to Palestine, 30
    from Poland, 109, 176
    political reaction to, 129–30
    from Romania, 176–77
    from Russia, 29, 84
    from Soviet Union, 118, 177
    to United States, 18, 84, 95, 142–43
    from Western Europe, 61
Engels, Friedrich, 179
England, 54, 56, 76, 162. *See also* Britain
Enlightenment, 31, 71–79, 160, 171, 179
Enlightenment, Jewish (Haskalah), 82
equality, 179–80
Erasmus, 63
essentialist explanation of antisemitism, 45
Esther, book of, 39
eternal antisemitism theory, 33
ethnography, 92
eugenics, 94
Europe. *See also specific countries and regions*
    assimilation of Jews, 2
    attitudes toward Jews, 128, 149
    and Black Death, 60–62
    borders, 149
    and Communism, 30

demographics, 10–12
    and exodus of Jewry, 27
    and Holocaust, 117, 122–23
    immigration, 11, 126
    and Islamist antisemitism, 199–200
    Jewish population, 125, 126, 141, 172
    legislation, anti-racialist, 131
    in Middle Ages, 3–4, 50–62
    and Middle East, 15
    Muslim population, 10–13, 15–16
    regional variations in antisemitism, 66, 69
    socialism, 25
    sources of antisemitism, 196, 197
    status of Jews, 51–52, 172
    trends in antisemitism, 10
    violence against Jews, 38 (*see also* pogroms and massacres)
European Monitoring Centre on Racism and Xenophobia, 131
evil, Jews associated with, 149
Evola, Giulio, 129
exodus from Egypt, 40, 42, 44
exploitation of non-Jews, 157
expulsions of Jews
    from Arab peninsula, 68
    from Belgium, 54
    from Bohemia, 65
    from Britain, 36
    and denials of Holocaust, 141
    from England, 54
    from France, 36, 50, 54
    from Italy, 50
    from Poland, 103, 134
    from Portugal, 54, 69
    from Russia, 79

from Spain, 36, 50, 54, 69
    from Ukraine, 79
    extermination camps, 119, 121, 135, 136, 141

Farrakhan, Louis, 146, 184
fascism, 10, 112–13, 125, 127, 129
Fatimids, 68
Faurisson, Robert, 136, 183
feminism, 148–49
Fez pogroms, 193
Fichte, Johann, 74, 75
Fini, Gianfranco, 127
First Crusade, 38, 51, 52–53
fiscus judaicus tax, 44–45
Flagellants, 55, 61–62
Flatow, Alfred, 162
Flatow, Gustav, 162
Ford, Henry, 99, 143
Fourier, Charles, 24, 79
Fourth Lateran Council in 1215, 54, 57
France
    and Action Française, 87
    assimilation of Jews, 151
    attacks on Jews, 38, 51, 57, 77, 127–28
    attitudes toward Jews, 65, 126, 150
    and Black Death, 60
    blood libel cases, 56
    consular agents, 195
    and Crusades, 52
    and defenses against antisemitism, 163
    demographics, 11, 13
    Dreyfus case, 101–2
    in Enlightenment era, 72
    expulsions of Jews, 36, 50, 54, 62
    and Freemasons, 73
    French Revolution, 95–96, 171, 179
    ghettos, 71
    and Holocaust, 120

France (continued)
    imperialism, 177
    Jewish population, 29,
        66, 125, 127
    legislation, anti-racialist,
        131
    legislation, antisemitic,
        110
    literature on
        antisemitism, 23
    Muslim population, 19,
        126, 127–28
    philosophers, 75
    and Protocols of the
        Elders of Zion, 85
    and religious sectarian-
        ism, 91
    riots, 207
    status of Jews, 154
    transition to modern
        antisemitism, 5
Franco, Francisco, 113,
    134
Frank, Ludwig, 162
Frankfurt, Germany, 37, 76
Frankfurt school of
    critical theory, 31, 32
Freemasons, 73, 95, 98,
    113
French Revolution, 95–
    96, 171, 179
Freud, Sigmund, 37, 164,
    166
Friedrich, Carl, 34
Fromm, Erich, 32
functionalist explanation
    of antisemitism, 45
fundamentalism, religious,
    15, 182, 191, 198, 205

Gager, John, 33
Galton, Francis, 92
Garaudy, Roger, 130, 141,
    183
Gaza, 183
Geremek, Bronislav, 134
Germany
    assimilation of Jews,
        151
    associations defending
        Jews, 23

attacks on Jews, 51, 57
attitudes toward Jews,
    65, 128, 150, 160
Berlin Olympic Games,
    116
and Black Death, 60
blood libel cases, 56
and Crusades, 52
and defenses against
    antisemitism, 163
demographics, 11
and emancipation of
    Jews, 73, 76
emigration, 95, 116
expulsions of Jews, 138
financial restitution,
    128, 176
foreign policy, 116
"German ideology," 94–
    95
ghettos, 71
Green party, 185
and Holocaust, 118,
    122, 135
and Jewish identity, 166
Jewish population, 23–
    24, 66, 93, 164
legislation, anti-racialist,
    131
legislation, antisemitic,
    115
Muslim population, 126
nationalism, 34
and Nazism, 31, 36, 100,
    107, 113, 114–20, 125
philosophers, 74
pogroms, 117
population trends, 10,
    36–37
and Protocols of the
    Elders of Zion, 98
and religious sectarian-
    ism, 91
socialism, 25
sources of antisemitism,
    114
study of antisemitism in,
    35
transition to modern
    antisemitism, 5
and Wilhelm Marr, 21

Gerstein, Kurt, 137
ghettos
    and church, 62–63
    effects on Jews, 37
    in Enlightenment era, 71
    establishment, 62–63
    expansion of, 129
    in Middle Ages, 3
    in modern era, 76, 77
    and Nazism, 118, 119
    for Palestinians, 187
    resistance, 119–20
    and Zionism, 168
globalism, 15
Gobineau, Joseph, 92
Goebbels, Josef, 22
Goedsche, Hermann, 96
Goga, Octavio, 112
Gombos, Julius, 111
Granada, 68
Great Depression, 143–44
Greece, ancient, 2, 3, 41,
    43–44
Greece, modern
    attitudes toward Jews,
        129
    consular agents, 195
    and Holocaust, 120, 122
    Jewish population, 128–
        29
    religious antisemitism,
        10
Green party, 185
Gregory IX, 54, 58
Gregory X, 56
Granada pogroms, 193
Grimm's Fairy Tales, 56
Gruenbaum, Isaac, 109

hadith, 67, 68
Haecateus of Abdera, 41
Haider, Jörg, 130
hair length, 43
Haman, 39
Hamas, 192
Harkabi, Yehoshafat, 196
Harwood, Richard, 136
Haskalah (Jewish
    Enlightenment), 82
Hebrew language, 109,
    168, 191

Hebron massacre, 196
Hegel, Georg Wilhelm
  Friedrich, 74–75
Heine, Heinrich, 165
Hellenistic period, 41
Hep Hep disturbances, 76,
  78
Herder, Johann, 75
Herzl, Theodor, 27, 29,
  33, 164, 169
Heydrich, Reinhard, 118
Himmler, Heinrich, 118–
  19, 135
Hitler, Adolf. See also
  Holocaust; Nazis
  announcement of
    intentions, 117, 135
  and Chamberlain, 94
  and "final solution,"
    119–22
  ideology, 114
  on Kristallnacht
    pogrom, 117
  leadership, 110, 115–16
  propaganda, 113–14,
    115
  and Protocols of the
    Elders of Zion, 100
  and resistance, 123
  and revisionism, 137
  sympathizers, 140, 141,
    145, 187
  and Zionist-collabora-
    tion theory, 200
Hobsbawm, Eric, ix
Hoess, Rudolf, 137, 141
Hofjuden (court Jews), 65
Holbach, Paul-Henri,
  baron d', 72
Holland, 76, 129, 138
Hollywood, 143
Holocaust. See also Hitler,
  Adolf; Nazis
  Arab and Muslim
    attitudes, 139
  and assimilation of
    Jews, 2
  concentration camps,
    115, 117, 119, 121
  denials of, 125, 134,
    135–41, 184–85, 197

discussion of, 150
"final solution," 118–24,
  137
impact 28, 123–24, 207
  Jewish casualties, 121–
    22, 138
  and persecution by
    Jews, 6
  resistance, 122
  significance, 149
  and study of
    antisemitism, 35
  as unique event, 123–24
Holy Sepulcher, 52
Homel pogrom, 85–86
homosexuals, 124, 198
Horkheimer, Max, 31
Horthy, Miklós, 110, 111
Howard, Michael, 149
Hugh of Lincoln, 56
Hungary
  Arrow Cross, 107, 112,
    121
  assimilation of Jews,
    109–10
  attitudes toward
    Hungarians, 179
  Black Death in, 60
  and Communist
    leadership, 176
  and defenses against
    antisemitism, 163
  and emancipation of
    Jews, 76
  emigration, 176
  and Holocaust, 121,
    122, 123
  Jewish population, 107,
    110, 128, 133
  legislation, antisemitic,
    111
  and neofascism, 134
  pogroms, 30
  political parties, 30
  revolutionary coups, 99
  riots, 108
  status of Jews, 167
Hussein, Saddam, 130

Iberian peninsula, 92
identity of Jews, 33–34,
  165–66, 172–73

Ignacio de Loyola, 70
Illuminati, 95
immigration. See
  emigration and
  immigration
imperialism, 33, 177, 179,
  187–88, 199
Imredi, Bela, 111
India, 204
Innocent III, 54
Innocent IV, 56
Inquisition, 62–63, 70
internationalism, 149, 182
Internet, 17, 130
Intifada, 14
intolerance among Jews,
  40, 42, 44
Iran, 11, 140, 198, 201
Iraq, 188, 193, 196
Iron Guard of Romania,
  107, 111, 112
Irving, David, 136
Islam. See also Muslims
  and Christianity, 19, 52,
    67–68, 192
  and European
    antisemitism, 199–200
  fundamentalism, 182,
    191, 198, 205
  hadith, 67, 68
  Jews under rule of, 51,
    67, 192–93
  jihad, 192
  Judaism's rejection of,
    1, 36, 151, 191–92,
    193, 194
  Koran, 59, 67–68, 147,
    191–92, 193, 199
  militancy, 205–6
  and references to Jews, 6
  and sources of
    antisemitism, 5, 197–
    98
  status of Jews, 67–69
  and Trotskyism, 186
  Voltaire on, 71
Israel. See also anti-
  Zionism; Zionism
  anti-Israelism, 5–6, 7, 9
    (see also anti-Zionism)
  and Arabs, 196–97, 202,
    204–5

Israel (*continued*)
and Christianity, 45
criticisms, 6–7, 8
founding, 160, 182, 184
integration, 15
Israeli-Palestinian
conflict, 8–10, 19–20,
187, 200, 203–5
Jewish population, 209
and left-wing opposi-
tion, 147–48
and Palestinians, 187
religious nationalism,
15, 205
Six-Day War, 181, 183,
204
and sources of
antisemitism, 203
status, 14
as threat to world peace,
ix, 7–8, 149, 186–87
and United States, 15,
17–18, 200
Israelitische Allianz, 160
Italy
attacks on Jews, 77
attitudes toward Jews,
150, 160
demographics, 10
expulsions of Jews, 50
and fascism, 112
and Holocaust, 120, 122
Jewish population, 66,
127
legislation, antisemitic,
113
and neofascism, 127
propaganda, 10

Japan, 86, 177
Jehovah's Witnesses, 124
Jerusalem, 50, 192, 203,
205
Jesus Christ, 45–46, 74,
93, 151, 192
Jewish antisemitism, 159,
166, 176
Jewish Enlightenment
(Haskalah), 82
Jewish identity, 33–34,
165–66, 172–73

"Jewish question," 23–25,
27, 29, 30
"Jewish spirit," 21, 25
"The Jews and Their Lies"
(Luther), 63–64
jihad, 192
John, book of, 47
John Chrysostom, 47–48,
49
Joly, Maurice, 96
Josef II, 76
Josephus, Flavius, 40, 41
*Journal of Historical
Review*, 136
Judaizers, 48
Judas Iscariot, 48
Judeophobia, 5, 20, 22,
26, 201
Justin Martyr, 45, 47
Justinian I, 50
Juvenal, 43

Kaganovitch, Lazar, 30
Kallinikon, 50
Kant, Immanuel, 74, 75
Kautsky, Karl, 173, 180
Keynes, John Maynard,
155
Khomeinists, 198
King, Martin Luther, 145
Kishinev pogrom, 78, 85–
86, 168
Kniga Kahala (Brafman),
82
Korherr, Richard, 121
Kristallnacht pogrom,
117, 147
Kun, Bela, 108, 110
Kunzelmann, Dieter, 147
Kurds, 2

La vieille taupe (the Old
Mole), 137, 183
Lagarde, Paul, 22, 93
land ownership, 155
Landau, Ben, 200
Lassalle, Ferdinand, 172,
173
Latvia, 105
Lazare, Bernard, 27–29,
102
Le Monde, 13

Le Pen, Jean-Marie, 127,
130
League of Nations, 110,
116
left wing, 147–50. *See
also* Communism
Friedrich on, 34
on Holocaust, 17
ideology, 15
and political parties,
185–86
on Zionism, 17, 150, 182
legal status of Jews
in Middle Ages, 3
in Muslim world, 193–
94
in Poland, 81
in Roman civilization,
50
in Spain's Golden Age,
69
Legion of Archangel
Michael. *See* Iron
Guard of Romania
legislation, anti-racialist,
131, 160
legislation, antisemitic
in Eastern Europe, 30
in Germany, 115
in Hungary, 111
in Italy, 113
opposition to, 110
in Poland, 109
Lenin, Vladimir Il'ich,
132, 173, 174
Leninism, 179–80, 182
Leo III, 50
Leon, Abram, 174
Leonard, Benny, 162–63
lepers, Jews as, 40, 42, 44
Lessing, Gotthold, 73
Lettwin, Oliver, 149
Leuchter, Fred, 136
Lewinsky, Monica, 201
Lewis, Bernard, 68
libel against Jews, 54. *See
also* blood libel
Libya, 196
limpieza de sangre (purity
of blood), 22, 70, 91–
92, 159–60

literature, antisemitic, 65, 76, 96–101, 132, 174
literature on antisemitism, 22–23, 30–36
Lithuania, 80, 81, 103
Livingstone, Ken, 13
Lodz ghetto, 119, 120
Lombards, 154
London, England, 60
Louis, George, 87
Low Countries of Europe, 70
Lowther, Sir Gerald, 195
Lueger, Karl, 78
luftmenschen status, 167
Luke, book of, 46
Luther, Martin, 55, 63–64
Luxemburg, Rosa, 156, 173
Lvov, Poland, 107
Lysimachus, 41

Madagascar, 93, 109
Mahler, Horst, 129, 130, 183–84
Mainz, Germany, 52
Majdanek extermination camp, 119, 136
Makhno, Nestor, 104
Malik, Charles, 140–41
Manetho, 40
Manifestations of Antisemitism in the EU 2002–2003, 131
Manifesto group, 127
Maria Theresa, 65
Marr, Wilhelm, 21, 93
marriage, 50, 51, 115, 134, 193
Martial, 43
Marx, Karl, 24, 79, 157, 172, 173
Marxism, 31, 179–80, 182
Marxist Social Democrats, 79
Masons, 73, 95, 98, 113
Matthew, book of, 46
Mein Kampf (Hitler), 114
Mendoza, Daniel, 162

Mensheviks, 83, 105
Menuhin, Yehudi, 124
Merker, Paul, 175–76
Middle Ages, 50–62
  conspiracy theories, 101
  expulsions of Jews, 3–4
  prosperity of Jews, 192–93, 194
  and rule of Islam, 67
  sources of antisemitism, 151–52, 153
middle class, 4, 34, 105
Middle East, 15, 126, 130, 141, 203
military conscription, 81, 82, 86
Minc, Hilari, 176
minorities, non-Jewish, 8, 77–78, 107, 144–45, 179–80
minority, Jews as, 1–2, 35
Minsk ghetto, 119
"The Mirror of the Jews" (Pfefferkorn), 63
missionary efforts of Jews, 42–43, 49
Mohamad, Mahathir, 198–99
monotheism, 3, 37, 40, 42, 44
Moses, 41, 42, 58, 192
Mossad, 200
Mueller, Max, 92
Muhammad, 67, 151, 191–92, 193, 194
Munich Olympic Games, 183
Muskeljudentum (physical fitness), 168
Muslim Brotherhood, 186, 198
Muslims. See also Islam
  antisemitic activity, 131
  anti-Zionism, 198
  and Black Death, 61
  and Christianity, 52
  conspiracy theories, 20
  and critics of Jews, 148
  and Crusades, 52
  in Europe, 10–13, 15–16

and Fourth Lateran Council, 54
  in France, 19, 126, 127–28
  and Holocaust, 139, 140–42
  immigration, 11, 12, 127, 201–2
  legal status of Jews, 193–94
  political influence, 149–50
  and prosperity of Jews, 194
  relationships with Jews, 12–14, 18–19, 125, 128
  and Russia, 16
  sources of antisemitism, 201–2
  in United States, 18
  voting rights, 12
Mussert movement, 113
Mussolini, Benito, 120

Napoleon, 76
Narodniki groups, 83
Nasser, Gamal Abdel, 141, 198
Nasser, Najib, 195
Nation of Islam, 145, 184
National Alliance, 127
National Association for the Advancement of Colored People (NAACP), 145
National Bolshevism, 129
National Democrats, 109
National Front, 127, 128
National Socialism, 179
nationalism
  of Arabs, 182
  and Nazism, 113
  and neofascism, 127, 134
  in nineteenth century, 171
  religious nationalism, 15, 107, 205
  and violence against Jews, 77

Nazis. *See also* Hitler,
  Adolf; Holocaust
  and "antisemitism" term,
    22
  and Christianity, 144
  concentration camps,
    115, 117, 119, 121
  cover-up of mass
    murders, 121, 135
  current influence, 10
  extermination camps,
    119, 121, 135
  "final solution," 118–24,
    137
  and financial restitution,
    128, 176
  Friedrich on, 34
  in Germany, 31, 36, 100,
    107, 113, 114–20, 125
  and ghettoization, 93
  in Italy, 113
  Jews acceptable to
    Nazis, 159
  Jews under rule of, 118
  and minorities, 111
  neo-Nazism, 10, 17,
    183, 209
  opposition, 145
  and Polish population,
    134
  propaganda, 113–14,
    115
  and *Protocols of the
    Elders of Zion*, 100
  rise of, 107, 111
  and St. John
    Chrysostom, 48
  and study of
    antisemitism, 31, 35
  and Zionist-collabora-
    tion theory, 137, 141,
    200
Near East, 70
negationism, 125, 134,
  135–41, 184–85, 197
neoconservativism, 188
neofascism
  and decline of
    antisemitism, 130
  emergence, 126–27,
    133–34

and fascism, 127
and immigration, 11
influence, 10
neo-Nazism, 10, 17, 183,
  209
Netherlands, 64, 113, 120,
  122
Neumann, Franz, 31
Neumann, Michael, 149
"new antisemitism"
  (term), 5, 7, 9, 16, 189
New York Times, 143
Nicholas I, 81
Nicholas IV, 54, 56
Nietzsche, Friedrich
  Wilhelm, 93, 167
Nobel Prizes, 23, 162
Nordau, Max, 94, 168
North Africa, 127, 185,
  193, 203
Northern League, 127
numerus clausus (quotas),
  82

October Manifesto, 88
oil, 15
Oklahoma City federal
  building bombing, 144
Olympic Games, 116,
  162, 183
Oppenheimer, Joseph
  Suess, 36
"Orat mater ecclesia"
  papal bull, 56
organ transplantation, 140
organized crime, 158
Oriental Jewry, 67
orientalization of Israel, 15
Origen, 47
*The Origins of Totalitari-
  anism* (Arendt), 32–33
Orthodox Church, 80,
  132, 178, 195
Ottoman empire, 13–14

Pakistan, 209
Pale of Settlement, 81–82,
  86, 128
Palestine
  and American blacks,
    202
  anti-Zionism, 195–96

British Mandate, 30
immigration, 84, 109
insurgencies, 182
Israeli-Palestinian
  conflict, 8–10, 19–20,
  187, 200, 203–5
and Jewish colonization,
  195
and Jewish conspiracies,
  140
and Jewish zealots, 44
loss of homeland, 196–
  97, 202, 203–5
restrictions on Judaism,
  50
sacrifice of, 141
and sources of
  antisemitism, 203–5
and Zionism, 27, 167,
  169
Pamyat antisemitic group,
  132
Parkes, James, 31
Parsons, Talcott, 34–35
Pascal, Blaise, 166
patricide, 37
patriotism, 160, 161
Pauker, Ana, 176
Paulus, 45
Pearl, Daniel, 201
Pearson, Karl, 92
peasantry, Jewish, 24, 168
Pelley, William Dudley,
  144
People of the Book (*ahl
  al-kitab*), 68, 192
People's Democracies,
  175, 177, 178
People's Will party, 173
Pernersdorfer, Engelbert,
  173
persecutors, Jews as, 6
Persians, 40
Peter the Hermit, 52
Peter the Venerable, 50
Petlyura, Symon, 104
Petronius, 43
Pfefferkorn, Johannes, 63
philology, 92
physical appearance of
  Jews, 43, 54, 80–81,
  158–59, 168, 193

Pilate, Pontius, 46, 47, 48
Pilsudski, Joseph, 108, 109, 111
Pinsker, Leon, 26–27, 29
Plehve, V. K., 85
Pobedonostsev, Konstantin, 84
pogroms and massacres. *See also* Holocaust
  in Algeria, 196
  in Baghdad-Farhud, 196
  during Black Death era, 38, 54, 60–62, 67
  Chmielnicki massacre, 69
  Crusades, 38, 51, 52–53
  in Eastern Europe, 78
  in Fez, 193
  by Flagellants, 55
  in Germany, 117, 147
  in Granada, 193
  in Hebron community, 196
  in Hungary, 30
  in Libya, 196
  in North Africa, 193
  in Romania, 30, 120
  in Russia, 27, 29, 30, 38, 78, 83–89, 104, 105, 168
  in Ukraine, 30
Poland
  assimilation of Jews, 80–81
  attacks on Jews, 57
  attitudes toward Poles, 179
  blood libel cases, 80
  and Communist leadership, 176
  and defenses against antisemitism, 163
  emigration, 109, 176
  expulsions of Jews, 103, 134
  ghettos, 119, 120
  and Holocaust, 117–18, 119, 121
  Jewish population, 66, 79, 80, 81, 107
  and "Jewish question," 27

land ownership, 155
literature on antisemitism, 22
racialist antisemitism, 111
social tensions, 36
sources of antisemitism, 4
status of Jews, 65–66, 167
"street antisemitism," 108
trades, 108
virulence of antisemitism, 108–9
Poliakov, Leon, 66
political antisemitism, 23, 77, 78, 126
political explanations of antisemitism, 49
political influence of Jews, 143, 156–57
political parties, 11, 30, 109, 185–86. *See also specific parties*
politics, Jews in, 77
popes, 53, 54, 56–57, 61
population trends, 10–11, 36–37. *See also specific regions and countries*
Populism, 142, 171, 173, 181–82
Portugal, 54, 62, 69–70, 146, 193
Posidonius, 41
post-racialist antisemitism, 20
poverty, 36, 84
Powell, Adam Clayton, 145
professions of Jews. *See also usury*
  in Austria, 78
  competitors, Jews as, 77, 95, 143, 154
  entrepreneurship of Jews, 157
  as estate managers, 79–80
  in Hungary, 110

and Nazism, 115–16
  in Poland, 108
  restrictions on Jews, 3, 65, 66, 154
  success of Jews in, 157–58
  in United States, 142
proletariat, 185
propaganda. *See also Protocols of the Elders of Zion*
  anti-Islamic propaganda, 198
  of Arab world, 198, 203
  and denials of Holocaust, 184
  in Eastern Europe, 134, 175
  of Henry Ford, 143
  of Nazis, 115
  political propaganda, 144
  prevalence, 65, 76, 120
  on Russia and Communism, 175
  of Soviet Union, 178
Proskurov pogrom, 104
prosperity of Jews, 62, 157, 171, 194, 202
prostitution, 158, 187
Protestantism, 64, 91
The Protocols of the Elders of Zion, 96–101
  and American policies, 188
  in Arab world, 197
  distribution, 105, 198
  Ford's distribution of, 143
  influence, 29, 82, 85
  modern interpretation, 9
  in Spain, 113
Proudhon, Pierre, 24, 79
psychological explanations of antisemitism, 32, 37, 172
public office, 68, 75, 76, 176, 193
Puritanism, 25
purity of blood (*limpieza de sangre*), 22, 70, 91–92, 159–60

Qaradhawi, Youssef el, 199
Quintilianus, 42
Qutb, Sayyid, 198

race theory, 92–94
racialist antisemitism, 4–5, 22, 70, 91–95, 111
Rakosi, Matias, 176
Rashi, 154
Rassinier, Paul, 135–36
Rathenau, Walther, 159
Ree, Paul, 164
Reich Citizenship Law, 115
Reinhardt, Django, 124
religiosity of Jews, 2
religious sources of antisemitism, 36, 54
  in Arab world, 196
  and assimilation of Jews, 151
  attitude of church, 66
  and Black Death, 61–62
  in Eastern Europe, 107
  in Middle Ages, 151–52
  in United States, 142
Renan, Ernest, 92
Republican party, 181
restitution, financial, 128, 176
Retcliffe, Sir John, 96
Reuchlin, Johann, 63
Revelation, book of, 46–47
revisionism, 125, 134, 135–41, 184–85, 197
Rhineland, Germany, 38, 52
Rhodes, Cecil, 33
Riga ghetto, 119
right wing, 10, 11, 17, 171, 172. See also specific groups, including Nazis
rights of Jews. See emancipation
riots, 76, 77, 83, 107–8
Rodinson, Maxime, 174
Rohling, August, 195
Roman, Petre, 134

Roman civilization, 2, 3, 41–44, 49, 50
Romania
  and defenses against antisemitism, 163
  emigration, 176–77
  and Holocaust, 121, 122, 134
  and Ion Antonescu, 134
  Iron Guard, 107, 111, 112
  Jewish population, 107, 128
  legionnaires, 121
  literature on antisemitism, 23
  and neofascism, 134
  pogroms, 30, 120
  virulence of antisemitism, 111–12
Roosevelt, Franklin D., 144, 187
Roosevelt, Theodore, 94
Rosenberg, Alfred, 99
Rosenblum, Maxie, 163
Rosenzweig, Franz, 164
Ross, Barney, 163
Rotfeld, Adam, 134
Rothschild family, 25, 79, 142, 157
Rousseau, Jean-Jacques, 75
Russia
  antisemitic activity, 131–33
  and Arab societies, 16
  assimilation of Jews, 81–83
  attitudes toward Jews, 128
  attitudes toward Russians, 179–80
  blood libel cases, 89
  and Chechnya, 7, 133, 134, 204
  and communism, 150
  and defenses against antisemitism, 163
  expulsions of Jews, 103
  and Holocaust, 118, 120
  and Japan, 86

Jewish population, 16–17, 66, 79
  literature on antisemitism, 22
  and Muslims, 16, 126
  pogroms, 27, 29, 30, 38, 78, 83–89, 104, 105, 168
  population trends, 11
  propaganda, 10, 175
  and Protocols of the Elders of Zion, 29, 85, 98, 100
  revolution, 30, 98–99, 104–5 (see also Bolshevism)
  social tensions, 36
  socialism, 25
  sources of antisemitism, 4
  status of Jews, 167
Russian Orthodox church, 80, 178

Sabbath ritual, 43, 44
Sachs, Maurice, 166
sacrifices, 40, 42
Sahih, 192
Saint-Simonians, 79
Salome, Lou Andreas, 164
Samuel, Maurice, 34
Sanacja political movement, 109
Saracens, 54
Sartre, Jean-Paul, 33–34, 147
Satan, 55, 199
scapegoats, 1, 33
Schelling, Friedrich Wilhelm Joseph von, 75
segregation of Jews, 115. See also ghettos
self-hatred of Jews, 165–66
Semitic language, 21–22, 191
Seneca, 42–43
September 11th terrorist attacks, 200
sexual relationships, 115, 158, 193

Sharon, Ariel, 14, 186
Sharpton, Al, 184
Shaw, George Bernard, 94
Shi'a Muslims, 19, 69
shtetl, 168
Six-Day War, 181, 183, 204
skinheads, 130. *See also* neo-Nazism
Slansky trial, 134, 175
slave trade, 146, 158, 184, 187
Slovakia, 76
Smith, Adam, 155
Smith, Gerald, 144
Sobibor extermination camp, 119, 136
social Darwinism, 94
Social Democrats, 83, 94, 173, 184
social explanations of antisemitism, 36, 79, 157
Social Revolutionaries, 83, 105
socialism
and capitalism, 28, 79, 172
emergence, 78
leadership, 24–25
and working class, 185
Socrates of Constantinople, 48
Sombart, Werner, 25
South Africa, 84, 95, 103, 162
Southern Europe, 69
Soviet Union. *See also* Bolshevism
and Arabs, 197
and conspiracy theories, 177–78
emigration, 118, 177
expulsions of Jews, 138
fall of, 132, 180, 181
and Holocaust, 122, 139
Jewish population, 175, 209
propaganda, 178
racialist antisemitism, 179
Stalinism, 174

Spain
assimilation of Jews, 151
attitudes toward Jews, 150, 160
blood libel cases, 56
expulsions of Jews, 36, 50, 54, 62, 69
fascism, 113
Golden Age, 69
Jewish population, 128–29, 192–93
limpieza de sangre, 22, 70
persecution of Jews, 38, 68
population trends, 10–11
racialist antisemitism, 4
restrictions on Jews, 154
state-supervised antisemitism, 69
status of Jews, 53, 154
Speer, Albert, 114
Spinoza, Benedictus de, 28, 72
sports, Jews in, 162–63
St. Augustine of Hippo, 47, 48
St. Cyril, 50
St. Simon, 57
St. William of Norwich, 55
Stahl, Friedrich, 156
Stalin, Joseph, 30, 62, 105, 175, 177
Stalinism, 174, 186
stereotypes, 37, 158–59, 172, 175
Strauss, Leo, 188, 201
"street antisemitism," 108
Streicher, Julius, 25–26
suicides of Jews, 52, 122
Summers, Lawrence, ix
Sunni Muslims, 19, 69
Sweden, 120
Switzerland, 76, 113, 150
Synod of Claremont, 50

Tacitus, 42, 43, 44
Talmud
anti-Christian references, 48–49, 152

and antisemites, 152–53
and conspiracy theories, 82
Eisenmenger on, 58–60
influence, 28
Pfefferkorn on, 63
The Talmud Jew (Rohling), 195, 197
"Talmud Jews," 57–60
Tantawi, Muhammad Sayyed, 199
taxes on Jews
and the church, 53
in Germany, 116
in Muslim world, 68, 193
in Poland, 109
in Rome, 44–45
temples, destruction of, 39–40, 50
terrorism, 126, 144, 200
Theobald, 55
Theodorakis, Mikis, 9, 129, 149
Theodosius, 50
Theophrast, 40
Third Reich. *See* Nazis
third world, 15
Thiriart, Jean François, 129
Tiberius, 44
Tito, Josip Broz, 175
Tomaso, Pater, 194
trades of Jews. *See* professions of Jews
Transnistria, 120
Trebitsch, Arthur, 166
Treblinka extermination camp, 119
Trotsky, Leon, 30, 173, 174
Trotskyism, 174, 181, 185–86
Turkey, 11, 70, 185
Turner Diaries (MacDonald), 144

Uighurs, 8
Ukraine
blood libel cases, 80
expulsions of Jews, 79

Ukraine (continued)
  and Holocaust, 121
  Jewish population, 66,
    81, 132
  pogroms, 30, 38, 83–84,
    104
United Kingdom. See
  Britain
United Nations, 8
United States
  and anti-Americanism,
    14, 17, 129, 187–88
  and Communism, 177
  and East Germany, 179
  foreign policy, 17–18,
    188
  immigration, 18, 84, 95,
    142–43, 162
  imperialism, 187–88
  and Israel, 15, 17–18, 200
  Jewish population, 209
  and Jewish spirit, 25
  legislation, antisemitic,
    110
  literature on
    antisemitism, 23
  political affiliation of
    Jews, 181
  prevalence of
    antisemitism, 142–47
Urban II, 52
usury
  interest rates, 155
  Leon on, 174
  modern equivalents, 9
  as primary profession of
    Jews, 28, 153–54
  resentment of, 3, 153–54

Valentin, Hugo, 31
Venice, Italy, 62
Verges, Jacques, 130
Vienna, Austria, 36
Vilna, Lithuania, 107
violence against Jews, 50.
  See also Holocaust;
  pogroms and
  massacres

Voevod, Vaida, 111–12
Volksgemeinschaft, 113
Voltaire, 71–72, 75
Von Rin, Anderl, 57

Wagner, Richard, 22, 93
Wales, 77
Wall Street banks, 177
Warburg, Max, 94
Warsaw ghetto, 119, 120
wealth of Jews, 62, 157,
  171, 194, 202
Weber, Max, 25
Weininger, Otto, 159, 166
Weishaupt, Adam, 95
wells, poisoning of, 60–61
West Bank, 181, 183
Western Europe. See also
  specific countries
  antisemitic activity, 131
  attitudes toward Jews,
    150
  and Holocaust, 123
  Jewish population, 107
  Muslim population,
    149–50
  propaganda, 203
  regional variations in
    antisemitism, 66, 69
  and socialism, 78
White Russia, 81, 99,
  104–5
Wiener Library in
  London, x
Wilhelm II, 93, 99
Williams, Lukyn, 31
Witte, Sergei, 87
women, 49
work of Jews. See
  professions of Jews
World Trade Center
  attacks, 200
World War I, 103–4, 110,
  114
World War II. See Hitler,
  Adolf; Holocaust;
  Nazis
Worms, Germany, 52

xenophobia, 2, 41, 126,
  127

Yavetz, Zvi, 42
Yemen, 193
Yiddish language, 109,
  168
youth groups, antisemitic,
  130–31
Yugoslavia, 122

Zambrowski, Roman, 176
Zealots, 43
"ZioNazis," 184
Zionism. See also anti-
  Zionism
  and assimilation of
    Jews, 169
  and Bolshevism, 180
  and colonization, 195
  and Communism, 180
  criticisms, 9
  influence, 210
  and Israel (state), 210
  and Lazare, 29
  left wing on, 17, 150,
    182
  and Marxist-Leninist
    doctrine, 180
  motivations, 166–68
  and Nazi-collaboration
    theory, 137, 141, 200
  opponents, 168
  and Pinsker's views, 27
  in Protocols of the
    Elders of Zion, 97
  and revisionism, 137
  and Soviet purges, 175
  term, 6, 179
Zionist Occupation
  Government (ZOG),
  17, 144
Zola, Emile, 102
Zuendel, Ernst, 136
Zunz, Leopold, 164

DATE DUE

9/20/07			